'A penetrating and confronting attempt to lift the veil into boardrooms, this work cuts to the chase as to what really drives the nominations processes, how directors develop and hold their sources of power, and why directors seek these roles in the first place. It gives essential guidance to Chairs, Directors and investors alike in Board construction and management.'

— Patricia Cross, Non-Executive Director, Aviva plc (chair of the remuneration committee, member of both the nominations committee and audit committee), Senior Independent Director, Aviva Investors; Chair, Commonwealth Superannuation Corporation. Previously Non-Executive Director, Macquarie Group Ltd

'Having recently made the transition from executive leadership to non-executive oversight, I found the book enormously helpful. It provides well researched insight into behaviour around the board table that will be of value to any director who wishes to comprehend the board environment and contribute more effectively. Not least because the book encourages reflection upon one's own style and influence.'

— James Darkins, Non-Executive Director, The Crown Estate, previously CEO, TIAA-Henderson Real Estate and Managing Director Property, Henderson Global Investors

'A very timely book that any board member can benefit from reading. The human factor is not talked about enough and often its effect on board effectiveness and decision making processes is under-estimated. No amount of good corporate governance can make a board effective if the individuals around the table are not functioning well individually and/or together. This book provides insightful guidance on developing a superior board culture.'

— Charlotte Valeur, Chair, Institute of Company Directors, United Kingdom; Member, Primary Markets Group, London Stock Exchange; Non-Executive Director, Laing O'Rourke; Advisory Panel Member, Hampton-Alexander Review

Identity, Power and Influence in the Boardroom

Over the last decade, the role of the board of directors in deciding on potentially value-creating decisions has gained greater prominence. Following extensive board research into the origins, reasons, effects and consequences of boardroom influence of directors, this book prepares directors for playing a more influential role in shaping such decisions.

Boards are only as effective as the relationships their members have with each other. Despite this, many of the published guides on board work do not focus sufficiently on the human dimension of governance, nor has there been a comprehensive understanding of the effect that group membership has on the decision behaviour of the individual director, or vice versa.

The author offers the reader actionable strategies to successfully navigate the complex dynamics that are inevitable when a group of powerful individuals with strong individual identities has to work together. Without a realistic understanding of the silent risks that a suboptimal dynamic may pose to the processes of making critical decisions, boards may find their decision outcomes compromised. Despite the best intentions, such dynamics can have a chilling effect on an individual director's contribution, marginalising or diminishing the value of their contribution and their influence on the board.

This book will be a valuable resource guide for aspiring and experienced company directors wishing to strengthen their effectiveness in the advisory role and develop a more influential voice in shaping the strategic direction of their companies.

Meena Thuraisingham, Founder and Principal of BoardQ, a board-level advisory practice, has over 30 years of corporate and consulting experience with global organisations. As a qualified organisational psychologist, her work with top-team and board effectiveness, development and renewal is aimed at strengthening the way organisations are led and governed, and the cultures that result.

Identity, Power and Influence in the Boardroom

Actionable Strategies for Developing High Impact Directors and Boards

Meena Thuraisingham

Routledge
Taylor & Francis Group

LONDON AND NEW YORK

First published 2019
by Routledge
2 Park Square, Milton Park, Abingdon, Oxon OX14 4RN

and by Routledge
52 Vanderbilt Avenue, New York, NY 10017

Routledge is an imprint of the Taylor & Francis Group, an informa business

© 2019 Meena Thuraisingham

The right of Meena Thuraisingham to be identified as author of this work has been asserted by her in accordance with sections 77 and 78 of the Copyright, Designs and Patents Act 1988.

Trademark notice: Product or corporate names may be trademarks or registered trademarks, and are used only for identification and explanation without intent to infringe.

British Library Cataloguing-in-Publication Data
A catalogue record for this book is available from the British Library

Library of Congress Cataloging-in-Publication Data
A catalog record has been requested for this book

ISBN: 978-1-138-48878-6 (hbk)
ISBN: 978-1-351-03950-5 (ebk)

Typeset in Bembo
by codeMantra

MIX
Paper from
responsible sources
FSC
www.fsc.org   FSC® C013985

Printed in the United Kingdom
by Henry Ling Limited

Contents

Figures

Tables

About the author

Meena Thuraisingham is founder of and principal at BoardQ, an advisory practice that provides consulting to global clients on top team and board effectiveness. She brings over 30 years of experience across multiple sectors, including resources, retail, banking and professional services. During this time, she has been actively involved in leading major business change projects including organisational renewal, restructures, acquisitions and divestments, and the risks associated with any major business change. She has authored several books, including *The Secret Life of Decisions* (Routledge, 2013).

She holds an Honours Degree in Psychology from Manchester University, UK, and has a PhD in Management from RMIT University in Australia. She is a graduate member of the Australian Institute of Company Directors (AICD) and is on the AICD's preferred panel of coaches. She is on the board of The George Institute for Global Health. She is also a member of the International Women's Forum.

Acknowledgements

Joseph Healy Advice provided in Part 2 by Joseph Healy, a career international banker. Joseph is a co-founder of Judo Capital, a challenger bank servicing the business financing needs of Small Medium Enterprises (SMEs). He has held several executive roles in the financial services sector, including in risk management, debt and equity capital markets, advisory, client management and strategy. Joseph has a MSc in Finance, MBA, MSc in International Management and a MA in Contemporary Chinese Studies. He is a member of the Institute of Bankers in Scotland and authored a textbook, *Corporate Governance and Shareholder Wealth Creation 2003*.

Abbreviations

APRA	Australian Prudential Regulatory Authority
BCG	Boston Consulting Group
CBA	Commonwealth Bank of Australia
CEO	Chief executive officer
CFO	Chief financial officer
CSR	Corporate social responsibility
EPS	Earnings per share
FRC	Financial Reporting Council
GE	General Electric
GFC	Global financial crisis
HR	Human resources
ICGN	International Corporate Governance Network
ICI	Imperial Chemical Industries
M&A	Mergers and acquisitions
NED	Non-executive directors
NIFO	Nose in, fingers out
NPV	Net present value
SCT	Social categorisation theory
SIT	Social identity theory
TMT	Top management teams

Introduction

The governing of corporations, especially the influential role that board members play in determining corporate strategy, has long been a subject of considerable debate, not only among the business community, investors and regulators but also, more recently, by society at large. The topic continues to attract unwanted attention, given the many documented corporate disasters and industry-wide scandals. This book brings a fresh approach to understanding how strategic decisions are made in the board context, challenging the under-socialised view of non-executive directors' (NEDs) involvement in decision-making and, ultimately, how they exercise accountability in value creation. The book draws from the author's experience advising and consulting for boards and top teams, and recent doctoral-level research into the silent risks that sub-optimal dynamics may pose to board decision-making (Thuraisingham 2018).

A recent, detailed review of literature on the role that boards play in strategy (Pugliese, Bezemer & Zattoni 2009; Thuraisingham 2018) shows two major shifts over the last three decades. First, a shift in focus from a preoccupation with the monitoring or control elements of boards' roles (i.e., value preservation) to their equally important, but previously neglected, advisory role in decisions pertaining to the long-term strategic direction of companies and value creation responsibilities (Pugliese, Bezemer & Zattoni 2009). This shift experienced a setback as a result of the global financial crisis (GFC) in 2008, during which long-term investors and shareholder activists stepped up their scrutiny of the quality of decisions. In particular, questions were asked about the concept of shareholder value, interests of stakeholder groups, debt and risk governance, levels of chief executive officer (CEO) remuneration and the role of management incentives. During this time, boards themselves became more cautious and risk-averse, focussing on value preservation, particularly in industries subject to close regulatory oversight—this, despite trust and control not being mutually exclusive and board accountabilities spanning both value creation and value preservation.

Second, there was a shift from reliance on economic, rationalist-based explanations of the functioning of boards to more behaviourally based explanations led by process-research pioneers such as Pettigrew (1992, 2001).

Economic theories of corporate governance held sway for several decades, de-emphasising the human side of governance (Filatotchev 2008; Filatotchev, Jackson & Nakajima 2013), which may be better explicated by social psychology theories (Thuraisingham 2018). Seen through the prism of social psychology, boards can be viewed as complex social systems, with their own power structures, affiliations and stated and unstated goals. In this context there is much we do not know about the internal workings of boards; to a considerable extent, how board directors enact their duties is a 'black box' that has eluded many stakeholders who wish to promote corporate governance practice and reform.

Researchers, consultants and directors themselves have always recognised that board decision cultures can vary significantly. New research, grounded in the theory of group dynamics, sheds light on why this may be so and suggests that boards may only be as effective as the relationships their members have with each other (Thuraisingham 2018). Despite this, many published guides on board work do not focus sufficiently on the human dimension of governance, nor has there been a comprehensive understanding of the effect that group membership has on the decision-making behaviour of individual directors, and vice versa. Where books have been written on board dynamics, they have indirectly inferred board dynamics from demographic factors such as tenure, age, gender, qualifications and experience, and/or relied on surveys and questionnaires. As a result, a view of board life as 'under-socialised' has persisted. Explorative, inductive studies are few and far between (McNulty, Zattoni & Douglas 2013; Thuraisingham 2018).

It is undeniable that the capability of a board and, therefore, the influence it wields cannot be determined by simply sum-totaling the individual ability of each director to calculate the total capability of that group. The influence of a board may be greater (and sometimes less) than the sum of its parts. Few board studies have explored the relationship between an individual director and a collective action taken by a board and how this may augment or diminish the collective influence of the board. This is a critical question for all boards. This represents a key tension in corporate directorships because by law, directors are held to be individually accountable, but their actions at board level are clearly part of a collective. As is well known in the field of social psychology relating to the study of group behaviour, people acting together may do things they would never do alone.

Access to boards is often given as the key reason why so little is known about the internal workings of boards. Board directors generally operate under a code of confidentiality and are reluctant to comment on the workings of boards; therefore, little is known about what goes on in, and around, boardrooms. In a qualitative study of 32 directors of well-known US companies, Finkelstein and Mooney (2003) found no correlation between what they referred to as the 'usual suspects' and company performance. The 'usual suspects' referenced the majority of board studies that focussed on factors such as inside versus outside directors, board size and CEO duality. With other researchers, they called for a different direction in board studies, away from input-output studies, towards a focus on the inner workings of boards, the so-called 'black box' (Pye & Pettigrew 2005). Input-output studies ignore the effects of moderating group variables such as the nature of interpersonal interaction, cohesion, trust, power and conflict (Finkelstein & Mooney 2003; Gabrielsson & Huse 2004; Pye & Pettigrew 2005).

Additionally, inaccessibility to the 'live' workings of boards has led to studies that have extrapolated the behaviour of board members from top management teams (TMTs). However, boards differ from management teams in a number of material ways. They are not teams in a strict organisational sense. For example, boards comprise a group of autonomous equals—seasoned, credentialed and expert in one or more fields; therefore, power differentials are not as great as in management teams. Most directors have multiple demands on their time and have to choose where they spend it. Board members generally meet (as a group) episodically, usually six–twelve times a year; consequently, they do not have the interaction frequency enjoyed by many other teams, nor do they develop the team norms that build up with regular and frequent interaction. Board directors serve fixed terms, after which they may decide to move on to bigger boards or retire. Finally, the group's role is ambiguous in nature as much board tradition today has arisen out of norms derived from practice and regulatory codes that are largely based around the principal–agent paradigm, influential over many decades. For all these reasons, extrapolating the behavior of board directors from TMTs is not entirely helpful.

This book focusses on NEDs. Most NEDs have well-developed ties and networks quite independent of the company and, while having personalities and reputations that represent valuable diversity, possess an inherent potential for tension. Sometimes the tension felt by members remains at a subterranean level. This is because of a powerful and shared ideology—held in common by all members of a board and derived from a sense of group identity—that the board should function harmoniously. Where there are tensions, these are not allowed to spill into the public arena; a show of unity to the outside world is a critical part of group membership. This can serve as pressure for unity. Where tension exists, it is typically something to be sorted out behind the scenes, with the NED taken to one side, usually by an alert and observant chair. This shared ideology is variously related to the primacy of shareholders, the importance of stakeholders and the criticality of creating firm value, and can have a pervasive governing influence on the thinking of individual directors. It can belie some of the important nuances that exist within board groups: for example, in situations in which value creation may be a dominant schema within the board, but each member differs in their view about how and what strategies create the most value.

So, why are some boards not able to achieve their full potential as a group in shaping the strategic direction of the company? As directors serving on multiple boards can attest, boards, despite having identical structures and similar composition, can vary in their effectiveness because the effects of internal dynamics or culture perform quite differently depending on social systems and beliefs (Nadler 2004). Structures, composition and information flow can be designed and redesigned easily, but cultures that develop over time can persist because they tend to reward those who perpetuate them, making them difficult to change (Nadler 2004; Pye & Pettigrew 2005). For the purpose of this book, board culture is defined as a social system derived from the directors' shared beliefs about their roles in active preparation and participation, and their shared values in terms of personal responsibility for the company's prosperity. This, in turn, results in a history of interactions that generates behavioural norms and routines that shape the expectations and conduct of members. In essence, this is what the culture of a board is—a 'social reality' that provides real understanding of the complex context in which directors must exercise their accountabilities. It acknowledges that a board group is embedded in a complex web of relationships with unique power asymmetries and identity affects, and requires understanding and sensitivity to the identities, motivations and interactions between group members. By 'humanising' the process of governing public corporations, a clearer understanding of what goes on in and around the boardroom, and a more balanced and complete understanding of director and board effectiveness, can emerge.

Deep domain experience and accumulated reputations are not enough, nor are directors' skills in lively inquiry, engaged dialogue and attentive learning. A director's awareness and understanding of how this 'social reality', unique to each board, consciously and subconsciously shapes their behaviour, matters also. Despite the best intentions, suboptimal dynamics can have a chilling effect on an individual director's contribution, marginalising or diminishing the value of their contribution and their influence, both individually and collectively. Further, without a realistic understanding of the silent risks that such a dynamic may pose to the processes of making critical decisions, boards may find their decision outcomes compromised. Through new and extensive research into the origins, reasons, effects and consequences of the influence of boardroom directors, this book reveals the incipient effects of identity politics as a fact of board life and the dangers it poses to the quality of decision-making at board level (Thuraisingham 2018). It offers a well-researched psychosocial framework, setting out the case for a new take on the understanding of board functioning, by viewing the board as a complex social system and directors as social actors in this system. The framework suggests that informal practices of accountability may matter as much as more formal structural forms of accountability and offers actionable strategies to strengthen accountability and effectiveness.

This book also provides insights for board chairs on how a healthy dynamic and a vibrant culture may be developed and sustained. Rather than simply accepting board culture as something that exists and must be worked through, it reveals how and why board cultures differ and how board cultures can be changed.

In summary, corporate governance and the role of the board of directors has evolved, particularly over the last decade, to incorporate a larger role for the NED in shaping strategic direction. By 'humanising' the process by which directors shape and direct strategy, this book (through the words of and lived experiences of directors themselves) presents a unique insight into how director and board effectiveness may be strengthened. In a practical sense, it offers prescriptions for boards that have evolved beyond their conformance role in monitoring management and wish to play a more strategically active role in shaping and directing a firm's long-term direction and success. The book will act as a valuable resource guide for both aspiring and experienced board directors wishing to strengthen their effectiveness in the advisory role and develop a more influential voice in shaping the strategic direction of their companies. In addition to being a useful resource for directors, the book also offers insights for investors, shareholders, regulators and peak-business bodies interested in understanding the complexities involved in board work and the process by which accountability may be strengthened or weakened. In particular it suggests that the post-crisis tendencies of regulators to implement formal rules and structural change to achieve greater accountability may be misplaced.

In summary, the questions that this book then seeks to answer are: If the complexities of governing a corporation can be explained only in part by using economic and legal prescriptions, how do we get a fuller, richer understanding of the role of boards? How do we explain the variations in how each board and, indeed, each director takes up their role? What drives these variations, and how does this understanding help us strengthen the effectiveness of directors, both individually and collectively as members of a board?

To address these questions, the book is separated into two parts. Part 1 draws from recent and extensive research (Thuraisingham 2018) presenting compelling evidence for why humanising the governing of our corporations is important. Through the words of directors themselves, Part 1 reveals to the reader both the complex social reality into which NEDs must fit and, consequently, the behavioural patterns they often demonstrate while arriving at a decision with their board peers. It describes how social identity and power play a role in who influences whom and how such attempts are received and reacted to. These findings contrast with regulatory assumptions that a board's decision-making processes are characterised by rational action alone. Rational action theories and theories spawned from the economic research tradition cannot fully explain the lived experiences of directors.

Building on many of the important theoretical concepts and frameworks in Part 1, Part 2 examines the implications of these insights for board advisors, investors, regulators and peak-business bodies, using case studies to distil key lessons. End users of corporate governance practices, such as long-term shareholders and investors, may also have an interest in why the same or similar practices pursued by different boards can have such different consequences. Regulators, focussed on corporate governance reform agendas, may be interested in the way regulatory codes are variously practised in different companies due to the different behaviours of decision-making groups. Part 2 also examines the limitations of the Anglo-Saxon model of governance and asks what we might be able to learn from other models in light of changing societal expectations and as the social purpose of corporations is being vigorously debated.

References

Filatotchev I, 2008, 'Developing an organizational theory of corporate governance: comments on Henry L. Tosi, Jr. (2008) "Quo Vadis? Suggestions for future corporate governance research"', *Journal of Management and Governance*, vol. 12, no. 2, pp. 171–178.

Filatotchev, I, Jackson, G & Nakajima, C 2013, 'Corporate governance and national institutions: a review and emerging research agenda', *Asia Pacific Journal of Management*, vol. 30, pp. 965–986.

Finkelstein, S & Mooney, A 2003, 'Not the usual suspects: how to use board process to make boards better', *Academy of Management Executive*, vol. 17, no. 2, pp. 101–113.

Gabrielsson, J & Huse, M 2004, 'Context behaviour and evolution, challenges in research on boards and governance', *International Studies of Management and Organisation*, vol. 34, no. 2, pp. 11–36.

McNulty, T, Zattoni, A & Douglas, T 2013, 'Developing corporate governance research through qualitative methods: a review of previous studies', *Corporate Governance: An International Review*, vol. 21, no. 2, pp. 183–198.

Nadler, D 2004, 'Building better boards', *Harvard Business Review*, May 2004, pp. 102–111.

Pettigrew, A 1992, 'On studying managerial elites', *Strategic Management Journal*, vol. 13, pp. 163–182.

Pettigrew, A 2001, 'Andrew Pettigrew on executives and strategy: an interview with Kenneth Starkey', *European Management Journal*, vol. 20, no. 1, pp. 20–34.

Pugliese, A, Bezemer, PJ & Zattoni, A 2009, 'Boards of directors' contribution to strategy: a literature review and research agenda', *Corporate Governance: An International Review*, vol. 17, no. 3, pp. 292–306.

Pye, A & Pettigrew, A 2005, 'Studying board context, process and dynamics: some challenges for the future', *British Journal of Management*, vol. 16, pp. 27–38.

Thuraisingham, SM 2018, 'Exploring the social factors that influence the decision making behaviours of non-executive directors in Australian public companies', PhD thesis, RMIT University, Melbourne.

Part I

Part I, comprising five chapters, looks closely at the board's role in developing and deciding strategy. In doing so, it recognises that governance does not occur in a social vacuum. Boards are complex social systems, in which accountability is socially accomplished through shared expectations, beliefs, norms and routines. Through their history of interactions with one another on a given board, NEDs are continually reassessing their value and place in the group and adapt their influencing behaviour accordingly. The decision dynamic that results has a self-regulating nature and can enable or inhibit influencing behaviours. These insights have been drawn from extensive inductive, exploratory research into how directors approached the task of shaping and deciding on a transformative strategy in the 15 public companies studied.

The first chapter distinguishes between the theory and the reality in how boards actually exercise their accountability for developing and determining strategy. The remaining chapters draw the distinction between *hard* and *soft* governance: hard governance relating to formal instruments of governance such as codes, frameworks, charters, regulation and compliance regimes and structure; soft governance relating to the shared interactional history and ways of working that emerge in a group that has to work with each other, in particular the effects of identification and power distribution on director behaviour. Hard governance does not guarantee effectiveness it provides the conditions for good governace to take hold. Soft governance, on the other hand, determines effectiveness. Both are equally critical for good governance. Part I concludes by suggesting that to be truly effective as an NED and to develop high-impact, influential boards, directors and boards need to pay more attention to soft governance. Nominations committees in particular may be wise to consider the implications for how they go about selecting and on-boarding new directors.

1 The board's role and accountability in developing and deciding strategy

The theory and reality

This chapter in summary

This chapter describes established theories on the role of boards, especially in strategy, and poses a challenge to these conventions. In particular, it challenges the 'under-socialised' explanations that these theories promote, suggesting that they tell us little about how boards really function and even less about how the decision culture of boards can be strengthened. Drawing from extensive research conducted by the author, the chapter contrasts theory with reality that shows a wide variation in how NEDs involve themselves in strategy and the extent to which they engage in a genuinely co-creative process of determining strategy with management. In doing so, it reveals the exercising of board accountability as a relational process. For example, while NEDs might share similar beliefs about board accountability, they differ behaviourally in how they go about exercising this accountability.

Despite this, accountability is often viewed in organisations as a hierarchical process or tool for economic or operational control, and formal instruments of accountability, such as mandates, codes and charters, are often referred to when describing board accountability. This chapter challenges this conventional view that assumes agency prescribed definitions of shareholder rights and claims. A more nuanced view is presented in this chapter, recognising that boards are highly complex social systems and the process of accountability is contextual and socially accomplished through role expectation, routines and interactions between members of a given group.

The chapter concludes with actionable strategies that boards, and especially chairs and subcommittee chairs, can take to ensure that there is real clarity about NEDs' roles in developing and determining strategy, paying special attention to the social dimension in how accountability for strategy is exercised.

The very idea of a board is based on the belief that the task of governing a company is beyond the capacity and capability of one person and that the collective capability of a group of people is better placed to do the task. To put this another way, it is assumed that the knowledge, skills, insights and networks that directors collectively bring to bear on their decision-making tasks are much greater in value than that of a single individual, no matter how experienced they are. Combining this collective knowledge and these skills, insights and networks is also more likely to neutralise any implicit biases that a single individual's perspectives may bring.

That is to say that directing is a relational concept in which agency occurs through interactions with others and this process is dynamic rather than additive (Thuraisingham 2018). Part 1 of this book reports on research that addresses this issue of the antecedents and moderators of board influence from a behavioural perspective. First, an outline of the formal and legal conventions relating to the role of the board is necessary.

The role of the board—theory and practice

There are seven major theoretical streams used to describe the role of the board in governing the corporation. These are agency theory (Fama 1980; Fama & Jensen 1983; Zahra & Pearce 1989), stewardship theory (Hillman & Dalziel 2003), resource dependence theory (Gulati & Westphal 1999; Pfeffer & Salancik 1978), resource-based theory (Barney 1991), class hegemony theory (Filatotchev, Jackson & Nakajima 2013; Judge & Zeithaml 1992; Mace 1991), managerial hegemony theory (Stiles & Taylor 2001) and stakeholder theory (Donaldson & Preston 1995; Sternberg 1997).

None of these theories on their own can describe, capture or fully explain the complexity of governing a corporation. Further, at various stages of a corporation's life cycle, different perspectives may be more relevant in explaining what is happening. For example, the life cycle of a company, transformation within the sector, competitive forces, disruptive technologies and systemic sector risk may bring one or more aspects into prominence. Changing societal expectations and stakeholder expectations, financial conditions and crises that may trigger regulation or re-regulation may also require a board to play different roles at different times. What is the task that boards need to accomplish? Generally, the board of directors has three interrelated tasks they have to accomplish.

First, a board is involved in setting the strategic context by providing overall direction on corporate strategy, mission or vision and overseeing the strategic development of a company, including approving strategic proposals. This is often characterised in literature as an 'advisory role' (Demb & Neubauer 1992; Ruigrok, Peck & Keller 2006). Second, a board manages succession for a CEO role, both hiring and firing a CEO, evaluating performance and providing wise counsel to a CEO and executive directors based on their experience and expertise; this is characterised as a board's 'service role'. Third, a board controls, supervises or monitors progress towards its objectives, including overseeing financial and other forms of risk. This role, which is focussed on the protection of shareholder interests, is often characterised as the 'control role'. All three (advisory, service and control) components of a board's accountability require extensive communication and deliberation, and members must learn to trust each other's judgement and expertise. Following decades of focus on the control or monitoring role, researchers into board work and board life have started adding a deeper understanding of the inherent challenges associated with all roles and tasks of boards. Leading this movement were process researchers such as Pettigrew (1992, 2001), Pye (2002), Pye and Pettigrew (2005), Maitlis and Lawrence (2003) and Samra-Fredericks (2003), who adopted a 'social actor'-driven and context-rich explanation of board function to suggest that boards are only as effective as the relationships their members have with each other. They argued that board work is often characterised by uncertainty, incomplete information and interdependency and, hence, relationship trust is key (Pettigrew & McNulty 1995b; Pye & Pettigrew 2005).

However, there is a fourth role. This is related to the links that directors provide a company to its external environment, including performing functions to enhance a company's legitimacy. This is sometimes characterised as a director's 'resource provision role' and is explained by the resource dependence theory (Pearce & Zahra 1992; Ruigrok, Peck & Keller 2006). Recent research has examined how those external links enhance the director's legitimacy in the eyes of their peers, which determines how their attempts at influence are received and responded to (Thuraisingham 2018). These social effects and their consequences are explored more fully in Chapter 3.

Despite the somewhat 'linear' descriptions advanced by researchers and academics, the reality is more complex as directors are confronted with several paradoxes inherent in their roles. There are three paradoxes facing boards (regardless of governance jurisdiction) that reveal significant role and task complexity. The first paradox relates to board authority; in a relative sense, management exercises considerably more power through the control of infrastructure, information and knowledge than board members, regardless of how well informed they may try to be. Second, board members are expected to provide critical judgement on management performance. This presumes a depth of knowledge and intimacy with the workings of the company, and yet, at the same time, the board must assure that their judgement is independent, which requires detachment and distance from the workings of the company. The third paradox relates to the collective strength of the board as a close-knit group, yet members must be independent personalities resisting 'groupthink' by raising critical questions with their equally experienced peers. In relation to this third paradox, we know that just because NEDs are independent of the company does not presume they are independent minded.

These three paradoxes were succinctly captured by Roberts, McNulty and Stiles (2005) following an extensive study of UK-based directors and chairs that led to the Higgs review into board governance in the UK as three behavioural couplets: *engaged but non-executive, challenging but supportive, independent but involved.*

The author's own research has built on these 'couplets' reported in the McNulty et al (2005) study and reveals a rounded, fuller picture of the dilemmas directors face when shaping strategy. Dilemmas unlike problems cannot be solved, only managed. Therefore, it requires NEDs to use a skilled combination of behaviour to manage the many dilemmas they encounter when dealing with management and with each other:

When interacting with management with respect to exercising the board role

- Informed but Heedful
- Challenging but Supportive
- Detached but Involved

When interacting with board peers with respect to dealing with the collective task at hand

- Skill and will/courage
- Tenured experience and beginner's eye
- Allegiances/personal ties and independent mindedness

For instance, with regard to the skill and will balance when interacting with board peers, NEDs are faced with a power structure into which they must fit and it may demand some courage to challenge a view advocated by others who are perceived to have a more powerful place in the group by dent of their accumulated experience, reputation and connections. When NEDs are not able to manage this boardroom dilemma skilfully it can result in deviant views being more easily controlled and conflict potentially surpressed by more powerful or influential subgroups. Revisions of confidence, opinion conformity and self-censorship of divergent views of those in the out-group may result. At the same time, in-groups can engage with misplaced confidence, marginalisation or dismissal of valid concerns and intolerance for dissent or disagreement (sometimes using subtle non-verbal strategies). These findings from the author's study (detailed in Chapters 2 and 3) further add support for viewing the exercise of board accountability as a contextual and relational process, with trust between individuals at the core of such interactions.

The skill differences in how each director navigates these paradoxes and dilemmas (described more fully in Chapter 4), is compounded by will differences. This is because, within a given board context directors develop a history of successful interactions which, in turn, influences the expectations, conduct and routines (heuristics) associated with their board activities, creating a self-perpetuating system. Directors will differ in their willingness to 'buck the system'. That is to say they will differ in their willingness to act in ways that are counter to the weight of this interactional history. Therefore, the actual practice of corporate governance can deviate from prescribed principles enshrined in governance codes. Furthermore, the study of instruments of board governance, such as board meetings, strategy days, closed-door sessions, board field visits and extraordinary meetings, commonly found in most modern boards vary widely in the different institutional settings in which they are applied. As such, director interactions and practices associated with the routine use of such instruments of governance are best studied in the context of social and behavioural psychology.

Seen through this prism of social psychology, groups such as boards are complex social systems with their own power structures, affiliations and stated and unstated goals. This relatively recent acknowledgement that corporate governance does not occur in a social vacuum has resulted in an emerging area of study the author calls *behavioural or soft governance*. As the author's recent research has shown, social factors, in particular factors such as power and identity, influence the process of making major strategic decisions on which both the personal reputations of directors and the company rides (Thuraisingham 2018). What these effects are, how they occur and their consequences are fully discussed in the remaining chapters of Part 1. The next section focusses on both the theory and the reality of the role directors play in the strategy of the company.

Board contribution to strategy: the theory and the reality

While there is not much argument about the complex tasks facing directors, there continues to be controversy over the director's role in strategic decisions. This controversy relates to how boards actually fulfil this role, rather than how they should play a key role in determining corporate strategy (Brauer & Schmidt 2008; Daily, Dalton & Cannella 2003; Hendry, Kiel & Nicholson 2010; Nicholson & Newton 2010; Pye & Pettigrew 2005; Rindova 1999; Zahra & Pearce 1989). One reason for this lack of consensus is the limited real-time access to boards when they are deciding on large complex strategic decisions, which has resulted in the actual behaviour of an individual board director when enacting their strategy-shaping accountabilities remaining largely under-researched.

In the last decade, calls for a greater focus on the role of boards in shaping strategic proposals (beyond simply their monitoring responsibilities) have gathered pace and volume, particularly in the US and the UK. This is a consequence of several contributing factors, including several high-profile corporate failures that precipitated increased regulation—for example, the US Sarbanes–Oxley Act (SOX) of 2002 following the collapse of Enron (Ahrens, Filatotchev & Thomsen 2011; McNulty, Florackis & Omrod 2013). The rise of private equity and takeovers, the growing influence of institutional investors and the rise of a shareholder activism movement have also been significant factors. Additionally, calls for boards to play a greater role in strategy have extended beyond the UK and US to the rest of the world, including Australia (Kemp 2006).

Lapses in corporate governance in the UK and the US precipitated the Higgs (2003) review, an independent review of the role and effectiveness of UK NEDs, which included an extensive qualitative study of the behavioural dynamics of UK boards (Roberts, McNulty & Stiles 2005). In the first inductive study of its kind, in which 40 NEDs were interviewed in the UK, Roberts, McNulty and Stiles (2005) argued that, at best, board structure and composition conditions, rather than determines, board effectiveness. Instead, they suggested that the behavioural dynamics of a board, together with group and interpersonal relationships between NEDs and executive team members, has a more far-reaching effect on a board's ability to perform its tasks effectively.

Australia has also experienced corporate governance issues, as evidenced by high-profile corporate failures such as HIH Insurance, One.Tel, Pyramid, Storm Financial, Allco Financial Group, Opes Prime and the myriad of issues highlighted by the 2017–2018 Royal Commission into Misconduct in the Banking, Superannuation and Financial Services Industry. There have been no Higgs-type corporate behavioural studies in Australia other than the 1991 Bosch report on *Corporate practices and conduct*. Further, there have been no corporate governance reviews in Australia, apart from publications such as the Australian Stock Exchange (ASX) Corporate Governance Council's (2014) Corporate Governance Principles and Recommendations, currently under review.

Europe and the US have also had their fair share of examples of lapses in corporate governance. Some of these are described in Part 2. While there is recognition that not all corporate failures can be attributed to lack of board oversight of strategic decisions, there are growing calls from academic and business communities for studies into NED involvement in strategic decision-making processes (McNulty, Zattoni & Douglas 2013; Zattoni & Van Ees 2012). These calls are motivated by a desire to ensure a richer understanding of the strategic governance function of boards, thereby redressing a historical focus on their monitoring function.

A board's role in shaping strategy has also attracted the attention of directors themselves who are keen to optimise their personal contributions in an increasingly complex environment (McNulty et al. 2011; Pick 2007). The McKinsey & Company (2017) Global Survey of 1,100 directors covering both public and private company boards showed that, 52% of directors wanted to spend more time on strategy, although actual time spent on strategy was reported in this 2017 survey as not exceeding the 27% level that was reported in the prior survey in 2015. The survey also reported that high-impact boards—defined as those effective in exercising their key roles (i.e., control, advisory and service)—tended to engage more frequently in strategic behaviours such as assessing value drivers, portfolio synergies and debating and evaluating strategic alternatives with the board as well as with the CEO (McKinsey & Company 2017).

To meet their responsibilities in the oversight of strategy and optimise outcomes, NEDs are required to collaboratively contribute to strategic proposals brought to a board by management (McNulty & Pettigrew 1999; Roberts, McNulty & Stiles 2005).

During the complex process of a board decision, as in the case of an international expansion strategy (which typically occurs over several months), many micro-decisions are made that synthesise progressive NED contributions. This involves the gathering of information, analysis and clarification until a workable consensus is achieved. However, there are notable complexities in how this process plays out. First, the identification, development and selection of strategic options rarely follow a sequential pattern. Second, a board's opportunity to shape strategic decisions can vary from one board to the next. The next section gives a sense of this complexity through the lens of NEDs who recounted their recent experiences participating in shaping strategy proposals brought to the board (Thuraisingham 2108).

The decision context and opportunities to influence and shape strategy

To understand the involvement of directors in strategy, the strategy-shaping context they each encounter is a good place to start, specifically the extent to which directors and boards have real opportunities to influence the strategy of the company and effect changes to its direction. As the author's earlier research has shown, this is not as straightforward as it may appear (Thuraisingham 2018).

For example, when a transformative decision was an international acquisition, it was observed that international growth was a strategic option raised by management and debated with a board over a considerable period. Formal consideration of an internationalisation strategy was then put on the agenda of the annual off-site strategy meeting. As Director I reported:

> Generally, with these big investment decisions, there is a bucket of potential places we may go, grow and develop and they would have been shaken out during the strategy day, and so if it is on the list to be developed then it is to be looked at, so there is not really anyone around the table that starts with the view that we should not do this.

The data collected in the said study reflected four stages in the strategy-shaping process, taking (on average) up to 12 months, given the size of some acquisitions. The NEDs did not appear to engage in the strategy-shaping process from a neutral position—that is, without any prehistory. This prehistory was twofold. First, NEDs had experience of this particular 'board group at work', which included knowledge of discursive practices and the 'political positions' of their peers in the group—that is, they all had a mutual understanding (as distinct from a shared understanding) of the decision logic that each of their peers was likely to adopt and use in influence attempts. Second, their different business and functional experiences could result in different interpretations of internationalisation ambitions and transaction risks. Such differences could produce 'incompatible discourses', which, in some cases, resulted in unresolvable differences. For example, the 'we need to be in Asia' discourse was not shared by all NEDs on one board because some NEDs believed that domestic growth could be better leveraged than it was at the time. Different NED attitudes, viewpoints and narratives about acquisition ambition and plans beyond the domestic market were therefore likely to exist on a given board.

It was difficult to determine the exact starting point of the decision stories covered by this study. NEDs reported that major transformative decisions often do not just become more formalised discussion points at off-site strategy meetings, but germinate in the thinking of management through informal conversations CEOs may have with a chair and other directors. These initial conversations sometimes occurred outside formal board meetings during which management sought to test board thinking on a range of growth options. Some directors saw this as 'lobbying to secure the numbers'. When they were convinced that the board would support growth options, management assumed they had agreement (tacit or otherwise) to bring an offshore investment proposal to the board. The following four decision stages were found in all 15 decision cases studied (Thuraisingham 2018).

Stage 1: judging strategic fit

The first stage was a director taking a personal position on whether a proposal could create value and the extent to which it was judged to fit the formally stated growth strategy of their company. In the case of the latter, this was not always a straightforward process. While some NEDs indicated that the quality of debate at the off-site strategy meeting was a major contribution to the quality of proposals received, others took a less sequential view. They pointed to the reality that a strategy session held 12 months prior may have little bearing on a market that had turned or been disrupted by forces impossible to predict at the time. They recognised that a proposal may, at times, emerge opportunistically or that changing market dynamics could make a proposed acquisition more interesting at one point in time rather than another.

As noted, in all 15 decision cases, the opportunity to create value was judged by the directors on two levels: their perception of the strategic logic of a proposal (i.e., 'how does this deliver value') and their perception of its strategic coherence with the broader growth strategy of a company (i.e., 'how does this fit'). The latter question related to alignment with the outcomes of the annual strategy retreat that all NEDs attended. All except one of the 15 boards represented by the NEDs had a regular annual strategy day during which they had a broad discussion and agreement about the overall strategic direction of a company. NEDs reported a range of experiences of annual strategy days. Some NEDs narrated their experience of a heavily backgrounded day packed with presentation after presentation from divisional managing directors with partly or fully formed strategies and business plans. Hence, there was little time for unstructured discussion, debate or contention about options facing a company. Other NEDs described a much improved format for a strategy retreat that had evolved over time, which provided NEDs with an opportunity for robust debate and an emergent sense of the strategic options and choices facing a company.

Some boards invested time beforehand, discussing the specific conditions under which a transaction or acquisition would be considered (some NEDs referred to this as 'go-no-go' hurdles). However, in a majority of cases, this was not done until a transaction actually emerged and discussions were at a mature enough stage for management to feel comfortable in bringing a transaction to a board for discussion. Even then, formal decision 'gates' or 'go-no-go' criteria were not used universally to evaluate transactions. As Director B reported:

'nothing formal ... [I]t would generally be a conversation about the country (of the target entity) being too heavily regulated or the costs of the acquisition being three or four times book or other reasons'.

Stage 2: judging the opportunity to shape strategy

The second stage was the extent to which a director felt there was 'room' to shape a decision. This was a subjective call that each director made, often independently, as it was generally contingent upon their evaluation of CEO openness to involve directors in a material way in shaping a proposal. In the case of a small number of directors, they perceived a proposal to be so well formed and developed that there was little opportunity for the participating NED to be involved. Director A narrated his experience of making three attempts before a CEO understood that a board was 'not just a rubber stamp'. The director described his experience of the CEO's unwillingness to engage with a board on matters of strategy as a tactic by the CEO to control the balance of power between the CEO and the board. This disengagement evidenced in this author's study was consistent with research on 'social distancing' relating to the use of information asymmetry as a means of control by corporate elites (Westphal & Khanna 2003). Other directors also described their experience of the political behaviour of CEOs. This included subtle co-option by inquiring from one director (ahead of a board presentation) their opinion of another director's attitude to an already well-formed idea and, therefore, secure an agreeable board when a proposal was finally tabled. For example, Director H reported:

> While chatting, they may say 'what do you think John might think of this' or 'how do you think Sue will react on this point' ... this way they know how to tackle John ... This kind of socialising of the proposal beforehand is not helpful to having a really robust debate as a group. So, you have to be engaged with management but alert and indifferent at the same time.

This kind of political behaviour was regarded as neither constructive nor conducive to creating intra-boardroom trust nor helpful to a debate. It is further explored in Chapter 3.

However, not all ideas brought to a board were well formed beforehand. In the case of Director L, one proposal was so poorly developed and unformed that it created some confusion among NEDs about what the board was being asked to agree on and what the preferred strategic option was. Therefore, there is a delicate balance to be struck, which has to be managed by the chair. The chair's skills are examined in detail in Chapter 5.

Another factor influencing the 'opportunity to shape' was an NED's perception, either caused by a CEO's lack of awareness or disinterest in the skills available on a board, that their potential to contribute to a proposed strategy was ignored. The CEO's interest in, and recognition of, NED skills and their potential contribution was, from the point of view of the participating NED, based on their observations of the steps the CEO took to proactively and constructively engage with their expertise.

In summary, both Stages 1 and 2 were likely to generate 'role tensions'. That is, at these two stages, NED contribution was shaped by their perceptions of the role of a director and board vis-a-vis management. Further, NED narratives appeared to reflect a strong element of intuition in judging how 'made up' the mind of a CEO was, which, in turn, influenced the perceived strategy-shaping opportunity. The data from this study revealed both affective and dispositional explanations for the responses of NEDs when navigating these tensions, which are more fully described in Chapter 4.

Stage 3: participating in decision deliberations

The third stage involved sufficient deliberation for an NED to feel comfortable with a proposal. In all cases, in making a decision at a personal level, the NED was motivated by reaching a decision with which they felt they could live. Their judgement on this point was influenced by two motivations. First, the contribution a potential transaction would make, either to shareholder value or to strengthening a company's strategic options (described in Stage 1), was considered. Some NEDs described an internalised norm they applied to proposals or ideas to deal with the first of these motivations. As Director H reported:

> There are lots of good ideas ... no shortage of those. But the only ideas that are good for this company are those that management is fired up to achieve and that the board is really comfortable with the idea. Ideas that don't meet those two tests are worthless for this company. I know this is a bold statement ... but if the management has a rollicking good idea but the board is not keen on it, and vice versa, then don't do it.

The second motivation was the effect any decision could have on their relationship with other NEDs and management. This is consistent with research on group dynamics (Kets De Vries 1991, 2001; Turner 1987, 2005) and board process studies (Forbes & Milliken 1999; Minichilli et al. 2012; Pye 2002; Pye & Pettigrew 2005; Roberts 1991). Compounding this complex social reality were practical concerns board members had about a CEO's lack of confidence to successfully execute a strategy. As Director N reported:

> It was now no longer just our concerns with the strategy but in our lack of confidence in the CEO and his ability to deliver what he had promised to the board. He was pilloried every time he presented regular updates to the board. As things deteriorated, every meeting became more fractious, and he became increasingly more aggressive with the board, and he did not like some of the things the board was saying. We started seeing some character traits we had not seen before.

Regarding the effect of the decision on an individual in terms of group dynamics, the transformative decision chosen by an NED for inclusion in the study had the potential of being seen as a very large, discrete and anxiety-provoking event that required active coping mechanisms. As such decisions are generally complex (in that they reflect a web of interlocking choices) and time bound, some NEDs reporting that there was pressure on boards to work efficiently towards final 'go-no-go' decisions. As Director N reported: 'everyone had reservations ... some with deep reservations like me. No one felt confident ... everyone was nervous about it'.

However, as reported by Director B, some anxieties were not shared with boards as a whole:

> One director shared with me their personal anxiety about the way in which the shareholder value rationale, often bandied around by directors, was regrettably cast in a very narrow way ... because some strategic proposals may not have a compelling NPV [net present value] or in fact may not be EPS [earnings per share] accretive for some time yet ... but may still be critical for the company to pursue.

In two of the decision cases, there was a more process-driven board. In these cases, NEDs characterised the board decision culture as being chair-driven more by good time keeping than the quality of thinking or discussion. Moreover, in some cases, the culture revealed a greater reliance on how a board had solved similar problems in the past. NEDs reported that these practices led to less contention. They spoke of the dangers associated with racing to a consensus without fully exposing or exploring spoken or unspoken concerns along the way. In summary, while Stages 1 and 2 were likely to generate 'role tensions', Stage 3 was likely to generate 'task tensions'—that is, tensions associated with an actual decision task itself.

Stage 4: reaching a consensus

The final stage of the decisions related to securing a consensus. In several cases, a decision was not unanimous but NEDs agreed that it was one they were prepared to live with despite their concerns.

In respect of large transformative decisions, it was common for consensus to be built rather than votes taken. NEDs reported that it was very rare that anyone pushed their point of view or requested that their dissent be recorded. Instead, focus was on robust debate to arrive at a consensus. If a small minority was not comfortable with a deal, they could decide to accept it or record their formal dissent; however, some NEDs reported feeling concerned about the effect that formal dissent would have on future board harmony.

Regarding the process of arriving at a consensus, decision-makers were less likely to engage in slow sequential or linear thinking than simultaneously integrating key choices and tactical plans as they proceeded through each stage of a decision-making process. NEDs reported that anxiety was a major component driving a single decision from a complex set of interdependent choices and this underpinned each influence attempt.

Each case resulted in a decision. In fact, there were four possible decision-process outcomes across all 15 decision stories studied:

1   A proposal was accepted without change (not evidenced by this study).
2   A proposal was revised after NED input and shaping.
3   A proposal was rejected.
4   A proposal was rejected in favour of a more attractive option; for example, replacing the outright acquisition of an entity with a proposal in which to buy a material stake in the target entity.

The point at which an NED or board was ready to decide was described as intuitive, thus, suggesting that rational analysis was not the whole story. As Director B observed:

> I think it was a bit intuitive ... there comes a point that more data is [sic] not going to give you more insight. And you have got to jump. And that point comes when you feel you have enough mitigants in place to defray the risks and where you have convinced yourself that the worst of the risks are manageable and the size of the prize is worth having.

In summary, in the four stages described earlier, NEDs confront the three paradoxes inherent in the role of directing, which, in turn, generates role and task tensions that are best understood through the prism of group dynamics. The following section makes the link to the end goal that shareholders and other stakeholders look to the board to deliver—namely, accountability for the corporation's decisions.

Accountability as a goal and a process

Corporate governance is the process by which corporations are made responsive to the rights and wishes of stakeholders (Demb & Neubauer 1992), and accountability is the process by which this is achieved. Roberts, McNulty and Stiles (2005) made an important distinction between accountability and 'creating accountability', using an empirical study of UK directors narrating their experiences. Their study concluded that 'creating accountability' is about bridging the gap between board role expectations and actual board task performance. Until then, board accountability was often discussed as board role expectations, that is, what should be done, by whom and how (Huse 2005). In their inductive study, Roberts McNulty and Stiles (2005) demonstrated that internal context is critical to the process of creating accountability through the study of actual interactions, behaviours, routines and norms (i.e., how accountability is practised). Role expectations, routines and interactions represent an element of the 'social reality' in and around the boardroom that may be difficult to delineate, even for those inside the boardroom. The remainder of this chapter takes a social reality approach to understanding the process of accountability as one that is accomplished through expectations, norms and relationships. In turn, the informal processes of accountability can themselves become sources of accountability and have a self-regulating effect on behaviour (Thuraisingham 2018). In the author's study (Thuraisingham 2018), NEDs who held multiple directorships reported different experiences of the process of accountability on different boards, even for largely similar tasks/decisions. The author refers to this as the process of 'soft governance', as contrasted with 'hard governance' which relates to the more formal sources of accountability that are typically structural and dictated by codes and other formal instruments of a regulatory regime. When the processes of soft governance are not operating as they should, decisions can be compromised because deviant views can be easily controlled and conflict potentially suppressed—an experience that many directors acknowledged. One may conclude, then, that the post-crisis tendencies of regulators to implement formal rules and structural change to achieve more accountability from organisations may be misplaced.

Formal and informal forms of accountability

The term accountability means the anticipation of an 'accounting' in response to others' explicit or implicit expectations. As such, it may be argued that it is contextual and relational and has an effect on a wide range of social judgements and choices (Lerner & Tetlock 1999). There are two sources of accountability—formal and informal. Academic research and business writing tend to focus on the former. Formal sources, or what the author refers to as hard goverance, are typically structural and embedded hierarchically such as is captured in employment contracts, terms and conditions, formally written mandates, performance and reward systems and codes of conduct. Informal sources of accountability, soft governance, are shaped by interpersonal relations between members of the group, recognition of a 'social reality' with trust at its heart. Importantly, this second source of accountability, rooted in dependence and relatedness, cannot be accounted for in traditional accounting or economic terms (Roberts 1991); therefore, it has implications for corporate governance reform.

In the last decade, the focus has moved away from a simple analytical, utility approach to board accountability, acknowledging that accountability between the actors in a social system (such as an organisation) is socially constructed. Accountability is at the root of any social system. Even the most primitive of tribal groups, let alone organisations, requires agreement on a set of expectations and roles guiding the behaviour of members of the group. However, in general, only those expectations that are socially valued and/ or seen as useful (instrumental) become codified in relationships as protocols and routines that shape notions of accountability. Routines are repetitive, recognisable patterns of interdependent actions, carried out by individuals and groups and are central features of human organising and a primary means of goal accomplishment (Brown & Lewis 2011). In the context of a board, routines (i.e., how we do things) habituate as a result of a history of director interactions and practices shaping how accountability is practiced over time.

Some board practices are more salient than others and, depending on the type of decision, can have positive and negative effects on NED behaviour (Thuraisingham 2018). For instance, how accountability is practised in the context of large 'bet the farm' decisions such as transformative acquisitions, may differ from how it is practised in relation to 'business as usual' decisions (Thuraisingham 2018). As Director L explained: 'Investment into new markets is about belief, desire, ambition and passion… not about facts, data or money and therefore demands a different model of governance'. These differences were reflected in how a range of practices, such as closed-door sessions, offline discussions and pre-meeting interactions with executives were actually conducted.

The more nuanced view of accountability described here advances the position that the process of accountability is socially accomplished through expectations, norms, routines and relationships, and has a self-regulating nature. The latter results from interactions and discussions in which trust is experienced, learned and reinforced between social actors (Roberts 2001). However, despite accountability being so central to how an organisation (as a social system) works, there has been surprisingly little research into understanding the processes of accountability and trust-based forms of 'soft governance' in the board context. The next section considers the relationship between accountability and power in a board context.

Board accountability, power and influence

In corporate governance theory, board accountability is often described in structural and hierarchical terms that are influenced by agency prescribed definitions of shareholder rights and claims. Accountability in this context is often viewed as a disciplinary mechanism of markets and powerful investor groups (Roberts 2001). To exercise vigilance over the CEO, the board, as the non-executive arm, needs power. Therefore, agency theory can be seen as a theory about power and control—in particular, how the shareholders (the principals) exercise power and control over the management of the company via the board (their agents), and board directors discharge their accountabilities acting for the principals. At its core, it assumes that management—as either 'shirkers of responsibility' or 'opportunistic' in exercising overreach—is to be constrained, reflecting a utilitarian approach to relationships that closely resembles McGregor's classic Theory X notion of the world.

The self-interested nature of human beings advanced by some agency theorists is somewhat overstated. In contrast to this, stewardship theory promotes the view that trust and control are not mutually exclusive. In line with this coexistence of trust and control, researchers have promoted a 'collaborative model of the board', arguing that boards can provide advice and counsel while at the same time engaging in control (Westphal 1999). How roles and accountabilities work in reality, how contributions are made and how the balance of power shapes these contributions is complex (Roberts, McNulty & Stiles 2005; Thuraisingham 2018). Recent research has shown that, while in theory, boards can provide advice and counsel at the same time as engaging in control, the reality may be harder to achieve, as directors possess a variety of relational and dispositional tendencies that make them more disposed one way or another (Thuraisingham 2018). This diversity of dispositions and their social effects is described more fully in Chapter 4.

The distinctive social realities that exist on different boards is not a new research revelation, nor will it be novel to NEDs who serve on multiple boards. NEDs' power is limited in three ways: position (by virtue of the non-executive nature of the role), expertise (by virtue of limited direct access to the specialist skills that executives have) and information (they are always working with less information than executive management). Given this limited power, exercising accountability (on behalf of the shareholders they represent) is achieved through relationship power, which is exercised behaviourally through skilful personal influence, either individually or collectively. It operates through processes and routines, and shaped norms or standards that produce an implicit understanding of the social order of things. This kind of power has an unwritten value attached to convergent social practices, routines and standards within the group—that is, the informal sources of accountability. Conformity is elicited through observation, evaluation and sanctions depending on how strongly people in the group associate with the shared expectations (Frink & Klimoski 2004; Roberts 2001; Thuraisingham 2018). Those in the group who are not regarded as meeting minimum, average or optimum standards feel guilt or shame, at a subconscious level, for not conforming and will adjust or correct behaviour to fit in with group norms (Forbes & Milliken 1999; Roberts 2001). Routines shape the character of a board; some boards are highly formal and procedural in their norms and routines around debate, while others are more engaged, actively challenging each other and encouraging contention of ideas and proposals (Thuraisingham 2018). This, then, becomes the norm for how that particular board operates and individual director behaviour is judged according to this group norm. As well as acting as a source of accountability, these routines also act as a standard against which individual NEDs assess how they are doing (Thuraisingham 2018). Through a history of NED interpersonal interactions, NEDs continually reassess their value to, and their place in the group and adapt their behaviour accordingly.

That is to say how I construe my identity in this board group influences my behaviours and actions, which contributes to the collective routines of a board, which, in turn, shapes what the board thinks is expected of them. Seen in this way, the process of accountability as a trust-based self-regulating process is a consequence of how self/group identity shapes behaviour, which generates routines that describe how things are done:

- Who I/we am/are (director construal) drives ...
- What I/we do (director behaviour) drives ...

- How I/we work (board routines) drives …
- What is expected of me/us (board accountability).

In conclusion

Since all strategies are cognitively complex, strategy proposals brought to the board are generally debatable and differences of views are inevitable. The role of director can be complex and is characterised by role and task tensions that have to be navigated. The practices that directors adopt over time to deal with this role and task complexity become routines, norms and conventions, which contributes to the social reality that is explored in the remaining chapters of Part 1.

As noted in this chapter, the role that boards play in shaping strategy is complex and involves testing ideas, questioning assumptions, evaluating (strategic) logic, raising concerns, weighing risks and offering encouragement. Each line of questioning posed by NEDs in this process effectively shapes a strategic outcome. Therefore, the process of shaping a strategic proposal and providing the required oversight is largely determined by NED behaviour. Despite this, a behavioural approach to the role of the board in terms of strategy has seldom been taken, a situation that this author has tried to rectify. The author set out to study director behaviour through the recollections of directors faced with large transformative decisions. Her study of the strategy-shaping process revealed not only evidence of variation in strategy-shaping behaviours of individual directors, but also factors that enabled and inhibited such behaviours (Thuraisingham 2018).

This chapter cautions the reader to consider both the formal and informal processes of accountability, essential to addressing both hard and soft governance, the latter holding the key to decision practices, norms and routines embed in each board. This is something that most current board effectiveness reviews fail to recognise. This point is dealt with more fully in Chapter 7. Especially in small elite groups such as boards, members are immersed in a web of expectations, norms and interactions between members with dependence, relatedness and interpersonal trust as key.

As members of a group develop an interactional history, mutual understandings and behavioural norms develop, as do expectations about approach and effectiveness. These understandings resemble a loose 'social contract' characterised by behavioural norms and expectations, which NEDs must negotiate through discourse with the required collective awareness of, and attentiveness to, social cues and application of social competence. Seen through the lens of the psychology of groups, accountability has been shown to be contextual and relational, showing also how the 'social reality' within a given board might affect how NEDs take up their roles and perform their duties, particularly what NEDs choose to say, who listens to who and the advice one chooses to heed. Chapter 2 describes the sources for director influence and how perceptions of relevance and legitimacy matter; and Chapter 3, delves into the invisible incipient forces at play during the strategy-shaping process.

Actionable strategies

Desired impact	Strategies the board may take collectively	Strategies the individual director may take
A robust process for determining strategy	Before a major transformative proposal is tabled, reaching an agreement with management on appropriate rules of engagement relating to the opportunity NEDs have to influence strategy	Openly testing one's internalised norm (with board colleagues) of how value is judged, making explicit one's thinking (before any major strategic proposal emerges)
An objective dispassionate stance on promised value creation	Agreeing the go-no-go parameters well before the pressure of an acquisitive deal and associated emotion is felt	Openly debating how this deal may be perceived as different or similar to a previous one that the director may have encountered on this board or another board so that differences in underlying assumptions and beliefs can be openly and vigorously debated with your peers
Genuine impact on board strategy—direction and content	Agreeing what constitutes room to shape and conveying a shared expectation to management	Using 'closed sessions' or if preferred private discussions with the chair, to raise concerns (supported by examples) if you do not believe your voice is being heard during strategy discussions/debates
Strengthening accountability	As part of the annual board effectiveness review, determining if there is a shared view of board accountability (i.e., what it constitutes and what it entails)	Asking yourself if you fully understand the expectations of your role—both those that have been formally communicated and those that are conveyed in conversations you had on appointment
Identifying informal processes of accountability	Acknowledgement that formal instruments of governance such as mandates, codes and charters (and the role expectations they imply) alone do not strengthen board accountability, and that the informal practices that a board adopts and persists with are also critical to review and should be part of any board review	Spotting and challenging routine behavioural patterns that are not reflected in formal mandates or charters but that may reveal an informal norm that has come to be accepted practice on a board, and questioning its efficacy in strengthening accountability

References

Ahrens, T, Filatotchev, I & Thomsen, S 2011, 'The research frontier in corporate governance', *Journal of Management Governance*, vol. 15, pp. 311–325.

Barney, J 1991, 'Firm resources and sustained competitive advantage', *Journal of Management*, vol. 17, no. 1, pp. 99–120.

Bosch 1991, The 1991 Bosch Report: *Corporate practices and conduct, Information Australia, Melbourne, 1991.*

Brauer, M & Schmidt, S 2008, 'Defining the strategic role of boards and measuring board's effectiveness in strategy implementation', *Corporate Governance*, vol. 8, no. 5, pp. 649–660.

Brown, AD & Lewis, MA 2011, 'Identities, disciplines & routines', *Organization Studies*, vol. 32, no. 7, pp. 871–895.

Daily, C, Dalton, D & Cannella, A 2003, 'Corporate governance: decades of dialogue and data', *Academy of Management Review*, vol. 28, no. 3, pp. 371–382.

Demb, A & Neubauer, FF 1992, 'The corporate board: confronting the paradoxes', *Long Range Planning*, vol. 25, no. 3, pp. 9–20.

Donaldson, T & Preston, LE 1995, 'The stakeholder theory of the corporation: concepts, evidence, and implications', *The Academy of Management Review*, vol. 20, no. 1, pp. 65–91.

Fama, EF 1980, 'Agency problems and the theory of the firm', *Journal of Political Economy*, vol. 88, no. 2, pp. 288–307.

Fama, EF & Jensen, MC 1983, 'Separation of ownership and control', *Journal of Law and Economics*, vol. 26, no. 2, pp. 301–325.

Filatotchev, I, Jackson, G & Nakajima, C 2013, 'Corporate governance and national institutions: a review and emerging research agenda', *Asia Pacific Journal of Management*, vol. 30, pp. 965–986.

Forbes, DP & Milliken, FJ 1999, 'Cognition and corporate governance: understanding boards of directors as strategic decision-making groups', *The Academy of Management Review*, vol. 24, no. 3, pp. 489–505.

Frink, D & Klimoski, R 2004, 'Advancing accountability theory and practice: introduction to the Human Resource Management Review special edition', *Human Resource Management Review*, vol. 14, pp. 1–17.

Gulati, R & Westphal, JD 1999, 'Cooperative or controlling? The effects of CEO-board relations and the content of interlocks on the formation of joint ventures', *Administrative Science Quarterly*, vol. 44, no. 3, pp. 473–506.

Hendry, KP, Kiel, GC & Nicholson, G 2010, 'How boards strategise: a strategy as practice view', *Long Range Planning*, vol. 43, pp. 33–56.

Higgs, D 2013, *Review of the role and effectiveness of non-executive directors.* www.dti.gov.uk/cld/non_exec_review.

Hillman, AJ & Dalziel, T 2003, 'Boards of directors and firm performance: integrating agency and resource dependence perspectives', *The Academy of Management Review*, vol. 28, no. 3, pp. 383–396.

Huse, M 2005, 'Accountability and creating accountability: a framework of exploring behavioural perspectives of corporate governance', *British Journal of Management*, vol. 16, pp. 65–79.

Judge, WQ & Zeithaml, CP 1992, 'Institutional and strategic choice perspectives on board involvement in the strategic decision process', *Academy of Management Journal*, vol. 35, pp. 766–794.

Kemp, S 2006, 'In the driver's seat or rubber stamp? The role of the board in providing strategic guidance in Australian boardrooms', *Management Decision*, vol. 44, no. 1, pp. 56–73.

Kets De Vries, M 1991, 'Whatever happened to the philosopher-king? The leader's addiction to power', *Journal of Management Studies*, vol. 28, no 4, pp. 339–351.

Kets De Vries, M 2001, *The hedgehog effect: the secret of building high performance teams*, John Wiley & Sons Ltd, West Sussex.

Lerner, JS & Tetlock, PE 1999, 'Accounting for the effects of accountability', *Psychological Bulletin*, vol. 125, no. 2, pp. 255–275.

Mace, BJ 1991, 'Full insurance in the presence of aggregate uncertainty', *Journal of Political Economy*, vol. 99, no. 5, pp. 928–956.

McKinsey & Company 2018, *Global Survey Results*. https://www.mckinsey.com/business-functions/strategy-and-corporate-finance/our-insights/a-time-for-boards-to-act.

McNulty, T, Florackis, C & Ormrod, P 2013, 'Boards of directors and financial risk during the credit crisis', *Corporate Governance: An International Review*, vol. 21, no. 1, pp. 58–78.

McNulty, T & Pettigrew, A 1999, 'Strategists on the board', *Organisational Studies*, vol. 20, no. 1, pp. 47–74.

McNulty, T, Pettigrew, A, Jobome, G & Morris, C 2011, 'The role, power and influence of company chairs', *Journal of Management and Governance*, vol. 15, pp. 91–121.

McNulty, T, Zattoni, A & Douglas, T 2013, 'Developing corporate governance research through qualitative methods: a review of previous studies', *Corporate Governance: An International Review*, vol. 21, no. 2, pp. 183–198.

Maitlis, S & Lawrence, T 2003, 'Orchestral manoeuvres in the dark: understanding failure in organisational strategizing', *Journal of Management Studies*, vol. 40, no. 1, pp. 109–139.

Minichilli, A, Zattoni, A, Nielsen, S & Huse, M 2012, 'Board task performance: an exploration of micro- and macro-level determinants of board effectiveness', *Journal of Organisational Behavior*, vol. 33, pp. 1913–215.

Nicholson, G & Newton, C 2010, 'The role of the board of directors: perceptions of managerial elites', *Journal of Management and Organization*, vol. 15, pp. 204–218.

Pearce, JA & Zahra, SA 1992, 'Board composition from a strategic contingency perspective', *Journal of Management Studies*, vol. 29, no. 4, pp. 411–438.

Pettigrew, A 1992, 'On studying managerial elites', *Strategic Management Journal*, vol. 13, pp. 163–182.

Pettigrew, A 2001, 'Andrew Pettigrew on executives and strategy: an interview with Kenneth Starkey', *European Management Journal*, vol. 20, no. 1, pp. 20–34.

Pettigrew, A & McNulty, T 1995b, 'Sources and uses of power in the boardroom', *European Journal of Work and Organizational Psychology*, vol. 7, no. 2, pp. 197–214.

Pfeffer, J & Salancik, GR 1978, *The external control of organizations: a resource dependence perspective*, Harper & Row, New York.

Pick, K 2007, 'Around the boardroom table: interactional aspects of governance', PhD thesis, Harvard University, Cambridge, MA.

Pye, A 2002, 'Corporate directing: governing, strategising and leading in action', *Corporate Directing*, vol. 10, no. 3, pp. 153–162.

Pye, A & Pettigrew, A 2005, 'Studying board context, process and dynamics: some challenges for the future', *British Journal of Management*, vol. 16, pp. 27–38.

Rindova, VP 1999, 'What corporate boards have to do with strategy: a cognitive perspective', *Journal of Management Studies*, vol. 36, no. 7, pp. 953–975.

Roberts, J 1991, 'The possibilities of accountabilities', *Accounting, Organizations and Society*, vol. 16, no. 4, pp. 355–368.

Roberts, J 2001, 'Trust and control in Anglo-American systems of corporate governance: the individualizing and socialising effects of processes of accountability', *Human Relations*, vol. 54, no. 12, pp. 1547–1572.

Roberts, R, McNulty, T & Stiles, S 2005, 'Beyond agency conceptions of the work of the non-executive director: creating accountability in the boardroom', *British Journal of Management*, vol. 16, pp. 5–26.

Ruigrok, W, Peck, SI & Keller, H 2006, 'Board characteristics and involvement in strategic decision making: evidence from Swiss companies', *Journal of Management Studies*, vol. 43, no. 5, pp. 1201–1226.

Samra-Fredericks, D 2003, 'Strategising as lived experience and strategies' everyday efforts to shape strategic direction', *Journal of Management Studies*, vol. 40, no.1, pp. 141–174.

Sternberg, RJ 1997, *Thinking styles*, Cambridge University Press, New York.

Stiles, P & Taylor, B 2001, *Boards at work: how directors view their roles and accountabilities*, Oxford University Press, Oxford.

Thuraisingham, SM 2018, 'Exploring the social factors that influence the decision making behaviours of non-executive directors in Australian public companies', PhD thesis, RMIT University, Melbourne.

Turner, JC 1987, 'A self-categorization theory', in JC Turner, MA Hogg, PJ Oakes, SD, Reicher & MS Wetherell (eds), *Rediscovering the social group: a self-categorization theory*, Blackwell, Oxford, pp. 42–67.

Turner, JC 2005, 'Explaining the nature of power: a three-process theory', *European Journal of Social Psychology*, vol. 35, pp. 1–22.

Westphal, JD 1999, 'Collaboration in the boardroom: behavioural and performance consequences of CEO-board social ties', *Academy of Management Journal*, vol. 42, no. 1, pp. 7–24.

Westphal, J & Khanna, P 2003, 'Keeping directors in line: social distancing as a social mechanics in the corporate elite', *Administrative Science Quarterly*, vol. 48, no. 3, pp. 361–398.

Zahra, SA & Pearce, JA 1989, 'Boards of directors and corporate financial performance: a review and integrative model', *Journal of Management*, vol. 15, pp. 291–334.

Zattoni, A & Van Ees, H 2012, 'How to contribute to the development of a global understanding of corporate governance? Reflections from submitted and published articles in CGIR', *Corporate Governance: An International Review*, vol. 20, pp. 106–118.

2 Board capital

The source of director influence, perceived relevance and legitimacy to influence

This chapter in summary

The identity of a director is bound up in their experience and career history, and shapes how they and their peers perceive the unique contribution they make in influencing the decision-making process.

This chapter introduces the reader to the notion of 'board capital', which describes what the director brings to the board in terms of influence within the group. Rather than simply defining a director's career experience and implied skill as a proxy for the value they bring to the board, the notion of board capital provides a more holistic approach to capturing the director's relative value, both cognitively and ideologically. In doing so, it shows how board capital (and its perceived relevance) acts as an 'internalised guide' to how a director responds to the influence attempts of other NEDs, potentially with material consequences on decision outcomes.

This understanding of board capital also provides a means for ensuring that board composition is fit for purpose and board renewal efforts are well targeted and future focussed. It shows that where and how board capital is acquired matters, posing the bigger question of the gene pools from which experienced directors are typically hired. However, the chapter cautions that board capital may be an imprecise proxy for influence, as the source of real influence is not the possession of board capital but how directors choose to use the board capital they possess it. The choice individuals make to utilise (or not utilise) the board capital they possess is largely dependent on their self-construal of their 'place' in the group (the hidden hierarchy that results is exposed and its effects described in Chapter 3).

This chapter concludes with a 'letter to the nominations committee', which contains advice offered to nominations committee members typically entrusted with the hiring of directors, board development and plans to renew and refresh board composition. It offers suggestions for how selection decisions might take into account the life cycle of the company, its strategic opportunities and challenges to deliver a 'fit for future' board.

The task of a director is largely cognitive in nature: to provide advice and counsel to executives. Implicit in the experience that each director brings are cognitive differences potentially resulting in multiple perspectives, divergent viewpoints and different world views. For instance, in contemplating acquisitions in new markets, there is significant complexity and uncertainty. Therefore, conflicting views are likely to emerge between the management team and NEDs. This is particularly so when management fails to fully acknowledge, recognise and actively utilise the depth and breadth of knowledge, expertise and networks that NEDs cumulatively bring to the table. The NEDs interviewed as part of the author's doctoral research, recounted conflicting perspectives and differences among their board peers—a consequence of cognitive or ideological differences within the board group. In this chapter, power is defined as the capacity to modify outcomes or the thinking and actions of others. A distinction is made between power and influence, influence being exercised when power is used. For instance, some may possess the capacity to influence through occupying a formal position in a hierarchy (structural power) or through the possession of expertise as in the case of directors (expert power), or through a position within a social network that accords a particular status to the individual (social power) but may choose not to use it.

Origins of and differentials in power between NEDs

> To strengthen the oversight function, boards need to have a process for ensuring optimal value is derived from the experience [or] skills that each director brings.
>
> (Director B)

To better understand the cognitive and ideological diversity that NEDs bring to the task of governing, this section asks: What are the origins and differences in an NED's power to influence? As noted in Chapter 1, which explored the role of NEDs, NEDs are not responsible for the execution of strategy and their contribution in and around a boardroom is almost entirely cognitive. Therefore, the 'cognitive history' (reflected in Figure 2.1) that NEDs bring as input to a decision-making process is relevant. The source of power lies in the NED's cognitive history, and it is an important part of their unique identity. Further, it has been shown that the extent to which similarities exist in cognitive history may indicate how much connection and learning occurs on a given board (Thuraisingham 2018).

Rindova's (1999) and Johnson, Schnatterly and Hill's (2013) elaboration of cognitive variety within a group offers a useful means to categorise and describe the cognitive history of individual NEDs. The cognitive history of directors varies in two ways. The first is the requisite variety derived from prior career experience and business reputations accumulated from that experience, for which the term 'human capital' has been applied (Johnson, Schnatterly & Hill 2013). The second, an external variety (known as 'social capital'), is derived from an NED's connections and corporate networks, such as multiple directorships (Johnson, Schnatterly & Hill 2013). This combination of

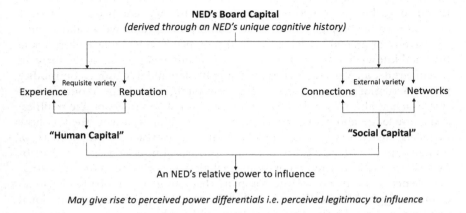

Figure 2.1 Cognitive history as a source of an NED power and capacity to influence.
Source: Thuraisingham (2018).

human and social capital represents an NED's relative capacity to influence others. The relationships between cognitive history and relative power of the NEDs are shown in Figure 2.1.

Both human and social capital combine to form the NED's unique identity, which, in turn, defines their source of power and influence relative to others of their peers. This in essence determines the extent of power differentials on a given board.

Cognitive diversity

Requisite variety: NED human capital

Differences in how members of top management teams (TMTs) perceive, process and respond to tasks are often attributed to diversity of career experience and knowledge networks (Prahalad & Bettis 1995; Ruigrok, Peck & Keller 2006). At the same time, research shows that the functional tracks of management, such as finance, law and marketing, can narrow cognitive horizons and impede strategic adaptation (Geletkanycz & Black 2001). In other words, prolonged experience in key functional domains fosters greater commitment to the existing strategic frameworks and a narrowing of strategic mindsets. Conversely, functional diversity results in breaking free of cognitive attachments to the status quo. Studies have shown that directors who have honed their experience in one industry can come armed with 'industry recipes' that do not work in other industries, and that this potentially becomes a thinking trap (Thuraisingham 2018). Therefore, a reliance on functional or industry specialisation carries warnings for boards that continue to rely on narrow notions of the skill-based board.

The requisite variety in cognitive history or human capital of NEDs was found to go beyond functional and industry history, comprising a broader combination of complex and alternative interpretive frameworks and 'cognitive givens' or mental models gained through prior career experiences. These included knowledge or assumptions about future events (such as the forward revenue trajectory of a target business, supply–demand dynamics, commodity price fluctuations and changes in cost of capital), knowledge about alternatives (such as alternative deal structures or alternative targets or geographies) and knowledge about the consequences of those alternatives (such as how investors, analysts, regulators or competitors may react). This diversity of human capital that NEDs brought into a boardroom (as a function of prior experience and associated reputations) included one or more of the following: experience as a CEO of a large company that had grown globally or had an acquisitive profile, specialisation in M&A economics, advisory or functional experience at top levels of advisory firms and public companies, an international career (either working in or running an international business), leading a functional team dispersed across multiple locations, or direct experience in internationalising a business or company across multiple jurisdictions. These differences in NED human capital and how they were perceived were significant because, as shown by the theories of social identification and self-categorisation discussed in Chapters 3 and 4, they formed the basis of how strongly NEDs identified with each other. How strongly directors identified with each other potentially determines the degree of agreement or disagreement there was on a given board.

Hence, NEDs' level of social identification and self-categorisation determined the relative value they placed on contributions of others and, in turn, the extent of the potential of others to influence. For example, NEDs participating in the author's study tended to place a higher value on their own type of career experiences (Thuraisingham 2018). In particular, Directors N and M, who had previously held CEO roles, remarked on the rise of professional directors who 'had not run a business before'. They believed a lack of experience could reduce the value of an NED's contribution, including the ability to challenge assumptions, alternatives or consequences relating to an acquisition proposal. Since Directors N and M had served as CEOs, it was not surprising that they would value the experience of running a business ahead of, for example, functional expertise in an accounting or legal firm. As Director N observed:

> I think operators who have spent their life battling in the trenches sometimes have a different perspective of how easy it is to drive change or turn around a company … as opposed to someone from the public sector or from an accounting firm where some of those views [put forward by management] may seem logical … In this case [referring to the acquisition under consideration], I could hear all the theory, but it smells like this is too tough.

Director M held a similar view:

> The legal person has had commercial experience but always from a legal point of view. This is valuable, but you always have your legal glasses on. But someone who has been a CEO of a business has had to deal with issues without a functional filter and that changes the conversation … this is the challenge of getting the board composition right.

However, other NEDs (mostly those who had not previously held CEO roles) disagreed. They observed that, when an NED had previous experience as a CEO, this challenged the transition to an NED role because of a 'healthy measure of arrogance' that comes with 'let me show you how'. They also recalled that, when things do not go well, there is a propensity for ex-CEOs to jump into the details and try to run a company.

These differing perspectives reinforce the conclusion that NEDs tend to place a higher value on their own career experiences and, therefore, value the contribution of those who were 'like them'. It suggests that, at a subconscious level, NEDs were continually assessing how the human capital of their peers was like their own. In effect, this laid the foundation for how susceptible each NED was to the influence attempts of those most like them and how, in turn, they exercised their capacity to assert their influence during a strategy-shaping process. The findings of the author's study suggests that power, as the capacity to influence, worked through the processes of social identification (i.e., group membership can itself become a source of power). The effects of group identification are discussed further in Chapter 3.

External variety: NED social capital

In addition to similarities or differences in NED experiences, the diverse cognitive communities from which NEDs were drawn were also relevant to an individual NED's capacity to influence. As Director I explained:

> During the eighteen-month period of this deal here, my directorship with another company was maturing … so I was learning some interesting things from that board I was on, and they [the directors on this board] were looking to me as one of the people with expertise … so there was quite a bit of questioning of me outside the meetings about what was happening over there and how it was all going.

The external variety or 'embeddedness' of participating NEDs comprised their current and relevant connections and networks gained by association with and membership of diverse 'cognitive communities'. Embeddedness is a social science construct employed in a board context by Pettigrew (2001) to account for the dependence of a social phenomenon in the environment in which it occurs—that is, social action cannot be understood when dissociated from the social world in which it is embedded. Memberships in cognitive communities exposed NEDs to industry 'macro-cognitions' not acquired by career experience. These professional connections (which often included multiple directorships in completely different sectors) exposed NEDs to inter-industry perspectives, diverse business models, 'industry outsider' perspectives and diverse approaches to disruption in those sectors. Exposure to sectors outside one's own is key especially when the sector is facing disruption. If a company is going to be disrupted it is likely to come from outside the sector and some sectors are further up the curve on disruption. In this context, social capital becomes critical to how effectively a director can contribute to strategy discussions and debates.

Social capital also constituted an array of networks with corporate and proxy advisors, investor groups, consultants and other 'outsider' groups, and, therefore, provided access to relevant, up-to-date knowledge, connections and information. In effect, the strength of an NED's external networks provided them with legitimacy in the eyes of their peers, which gave them greater power to influence.

The author's study found that NEDs' connections within the broader director community served four purposes: securing board appointments, access to knowledge that allowed them to cross-calibrate information from management, door opening for management and access to resources for a company.

In recounting how they joined a board, most participating NEDs reported that, although an appointment process was formalised through a search firm, initial contact was established through their personal networks. Hence, it may be inferred that an NED's embeddedness in networks and connections was significant in securing other board roles. As Directors L and K explained:

> I was invited to join by the chairman ... to consider joining in and then went through the process of interviews ... [E]essentially, I was known to the CEO and chair over a number of many years of interaction ... the CEO for about 25 years as a peer and [in] various business relationships.
>
> (Director L)

> The chair and I were on the board of Company X [names the company] together ... we had enjoyed ... [and] had a good rapport there. So, when I came back [to Australia], he contacted me and said come in for an interview ... and that's how I came to be on this board.
>
> (Director K)

Previous research suggests that personal ties and NED embeddedness may result in strong identification with a group, which may be socialised into shared notions of accountability and normative expectations of how one behaves in a group (Westphal 1999). This raises questions about how the effects of social ties and past associations may generate an informal set of expectations, even if operating at a subconscious level, compared to no prior personal relationship. It also raises questions about the extent to which a degree of agreeableness may emerge during discourse through the norms of reciprocity that are created and, therefore, inhibit necessary boardroom contention (Thuraisingham 2018; Westphal & Zajac 1997). Additionally, past personal associations and ties may lead to cognitive and behavioural convergence at a board level because of the narrowness of the cognitive pools from which NEDs are selected (Geletkanycz & Black 2001; Thuraisingham 2018). These issues are revisited in Chapter 3.

Second, an NED's embeddedness, characterised by inter-organisational and inter-sectoral links, facilitated information flow and knowledge exchange between directors and boards. In turn, this allowed NEDs to calibrate and verify market information provided by management with peers sitting on other boards, and by tapping into different networks of advisors used by other boards. Research on industry macro-cognitions suggests that executives from outside a specific industry are more likely to challenge 'industry recipes' (Rindova 1999; Spender 1989; Thuraisingham 2018). Moreover, provided it was accompanied by pattern recognition skills, the value of an 'outsider' view was supported by Director B, who held four ASX directorships:

> I have particular and strong views about this. Sector should not matter as much it is how one thinks about the business that matters more. So, for example, with W and X [refers to two of his current directorships], despite being in very different sectors, are both large branch-based distributed businesses and highly technology driven … The same with Y and Z [refers to two of his other current directorships] … although they are both in different sectors, the issues relating to physical risk and the impact of environment issues are very similar … My cross-sector experience is useful because I am able to extrapolate. Valuable lessons can be taken from one sector into another. But it requires you to step back from the sector and consider what are the issues by thinking laterally and transformatively … [using] pattern recognition skills.

Finally, this author's study found that the extent of an NED's social capital served the purpose of both door opening for management and access to relevant resources when a company was acquisitive. As Directors C and M observed:

> Someone has information that has subsequently come to the attention of the NED and may be relevant … it happens in big M&A scenarios

because there are always people wanting to talk to you ... [Y]ou are be-
sieged from everywhere.

(Director C)

We [referring to himself and one other NED on a risk committee] had
connections with people in regulatory agencies, government and so
on ... [W]e were able to talk to them and open the door to having a
discussion with management about this issue ... Sometimes it is difficult
[for management] to make a cold-call on something a bit out of the box
[referring to a unique restructuring of assets that had no prior precedence
and would have needed regulatory approval].

(Director M)

In summary, a director's cognitive history comprised both human and social capital. However, before considering the effects of variations in NED
cognitive history, it is useful to consider how each NED judged (relative to
their own cognitive history) who was most like them, which, as we will see
in Chapter 3, determined who they paid the most attention to. There were
three ways in which these 'like me'/'not like me' judgements were made: past
associations and personal ties, common cognitive histories and shared values,
and implicit beliefs. These are described in the following.

Perceived legitimacy of one's cognitive history

This section describes the judgements each NED made about who was most
like them and the legitimacy they attributed to that cognitive history. This
phenomenon has been well investigated in social psychology and describes
how an NED's sense of shared identity with the group shapes how they interact and participate in the process of decision-making. Social identity theory
(SIT) and social categorisation theory (SCT) show how groups can fundamentally change and transform an individual's psychology and behaviour
(Turner 1982; Turner & Reynolds 2012). SIT describes how group membership assists people to define themselves and, therefore, provides the salience
of the social context in which an NED must perform their duties. SIT and
SCT describe two group identity-related processes that contribute to the
strength of group identification: first, through a process of 'like me' and
'not like me' self-categorisation; second, through a subjective validation of
one's own and others' legitimacy to mount influence attempts. An influence
attempt is defined here as a specific intervention initiated by one or more
NEDs designed to make an effective contribution to the direction and nature
of a debate about a decision. This section proceeds by describing the themes
that emerged from the author's study from each of these two identity-related
processes (Thuraisingham 2018). Three themes emerged from the subjective
judgements NEDs made about who they most associated or affiliated with in
a group. These related to past associations and personal ties, common cognitive histories, and shared values and implicit beliefs.

Past associations and personal ties

The power of past associations and ties in regulating social behaviour has been observed by Pick (2007). Personal ties are important becuase they create an informal set of expectations and obligations that can influence behaviours. Although NEDs considered personal ties to have precipitated their board membership by lending legitimacy to their appointments, the NEDs in this author's study did not claim pre-existing ties were more than an introduction to a board. However, despite this, some statements suggested that NEDs looked on these relationships positively, reflecting the value they placed on continuing rapport. Further, NEDs were generally more open to interacting and exchanging viewpoints with these peers (who they knew well) outside formal board meetings. As Directors G, J and K observed:

> The CEO of the investment bank that had been involved in advising on the recapitalisation of the business approached me (I had known him previously). I also knew the incoming CEO whom I thought was a good guy ... competent.
>
> (Director G)

> I was approached by the chairman of the board to see if I would be interested in speaking to him and to the CEO about becoming a director ... I knew some of the other directors as part of my professional personal network. Obviously, I don't know how this actually came about as I was not there, and there is a nominations committee meeting ... but they were looking for skills I had, and I was known to other board directors.
>
> (Director J)

> The chair and I were on the board of Co X together ... we had enjoyed ... had a good rapport there.
>
> (Director K)

Common cognitive histories

Director comparisons related to both requisite and external varieties of cognitive history. In the case of the requisite variety (human capital), comparisons were made in relation to experience in terms of role, function, sector or industry. As portrayed in this following quotation, NEDs with different cognitive histories were not always regarded positively. Comparisons were not only used as guides to determine who to pay attention to, but also the reverse. As Director G reported:

> I had assumed they were all CFO [chief financial officer] types ... a cabal ... who thought in a particular way, but in fact, they also had reached the same conclusion as I had. I have my prejudices about CFO types ... [T]hat they are unable to see past the numbers and do not understand strategy.

Director G continued to recount his experience by naming another board of which he had previously been a member. There, his view about 'CFO types' was shared by other directors like him who had previously run businesses.

Shared values and implicit beliefs

Support for shared values and beliefs appeared to be important to some participating NEDs, as it generated a greater sense of 'we' and 'us' collectivism. This was evidenced in some of the stories about decision-making in which NEDs expressed confidence in the contributions of board members, as they perceived them to have shared values.

How threats to implicit beliefs were responded to was identified from the interview transcripts (in the author's study) at both individual and subgroup levels. For example, identification acted as a form of group control and the sanctioning of a member deemed to be 'unlike' the majority (Thuraisingham 2018). These findings confirm other research into boards (Westphal & Bednar 2005; Westphal & Khanna 2003). The author found evidence that new-to-the-board directors and others who sought to exercise influence in debates over decisions were likely to be socially sanctioned (often in private) when perceived to violate in-group values or beliefs. This was evidenced by Director A, who, after her initial board meetings, was sanctioned:

> The chairman was very alpha-dog (he has now moved on). It was very polite … in fact, a board member after the first few board meetings took me aside and said, 'you can be awfully blunt'. They were old-fashioned and very polite, and I had come from an organisation that was hard-headed and where the motto was 'think straight talk straight' … [O]nce he [the chair] pronounced, it was difficult to disagree with anything he raised … he was very much the man in charge … [O]nce he said what he thought, there was very little further discussion.

While board cohesion is important for process effectiveness, it also has the potential to create self-censorship, acting as a 'mind guard' by creating and subtly enforcing social norms that can pressure deviant thinkers, as evidenced in Director A's and Director B's interview transcripts. In at least one decision story recounted by Director O, threats to implicit beliefs and values of two subgroups (one that supported the internationalisation transaction going ahead and another that was strongly against it) resulted in a split board. In a decision story recounted by Director G, the eventual departure of a chair and CEO were the result of their fundamental disagreements. Essentially, the basis of these divided boards were differences in beliefs about the importance of value creation (not just value preservation), notions of risk and the relevance of acquisitive activity. Based on these two case study examples, it may be suggested that shared values and beliefs are not only important for the functioning of a board but also may act as a source of power. Differences on fundamental matters, such as values and beliefs, may result in a loss of confidence and cohesion. Internally posed threats to shared values may also evoke swift action by an in-group (like-minded directors) to close down contention or disagreement, as illustrated by the two cases mentioned earlier. Board factions can emerge as a result, breaking down trust and leaving a board divided, as described by Directors G and O.

Regarding the significance of shared values and implicit beliefs, as was noted earlier in 'Cognitive diversity', there was a clear tendency of NEDs to value their own experience and to attach a higher relative value to the 'cognitive communities' from which they came above that of others. This 'like me' tendency is important, as it may have implications for the attention participating NEDs paid to the perspectives of others or the weight they gave to the contributions of others 'unlike me', even to the extent of discounting those contributions, as observed by some NEDs (Thuraisingham 2018). It follows that cognitive similarities may create 'people like me' groupings and result in tensions when issues of role, ideology, beliefs and values are perceived to be at stake during a decision-making process. These findings provide confirmation of Magee and Smith's (2013) recent work on the social distance theory, which articulates predictions about how power affects social comparison, susceptibility to influence, and emotions.

These themes relating to self-categorisation examined here have important implications for questions about why, when and how NEDs mount influence attempts and how they respond to the influence of others. These implications are discussed in detail in Chapter 3.

As noted in Chapter 1, self-construal matters in how accountability is practised. Therefore the original motivations of why directors joined boards in the first place may hold a clue to this self-construal (Thuraisingham 2018). This final section draws from the evidence from the author's research pertaining to the motivations of NEDs in joining their boards. It reveals rich insights into how NEDs defined their distinctiveness with respect to their peers and provides a glimpse into how individual NEDs construed their distinctiveness and articulated the contributions they made. As will be seen in the remaining chapters of Part 1, this, in turn, shaped how they approached their accountabilities, revealing the social and relational aspects of accountability.

Director motivations: 'why I joined' and how it shapes the process of accountability

Based on the author's study, motivations for joining a board appeared to fall into four categories, although NEDs often cited more than one reason: an opportunity to add value, belong to a successful company, join a board that was respected, and work with great people and culture (Thuraisingham 2018). Critically, it was found that, while some of these motivations may be viewed as adding significant cognitive diversity to a group, in other cases they may contribute to a narrowing of cognitive horizons, which may drive strategic persistence, providing support for hypotheses put forward by other researchers (Sundaramurthy & Lewis 2003; Westphal 1999). Further, the author found that cognitive diversity fostered good debate up to a point; however, a divergence of views could prove unproductive and detrimental to collaboration. This section explicates these four motivational themes and theorises what they say about NEDs' construals of board capital they bring to their boards. As will be shown in Chapters 3 and 4, these construals to some extent influenced the choices NEDs made to mount influence attempts, determined the degree of contention that existed on the board and how accountability was exercised.

Opportunity to add value

For those NEDs who spoke about their excitement at joining a board and the value they could add, a board represented an opportunity to engage in decision-making in a meaningful and unique way. In several cases, NEDs identified the unique expertise they could bring to a board. This included international mergers and acquisitions (M&A) or start-up experience, and was not unexpected, as the decision scenario selected for study was a transformative decision. In situations in which an NED was hired expressly for the unique experience they could add to a board, there was evidence that that experience was being used to challenge board thinking. For example, Director C had previously run a large business in Asia. She had reported that the new board viewed her as uniquely placed to guide their thinking on a major Asian investment:

> It is one of Australia's largest iconic companies. It is very complex and does a whole range of very different things ... and also [sic], it is global. It has operations all over the world ... and had been reasonably successful overseas ... but not as successful in Asia. This was one of the reasons they were attracted to me, and I was attracted to this particular company. They were looking at doing significant expansion in Asia ... they had done a few stop-start attempts. This is where my experience lies in this particular part of Asia.

Directors L and D also reported bringing unique expertise to a board:

> I was a CEO previously of a company and I know what it is like to operate from zero market and zero revenue and go from that to something big ... [W]hen everyone said it could not be done ... but I have lived it ... and not afraid of it and that in a sense is what I bring to this board.
>
> (Director L)

> The role they expect from me is a heavy engineering operational guy running big businesses ... as well as my Asian experience and US experience

for that matter. Most [other directors] had been involved in M&A, but I had this heavy plant experience also.

(Director D)

However, two NEDs also expressed anxiety about whether they were adding value by their appointment. This may suggest that the environmental context matters in terms of the perceived value that NEDs believe they are bringing to a board and, consequently, the degree of influence NEDs feel they can wield in and around a boardroom, especially when a company faces significant challenges. Directors P and N both expressed these reservations:

It worried me greatly that in my first couple of years ... [I] was not contributing ... but in a sense that I was saying I could not see how I was adding value. It worried me greatly ... all the time examining your own performance. In smaller companies or medium-sized companies ... when you sit around the table, they really need you. They can't afford to bring in specific skills they need into the executive ranks across the board, so they rely on board directors much more ... So let's contrast this with this [a] large company where you have [a] highly paid, highly skilled executive team ... where if you have a gap you simply hire it in, so they don't rely in a business sense or an everyday sense on the board. And when things are going swimmingly well, you sit back and wonder what value am I really adding when you sit on bigger boards?

(Director P)

I don't know how much we add as a board to strategy from a forward-thinking sense. Where we add value is when management brings a whole bunch of strategic decisions to us ... we play the role of filtering them out and add value in holding management accountable to driving what they said the strategy will deliver ... Additionally, the board really comes into its own when management has failed, or there is a big change or something like that ... When a company is going well, a board does not add value at all. Management says we are going to do this and do that and we say it sounds all right, and we double-check and then go away again. But when a company is in trouble or has to change the CEO or make decisions for the next generation, those are the times when a board really comes into its own.

(Director N)

As noted, some directors who were new to board life and had recently transitioned from executive to non-executive roles spoke about their attraction to a board because of the perceived ability to add immediate value. However, others felt more comfortable on the boards they had been on the longest. They cited the time it took to understand a business, get to know its different personalities—executives, shareholders and customers—and what their issues were. As Directors M, A, and E, respectively, reported:

I thought given my background ... I was a good match ... I could see this is somewhere I could add immediate value. When you are a NED, you have to believe you can add value. So, it was a large cap, capital-intensive, Australian-based, but international and, therefore, fitted the profile where I thought I could add value ... and they were looking for someone with a finance background and skills, which I think I bring.

(Director M)

in my case, I had an understanding of strategy at a major company ... so I brought a way of thinking about how you build sustainable companies. It is always attractive for someone like me with my financial background to be part of an audit committee for instance. But once you are on that board, then other dimensions of your experience come into play in addition to the initial dimensions that may have made you attractive to that board. This becomes evident through early board interactions.

(Director A)

I wanted a diverse range of boards ... while at that time [I] had no experience in this sector, I had enough different experience to be of value ... and at that time there were some people on this board with sector expertise, so my general business experience and CEO experience was seen as a complement to those people with sector experience.

(Director E)

In summary, it appeared that the way in which an NED construed their opportunity to add value to a board in a business, functional or process sense might affect how they perceived they could contribute, interpret the influence attempts of others and respond to those interpretations in their own influence attempts.

Opportunity to belong to a successful company, challenging business and vital sector

The lure of a particular sector or industry, a company experiencing change or one of vital importance to society, were other motivations cited by NEDs. The excitement they felt (in some cases, evident in their voices) was described in several ways. For example, a company was considered attractive if it was perceived as having a profound effect on day-to-day life or social materiality more generally. Businesses that were undergoing major disruption or facing major consolidation or disintermediation were also attractive. NEDs also mentioned the profile of a company and its success to date as motivating factors. Concerned with protecting their reputations as expert decision-makers, the research shows that NEDs would avoid serving on boards of lower quality firms. As Directors H, N, K and D reported:

What set this company apart was the style of the business they did, and some companies did not have businesses that were strategically sustainable ... [T]his one did. It had a reputation for honesty and probity and decent all around humanity. I don't mean sustainably in a green sense. What I mean by strategically sustainable is that they have got a business model that is going to work and does not have strategic weaknesses ... [I]t is not single-person sensitive and a business you would like to invest in.

(Director H)

It was a large, blue-chip successful company but had considerable challenges, and so the board had a real role to do to change the culture and the direction of the company. It was a meaty role ... in terms of it had pretty well everything you could want ahead of it ... big strategic decisions had to be made but also a lot of short-term tactical decisions had to be made ... fast-changing space where no two quarters were ever the same ... very evolving environment ... so it was an extremely interesting board to me and remains a really interesting board to me.

(Director N)

I was excited by this opportunity because of my scientific ... materials engineering background ... I understood the language, and I could walk around plants and understood it and was interested in it ... There were several things I wanted ... global reach in the US and here ... it was a leading player in this marketplace, and you get to deal with a particular level of problems. It felt as though there was some substance.

(Director K)

So, when I returned to Australia to pursue a non-executive career, I was approached ... and it exactly fitted my background in heavy industry ... and of course, it was an iconic company in that space.

(Director D)

Several NEDs cited the inherent complexity of the challenges facing particular sectors as being important motivators. While these responses could be part of a post-rationalisation of the reasons for joining, the espoused explanations were, nevertheless, meaningful to them. As Directors G and O observed:

I did not believe in doing turgid analysis about what boards I should join. It seemed to me that the business this company was involved in was a feature of the modern world. But, in the end, it is also about sociability ... how you are likely to get on with the people you work with.

(Director G)

It is a vitally important sector ... one that was important in all of our lives, impacting us all ... [I]t was strong in terms of its market position and its capacity to grow.

(Director O)

In summary, it may be assumed that an NED's desire to be associated with the boards of companies that they perceived as having a high profile and material effects on everyday life, and/or the complexity of the challenges it faced (e.g., through disruption), resulted in NEDs feeling the need to protect their identities and reputations as expert decision-makers. The extent to which the success of the company or the sector has the potential of breeding complacency in the thinking of directors is explored in Part 2 of this book.

Opportunity to join a respected board

Several NEDs pointed to the due diligence they undertook in relation to a board they were invited to join. Others spoke about the importance of a strong chair and their preference to join a board that could make a material difference in strategic decisions facing a company (i.e., that had influence over management). Several NEDs indicated that they would never join a board without first meeting its CEO and working out the nature of the dynamic between the chair and CEO. One NED spoke about deciding not to accept a high-profile board appointment because of a chair who was regarded by their peers as a bully. It is possible that, if an NED's view of a board before joining was positive, they might be more positively disposed to the board's decision-making processes and, hence, question these less. In this respect, comments made by Directors J, I, D and K were revealing in that it showed strong identification with members of that board:

> It clearly was a company that was performing very strongly … quite a unique culture, the board was a very strong board. It had a significant international side to the business, and in a sector I did not know a huge amount about … and so [I] thought I would learn a lot … The people on the board were highly respected for their achievements, and it also had several members of the board who were from overseas, and this attracted me.
>
> (Director J)

> The type of work that this board did was weighty and material enough to feel I was still meaningfully involved … [I]t had values that were very much aligned with my own … I was attracted by the people I was going to be sitting around the table with and the way the chair brings that group together.
>
> (Director I)

> A weak chairman and passive board … this is a frequent problem … You see papers not prepared on time because it is a low priority for the CEO … making decisions and then validating it with the board … but not on this board.
>
> (Director D)

I like boards where my fellow directors are engaged. Someone who has sleep apnoea and falls asleep at board meetings ... I have great difficulty with that. If you want to be around that table ... please be engaged ... The most important thing for me is the people on the board ... it makes a huge difference. ... I have enjoyed working on boards when people are clear about their intent ... they want to build a winning company ... to compete ... to make things better ... I like boards where my fellow directors are engaged.

(Director K)

In summary, when an NED is attracted to join a board because they identify strongly with the people on it, it is possible that they may, once on the board, be motivated by the desire to seek social support and acceptance from those individuals, which, in turn, may have an impact on independent mindedness.

The opportunity to work with great people and great culture

Directors spoke warmly about their positive associations, assessment and belief in the people they would become involved with on a board. These motivations are significant as an NED's positive perceptions of other board members are likely to contribute to greater cohesiveness and collaboration through the attribution of common understandings and shared values. This finding is consistent with the similarity–attraction syndrome known to define board ties, which has been extensively researched in social psychology (Westphal & Zajac 1997). It is also consistent with other studies (Forbes & Milliken 1999; Sundaramurthy & Lewis 2003). However, NEDs who identify with each other are also likely to share common ways of thinking and a cognitive schema that could lead to less robust challenging of each other in decision-making. As Director H observed:

The matters that the board considers are intellectually stimulating and interesting and opinions you offer of decisions you are part of are implemented ... and colleagues around the table are good to work with ... no smarty pants or put-down people ... [B]ut that is not to say they are in anyone's pockets, but everyone on this board are [sic] respectful of other people's knowledge and experience.

In summary, it seems that NEDs want to join reputable boards or companies that offer interesting challenges that might engage them and enable them to use their board capital, thereby facilitating intellectual and collegial stimulation. The reasons directors join boards and their keenness in describing the distinctiveness of their board capital was relevant in understanding the ways they categorised themselves relative to others on a board and construed their relative position in a social hierarchy (explored more fully in Chapter 3). NED self-construals of their unique board capital and the diversity it represented was found to influence their notions of what was expected of them and how they settled into effort norms and interaction patterns. The pervasive effects of group identification are discussed further in Chapter 3. Director motivations were significant in understanding potential allegiances that may develop on boards. NEDs' positive descriptions of boards they were invited to join implied they may be more positively disposed to the board's decision processes and, therefore, question them less. Finally, NEDs rely heavily on their networks and connections to obtain subsequent board appointments. This may affect how strongly they argue a point or adopt a minority position while shaping strategy. These effects and their consequences are discussed more fully in Chapters 3, 4 and 5.

In conclusion

Despite appearing to be homogenous groups when viewed from the outside, boards are internally differentiated in terms of the backgrounds, motivations, interests and beliefs their members bring to their work.

Prior career experience shaped the 'cognitive givens' each NED brought to a decision, such as knowledge, assumptions and mental models, and knowledge of alternatives and consequences of actions. A director's social embeddedness had the effect of exposing members to a range of macro-cognitions. These were broader cognitive strategies in decision-making, sense-making or problem-detection processes that generated various effective courses of action not determined by interactions they had experienced on other boards. When experienced, NEDs brought their exposure from multiple directorships or multi-sector experience, which others perceived as enriching the processes of strategic debate concerning options and possibilities. It prevented the over-reliance on narrow skill bases, specialisations or 'industry recipes'. Therefore, this social embeddedness and the exposure it provided had the effect of tempering a board member's tendency to reach for what had previously worked. Essentially, the findings showed that director networks could play a significant role in guarding against the narrowing of a director's cognitive horizons, thereby suggesting that multiple directorships hold value for broadening a director's strategic perspectives. There were significant variations in the mix of human and social capital NEDs brought to a board and their experience of influence in and around a boardroom. These variations in board capital among NEDs resulted in power differentials that strengthened or weakened group identification, which is explored more fully in Chapter 3.

It may be concluded then that motivations for joining the board held important clues to the perceptions of the relevance of others' board capital and acted as important markers for how board members related to each other. NED behaviour is affected by their self-construal of their place in the group (relative to the board capital they brought to a board, comprising a unique mix of experience, reputation, connections and networks). These relativities in the board capital of members led to 'like me' and 'not like me' comparisons, thus creating, in effect, a construed social reality into which an NED must fit. These comparisons, in themselves a source of power, led to validations that acted as internalised guides to an NED's own and others' legitimacy and relevance in decision-making interactions. This enabled NEDs to judge others' legitimacy to influence, providing a way to know 'whose opinion or viewpoint should I pay more attention to'. These internalised guides can be viewed as the 'psychosocial infrastructure' within which influence is enacted, potentially affecting the direction and strength of an NED's influence attempts. Furthermore, it affects the way in which those attempts are perceived and responded to by others. All of these invisible and subconscious processes contribute to a board culture and are more fully explored in Chapter 3.

Letter to the nominations committee

To: Nominations Committee

From: BoardQ Advisory

Re: Selection of board members

While you are aware that an effective board is not assured by simply assembling a group of individually experienced and expert NEDs, you also recognise that this is much easier said than done, and that effectiveness is not the same as an experienced board and that a large part of effectiveness comes from a healthy dynamic.

The skill-based board has long been a guiding paradigm for many nominations committees. However, we challenge what we have often witnessed as somewhat misguided application of this 'Noah's Ark' approach (of bringing diversity on to a board) for two reasons. First, expert skills, depending on where they are being hired from, may result in a narrowing of strategic perspectives and horizons on a board. While you have historically attempted to hire directors with a variety of expert skills needed for this board, these experts themselves have often been drawn from relatively narrow 'cognitive and social pools', which may result in ideological convergence (i.e., they operate with similar mental models and dominant logic from the sectors from which they are drawn). For example, in order to augment the legal, risk, audit and accounting skills on the board, you have generally turned to professional firms. Frequently, such experts have been hired after acting as advisors to the company/sector for several years, steeped and potentially trapped by the dominant logic within the firm/sector. This practice may not guard the company against the dangers associated with the effects of over-identification, including groupthink, opinion conformity, self-censoring of divergent views and silencing of dissent. Similarly, a sector head for banking from one of the professional services firms may, for example, be immersed in sector accepted norms or 'industry recipes' and that experience may potentially constrain thinking and prevent the challenging of these industry recipes and business models in the face of unprecedented disruption. As shown by the evidence from recent research, these are not just risks limited to recruits from professional services. It is true of all potential hires and questions such as how exposed they might be to disruptive forces outside the realm of their experience—new business models, new platforms, new technologies and so on.

Second, selection criteria heavily skewed to industry knowledge and expertise will not necessarily deliver an effective board. This is because a board that collectively has more board capital may not be more effective in influencing outcomes or strengthening the processes of accountability than one that possesses collectively less. Proof of the value the NED's board capital brings to the board is only evident in how they choose to use this board capital for influencing others and how their use of influence is perceived and supported by others. Therefore, while industry knowledge and expertise are important, mindsets, propensities and dispositions matter as much if you want to develop a strategically active board.

Therefore, nominations committees may need to reset their thinking on several fronts, rethinking the ways in which NED selection and on-boarding are conducted and how the effectiveness of boards is measured:

1   Replace the narrow conception of board skill and capability with the broader and more holistic concept of board capital.
2   Challenge the notion of the skills-based board by reviewing the cognitive and social pools from which directors have historically been hired, considering the career, social and life experiences of potential candidates, including the diversity of their social networks.
3   Develop a coherent and systematic approach to identifying the relational and dispositional attributes (see Chapter 4) required to complement the industry knowledge and expertise required.

Actionable strategies

Desired outcome	Strategies the board may take collectively	Strategies the individual director may take
Diverse cognitive histories	Chairs and nominations committees may wish to consider the cognitive history of current membership and consider how best to develop a more balanced mix, such as hiring new directors from diverse cognitive pools	Before joining a board, considering not just the composition of the board but where the directors have acquired their experience and the connections/networks they appear to have; this will be a good indication of the tendencies associated with strategic persistence or strategic adaptation likely to exist

Desired outcome	*Strategies the board may take collectively*	*Strategies the individual director may take*
Broadening strategic horizons	Challenging the notion of a skill-based board that may result in the functional tracks of directors potentially narrowing strategic horizons.	Seeking out and striking relationships with directors outside one's immediate circle in order to expose oneself to diverse cognitive perspectives
Strengthening independent mindedness	Widening the candidate pool from which new directors are hired to consider if and how past associations and personal ties may potentially result in opinion conformity, silencing of dissent and the self-censoring of divergent views	Being prepared to openly place the counter–position in the room and argue the case for it so that a balanced group view/ discussion emerges. Applying the 'pub test': would I/we still be comfortable with this decision if it became public

References

Geletkanycz, M & Black, S 2001, 'Bound by the past? Experience-based effects on the commitment to the strategic status quo', *Journal of Management*, vol. 27, no. 1, pp. 3–21.

Johnson, SG, Schnatterly, K & Hill, AD 2013, 'Board composition beyond independence: social capital, human capital and demographics', *Journal of Management*, vol. 39, no.1, pp. 232–262.

Magee, JC & Smith, PK 2013, 'The social distance theory of power', *Personality and Social Psychology Review*, vol. 17, no. 2, pp. 158–186.

Pettigrew, A 2001, 'Andrew Pettigrew on executives and strategy: an interview with Kenneth Starkey', *European Management Journal*, vol. 20, no. 1, pp. 20–34.

Pick, K 2007, 'Around the boardroom table: interactional aspects of governance', PhD thesis, Harvard University, Cambridge, MA.

Prahalad, CK & Bettis, RA 1995, 'The dominant logic: a new linkage between diversity and performance', *Strategic Management Journal*, vol. 16, pp. 5–14.

Rindova, VP 1999, 'What corporate boards have to do with strategy: a cognitive perspective', *Journal of Management Studies*, vol. 36, no. 7, pp. 953–975.

Ruigrok, W, Peck, SI & Keller, H 2006, 'Board characteristics and involvement in strategic decision making: evidence from Swiss companies', *Journal of Management Studies*, vol. 43, no. 5, pp. 1201–1226.

Spender, JC 1989, *Industry recipes: an inquiry into the nature and sources of managerial judgement*, Blackwell, Oxford.

Thuraisingham, SM 2018, 'Exploring the social factors that influence the decision making behaviours of non-executive directors in Australian public companies', PhD thesis, RMIT University, Melbourne.

Turner, JC 1982, 'Towards a cognitive redefinition of the social group', in H Tajfel (ed.), *Social identity and intergroup relationships*, Cambridge University Press, Cambridge, pp. 15–40.

Turner, JC & Reynolds, KJ 2012, 'Self-categorisation theory', in Van Lange, Kruglanski & Higgins (eds), *Handbook of theories in social psychology*, Sage Publications, London, pp. 399–417.

Westphal, JD 1999, 'Collaboration in the boardroom: behavioural and performance consequences of CEO-board social ties', *Academy of Management Journal*, vol. 42, no. 1, pp. 7–24.

Westphal, JD & Bednar, MK 2005, 'Pluralistic ignorance in corporate boards and firms' strategic persistence in response to low firm performance', *Administrative Science Quarterly*, vol. 50, no. 2, pp. 262–298.

Westphal, JD & Khanna, P 2003, 'Keeping directors in line: social distancing as a social mechanics in the corporate elite', *Administrative Science Quarterly*, vol. 48, no. 3, pp. 361–398.

Westphal, J & Zajac, E 1997, 'Defections from the inner circle: social exchange, reciprocity the diffusion of board independence', *Administrative Science Quarterly*, vol. 42, no. 1, pp. 161–183.

3 The boardroom

Decoding the hidden hierarchy and board culture

This chapter in summary

This chapter describes the largely invisible effects of group membership on the decision-making behaviour of individuals. An understanding of the psychology of groups reveals what really happens to the individual (in this case the director) when they join a group. How does the individual change and how does the group change? What does the individual gain and what do they give up on becoming a group member and how conscious are they of these processes? A group such as a board has an identity into which an individual has to fit. This is not a simple process either for the individual director or the board as a group. Subjective 'like me'/'not like me' categorisations, discussed in Chapter 2, may lead to self-censorship, silencing of doubt and revisions of confidence. These are only some of the behavioural changes that may be required to be accepted by the group. Strategies are offered for how to deal constructively when encountering their effects. While most directors understand that independent mindedness (contrasting with independence as a structural construct) is critical, the effects of group membership on independent mindedness can be pervasive.

For example, some directors will possess more board capital than others and, therefore, they may be perceived as having a greater legitimacy to influence. These power differentials may cause subgroups and coalitions to emerge that can materially effect the decision-making culture of the board. These director judgements, although wholly subjective, may have a direct or indirect effect on the director's behaviour towards a peer perceived to be more or less powerful. This chapter makes visible the hidden power structure that exists in every board through which some directors may be heard over others, potentially compromising the quality of decisions and outcomes. Identity politics (which is largely invisible and subjectively construes everyone's place in the group) determine if, how and when influence attempts are made or responded to, as well as who listens to who, making every board dynamic unique. Despite being wholly subjective, such perceptions may, at times, lead to unjustified support for the views of a powerful director or subgroup of directors, even if they hold minority views. The chapter also describes how a newly appointed director's desire for social support from, and acceptance by, the group can undermine their independent mindedness, the very role they were brought on board to discharge. Without a real understanding of this invisible psychosocial 'architecture'—how a board culture emerges and how it may be changed for the better—boards are unlikely to unlock their potential as strategically influential groups. This chapter is brought alive by director-lived experiences that reflect such political manoeuvrings. It also provides a typology of board culture that helps directors explain their experiences of board culture and what may be needed to transform it.

Other 'group effects', such as social distancing, groupthink, pluralistic ignorance, social loafing and social sanctioning, are also explained in the board context to reveal the complex realities of board life. The chapter offers prescriptions for how independent mindedness can be maintained and provides clear-eyed strategies for how these invisible forces can be overcome without compromising processes of influence or board accountability.

Directors do not operate in a social vacuum. As shown in this chapter, through being members of a board they are subject to group membership effects that can be pervasive—that is, when individuals get together in a group, they think and act in ways they may not have done on their own because of the effects of group membership.

As noted, when an individual joins a group, there are two subliminal and subjective processes that occur. The first process, which is largely intuitive, relates to a self-categorisation that the individual makes—a 'like me' or 'not like me' identification—in which a group derives comfort and confidence from associating with people most like them, resulting in affiliations. Such affiliations have been shown to result in subgroups being more open to the views of people they perceive as having common experiences. These affiliations are loose and exist as part of a social reality that provides a board member with a guide about where they fit into a board group. While this process of self-categorisation might determine feelings of affiliation, similarity and attraction, and the degree of openness to others' viewpoints, it does not necessarily affect the strength or direction of a director's influence attempts.

It is a second process, described in the following, that determines and defines the strength or direction of an NED's influence attempts. In this second process of identification, a director prejudges and validates the legitimacy of others to influence, and relies on their sensemaking of that legitimacy to influence, based on the three dependencies (Thuraisingham 2018): the competence and professional credibility of an influencer; the diversity of cognitive communities an influencer is connected to or embedded in; and shared perceptions of board work, particularly an NED's role in strategy. This subjective validation determines the importance that NEDs attach to the influence attempts of other NEDs and the withholding or granting of social support for the influence attempts of others, described in the next section.

Figure 3.1 depicts these largely subjective and sequential processes, which are critical to the processes of influence in and around the boardroom.

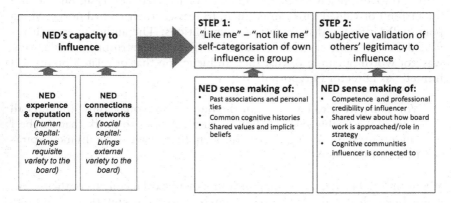

Figure 3.1 How self-categorisation and validation of others' power to influence occur in NED decision-making processes.
Source: Thuraisingham (2018).

The consequences of group identification: receiving and granting of social support

Chapter 2 described how NEDs identify with those they perceive to be most like them in terms of board capital (i.e., accumulated experience, reputations and embeddedness). This section describes the consequences associated with the second process of identification in which an NED subjectively validates their own legitimacy to influence, in turn, empowering or disempowering others in enacting their influence. The first part of this section examines the seeking of social support for an NED's own influence attempts; the second examines the decision to grant or withhold social support for the influence attempts of others.

Seeking social support from others for NED influence attempts

As discussed in Chapter 1, how an NED construes their role and accountabilities on a board shapes the contribution they make, influences how they view the contributions of others and ultimately affects a board dynamic (Hillman, Nicholson & Shropshire 2008; Thuraisingham 2018). For example, when an NED contributes by drawing on their business or functional skills, the way in which that contribution is responded to by other NEDs feeds back into self-construal and self-validation (Hillman, Nicholson & Shropshire 2008; Pick 2007; Thuraisingham 2018). Therefore, how convinced others are of this uniqueness matters and may, in some cases, result in a contribution being viewed as either disruptive and annoying or helpful and illuminating. Directors responded in several main ways if their contribution was not perceived to be positively received. Some concluded that their contribution was not understood or valued; this caused them to reassess their contribution, which potentially influenced their future contributions. The author's research revealed that, in some cases, this resulted in an NED determining that a point was not worth pursuing or that their influence on that or related points was limited. As Director N reported:

> You don't want to be a pain in the bum. Also, your fellow directors all seemed reasonably relaxed about it, and you start to think that maybe I am wrong and I don't feel that confident that I have some divine inspiration that they don't have.

When an NED had no social support from other board members for their view, it was likely that, if they identified strongly with the group, they were more likely to adopt, reflect or mirror the views of the in-group or self-censor their own reservations. The strength of numbers tended to be felt most acutely by new directors. This was reflected in the statement from Director N who was new to a board despite having considerable global experience as a CEO on acquisitions and divestments. His self-construal of his newness played a part in his reluctance to challenge robustly or hold firm on his divergent views.

On larger boards, strength derived from numbers can also result in 'offline huddles', usually after a formal board meeting has ended, such as packing up, during walks from or to a venue or by phone between board meetings—all intended to build informal 'coalitions' on a large board. As Director G explained:

> It just emerged from this discussion [referring to a discussion that took place between four of the most senior NEDs of a large board while packing up to leave after a board meeting had concluded] someone said something and then someone else said something else and so on and suddenly it was clear to us what needed to be done. That we would not be pushed into this ... that we would take control of this conversation ... which we did at the subsequent board meeting.

In this case, the formation of an 'offline coalition' was precipitated by shared views between a subgroup of NEDs about a board's responsibility, as well as beliefs about value creation. This subgroup appeared less prepared to voice their opinion until they felt they 'had the numbers'. In this and other similar narratives of participating NEDs, it was evident that subgroup influence attempts may be more salient than those of others on a board because of the construed importance or status accorded to their long- and well-established cognitive histories (Thuraisingham 2018).

Additionally, some NEDs used their identity as a source of self-definition and were motivated to maintain and promote a positive self-concept. The skills associated with seeking to maintain and promote a positive self-concept are detailed later in this chapter. Conversely, there was evidence that the contributions from 'people not like me' were subject to some 'discounting' during decision interactions—that is, attaching lesser importance to what 'people not like me' said. For example, Director C stated that 'I don't want to be one of those directors who just ask incessant questions without having a strategic intent' recalling a peer director that was prone to doing that. Granting or withholding social support for others' influence attempts was also evident. Director O observed that 'the perceived credibility of a director [in the eyes of their peers] determines the weight that will be given to their input'.

As described in Chapter 2, the comparative uniqueness of an NED's cognitive history acted as a form of personal validation of their purpose and role, prompting confident contributions to discourse and openness in influence attempts. Following on from this, it is important to examine when and how participating NEDs granted or withheld social support for others' influence attempts.

Granting or withholding social support for others' influence attempts

After engaging in a process of 'invisible' self-categorisation, participating NEDs tended to subjectively validate the cognitive history of others to determine their legitimacy to influence a given issue (Thuraisingham 2018). This subjective validation determined if an NED would give or withhold support for the influence attempts of their peers. Most NEDs made three, largely subconscious, determinations of competence and professional credibility of an influencer; the perception of a shared view of the work of a board, especially the role of the NED in strategy; and the perceived diversity of cognitive communities from which an influencer was embedded in or to which they were exposed. These are described in the following.

Perceptions of competence and professional credibility of an influencer

NEDs continually make judgements about the competence of their board peers. Every contribution is used to either confirm or disconfirm the competence of an individual director. In the author's study, NEDs who were new to directing or a board were particularly anxious to make a good impression with their peers. Wanting to be perceived as competent and wise, at times, they self-censored their own contributions to prevent them from being viewed as ill-judged or ill-informed. For example, referring to a proposal under consideration when he joined a board, Director G in the author's study was keen to create the right impression with his peers, withholding his own potential influence attempts and being receptive to the influence attempts of others based on their perceived competence and professional credibility. As he reported:

> I was new and was sitting back learning the competence of the individuals ... I did not have the confidence to say this [referring to a challenge about who would be the better owner of the business] at the time. It took me two to three meetings to notice particular individuals whose opinions you should pay attention to.

However, once an NED had established themselves, their response to influence attempts of others was motivated by a need to maintain a positive self-concept, such that they would be perceived as balanced, rational and wise. These social effects seemed to be subtle, unconscious and likely to be invisible to those outside a boardroom. As Director O reported, 'you should not be seen to blow with the wind or be stubborn or come to a meeting with what seems like a closed mind'. Similarly, Director D stated that 'if you say something often enough, it eventually washed over other people ... one must not appear to be too desperate'.

Shared view about the work of the board and the role in strategy

It is not uncommon to find a lack of a shared view among NEDs about their role in strategy (Simoes, Kakabadse & Ramos 2013; Thuraisingham 2018). Some NEDs are perceived by their peers as too involved in strategy, giving rise to unproductive interpersonal tension with management, while others are perceived as standing too much on the sidelines. In the author's study, NEDs continually made references to their observations about the convergence or divergence of their peers' view on the role of a board in strategy. For example, Director G stated:

> You see boards don't really understand their roles. There are only two critical roles they play: CEO succession and as an arbiter of strategy. The rest is really routine, for example, determining risks etcetera [sic] are all about how to achieve these two key things. The key issue for boards is to lock on to these two things. However, most CEO and directors don't understand strategy. What they think is strategy is simply tactical planning and budgeting.

The cross-case comparisons (in the study) showed some variation in when and how involved an NED was in strategy episodes. For example, Director G identified the failure to actively engage in strategy as a major ongoing issue in corporate Australia. As a current member of several boards, he described some NEDs who, in his experience, still believed they were there to 'endorse' strategy rather than 'determine' it in collaboration with management. As noted, he cited the determination of strategy and the selection of a CEO as being the two most critical aspects of board accountability.

Conversely, Director N observed that some director motivation was not always well placed:

> In these days with liabilities and things ... more and more of what the director is saying is how do we cover our backsides in case it goes wrong and we are sued ... Instead, we should be saying [sic], 'what is the best decision for the company' and then after that step back and consider the risks and liabilities.

Other NEDs described receiving limited background, incomplete information, experiencing a 'highly choreographed' strategy day or board papers that were late, which were taken as indicative of a CEO's attitude to a board's role in strategy. When faced with a resistant CEO, NEDs varied in the effort they applied in persisting with their desire to be more involved and in the tenacity with which they pursued their intention of being better informed (Thuraisingham 2018).

Diversity of cognitive communities of influence

In addition to shared or common histories, NEDs also have access to diverse cognitive communities, for example, by sitting on other boards together and having similar exposure to common external stakeholder groups. As Director I in the author's study noted: 'Multiple directorships (even across different sectors) can be useful because of the potential value of translating lessons and insights from one sector to another, in turn, strengthening [sic] the quality of oversight'. Directors who sat on multiple boards expressed the view that directors with experience in a particular sector were useful in a control role; by contrast, directors whose experience was drawn from diverse sectors were more useful in an advisory role—because of the value exposure to different business models, platforms and ways of creating added to a debate. To put this another way, there appeared to be a subtle but important distinction NEDs made between common and diverse cognitive histories.

Director M, who was chair of a finance, risk and audit committee, felt that he was the most exposed, should a transaction not go well. He recounted how he led discussions and involved himself with the regulators who were keen to know how the impairing of assets would be undertaken in the transaction. Significantly, he recounted that he had considerable experience with regulators from another period in his career. In his opinion, this made him the best placed director to be involved in steering the conversations with both regulators and the banks involved in a decision to free cash and continue as a viable entity by selling assets to a foreign joint-venture partner.

Director N recounted how his relationship with an institutional investor helped shape his thinking and subsequent pessimistic attitude towards the transformative decision that management had put forward to the board:

> I recall … one of our institutional investors whom I knew … a very smart guy predicted this completely … he had said to me, 'I predict if you don't sell it now you will be standing in front of us in a number of years' time, and you will be writing off shareholder value', and that's exactly what happened.

These findings show, especially when faced with complex cognitive tasks, how critical the links with external communities are because they offer a useful way of calibrating their judgements and solidifying positions.

As behaviours are often the consequence of cognition (i.e., how one thinks), the recounting by NEDs of their own thinking and the thinking of others (observed as more or less skilful than their own) was important in understanding the seeking, granting and withholding of social support in and around the boardroom. The recounting of their thinking and the thinking of others reflected how their human and social capital combined in dynamic ways to produce what participating directors perceived as 'practical wisdom' (from the Greek *phronesis*) and sound judgement. However, the findings showed this ability was a double-edged sword for board groups. While it increased the diversity of thinking at a board's disposal, it also had the potential of creating interaction difficulties and lower levels of collaboration. The perception of practical wisdom only affected a decision-making process when an NED possessed sufficient social skills to coherently or convincingly articulate the wisdom and judgement variously gained, sense the reactions of others and act on those reactions.

We may conclude that power differentials exist on every board, but only become salient under certain conditions—for example, when a task is complex and requires discernment, judgement and practical wisdom (Thuraisingham 2018). In some cases, while solving these cognitive tasks, such differences and resulting divergent viewpoints translate into tensions and conflicts between board members.

How the character and culture of a board emerges and thrives

As noted in Chapter 2 and in the foregoing, the consequences of identification are dynamic. Individual NEDs are not just passive recipients of social effects but are continually making subjective judgements and validations, modifying and adapting their original positions and influencing the positions of others during decision-making processes. Over time, through working with each other, NEDs become aware of the discursive practices, decision logic and 'political positions' that each of their peers is likely to adopt and use in influence attempts. A board represents a dynamic social reality in which consensus can ebb and flow over a decision-making process, as familiarity with the 'workings' of a group develops and as information, perspectives and insights emerge. These factors provide NEDs with the opportunity to actively judge the merits of new information, learn from each other and adjust their positions, in some cases discounting or rationalising away perspectives different from their own. This form of intra-group learning has rarely been explored by researchers. In all but two cases, it was found that, over the period of a transformative decision, trust and respect were continually being validated, earned and re-earned within a dynamic social structure that was shaped by the social support given or received for one another's influence attempts. Rather than mindless compliance with a group, members engage in conscious and deliberate attempts to gain the social approval of others to build rewarding relationships and in the process enhance self-esteem. This behaviour is enhanced or strengthened when threatened by the prospect (or actual occurrence) of not fitting within a group. This conscious and deliberate process was evident when NEDs described their early experience with new boards. It was also found to be true of NEDs with a shared history of working together (Thuraisingham 2018). Figure 3.2 captures these complex social effects at play and shows how the effects of power and identity can shape decision behaviour.

Finally, it was found that the consequences of decision-making were not simply a battle of numbers (Thuraisingham 2018). NEDs on large boards in this study (i.e., those with 10 or more members) reported that differences in viewpoints and the potential for disagreement were likely to emerge because of their greater cognitive diversity. By contrast, the differences that emerged in smaller groups, which were generally tighter knit—such as the conflict described by Director E that occurred with the chair of the audit committee—could be catastrophic, detrimentally affecting the continued functioning of a board. The number of NEDs with a majority view may not be salient to a decision dynamic. That is, even one NED, provided their cognitive history (a proxy for their boardroom influence) is regarded as highly credible, may sway a majority. This was exemplified by Director C, whose deep experience of North Asia was relied on almost exclusively by other members of a board, including its chair. Minorities (i.e., subgroups of directors with views that differ from the majority) can exist at the margins, as found in the transcript of Director G. That is to say, the bigger the power differentials between NEDs on a given board (a consequence of relativities in possessed board capital),

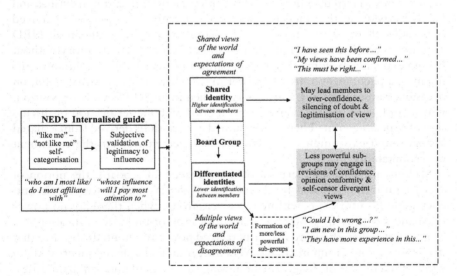

Figure 3.2 The hidden social hierarchy and the social context in which influence occurs.
Source: Thuraisingham (2018).

the greater the likelihood for disagreements to emerge and persist. This dynamic view of a board's social reality supports and extends the findings of the dynamic social impact theory (Latané 1996).

In recent years, there has been a marked shift towards a more dynamic explanation of social influence (Cialdini & Goldstein 2004). While research exploring the effects of 'like me' and 'not like me' categorisations exists (Oakes, Turner & Haslam 1991; Onorato & Turner 2004), studies into how these categorisations affect decision-making in boards or TMT processes are sparse. Equally, there has been little or no research on subgroup politics and how they might shape decision cultures and outcomes.

NEDs with multiple directorships reported tangibly different levels of engagement on each of their boards. Some boards were reported to be more formal and reserved, largely because of the concentration of power in the hands of a few (which is evidence of differentiated identities), while others were more open and engaged with power more evenly shared (which is evidence of shared identity). The shared history of NEDs also appeared to be influential in director decision behaviour through the mutual understanding and expectations of an agreement, not only due to board tenure but also through membership of the same boards. For example, NEDs who were on the same board and had a shared history on other boards developed expectations either through their committee or board experience—a reflection of the mutual understanding of how they would act under certain circumstances or in certain decision contexts. That is to say they developed a familiarity with each other's decision logic and cognition. The study also found evidence of how implicit expectations (referred to here as 'socialisation tactics') including routines and habits learned together increased the speed at which decisions were arrived at because of this shared mindset. This familiarity could result in an NED assuming a view or position of another director with a shared history without having explicitly explored this in the boardroom (which reflects pluralistic ignorance, a phenomenon discussed later in this chapter). Familiarity could, on occasion, result in missing a nuance contained in an NED's view or position, which could lead to unwarranted assumptions without verification or discussion of a specific point. Therefore, assumed expectations derived from a shared history could have implications for director effectiveness and the enactment of accountability.

Seeking a deeper appreciation of the character of a board, the notion of social equilibrium created by the effects of identity and power is relevant. Social equilibrium exists within any given group, when there are no power imbalances within the group. Over-identification or under-identification in a group exists when there are real or perceived power differentials/distance that may exist among group members. When a group had a shared identity, there was less likelihood of disagreement among members (Thuraisingham 2018). Over-identification or under-identification had the effect of creating 'constellations' of power within a group—that is, personally construed subgroups divided along the lines of those that possessed less or more board capital than oneself. NEDs reported being able to overcome the effects of more powerful subgroups through demonstrating effective uses of social competencies (comprising various social behaviours, described in Chapter 4), turning what limited power or social capital they had to carry out their preferred influence strategy.

In the context of the author's study (which was focussed on a large transformative decision that carried significant complexity and uncertainty), conflicting views were inevitable and likely to evolve dynamically through the decision-making process. However, the effects of identity and power were only salient when a director perceived there was little or no social support from other board members for his or her view. Therefore, social support can have a significant effect on the nature of agreement and contention in a group. When directors perceived large power differentials in a group, which implied less shared identity, they observed that members of some subgroups became more vocal, in some cases swaying the direction and content of a debate and frustrating the influence attempts of others.

To balance tensions and achieve social equilibrium, the most effective boards may, in fact, sometimes need to operate collectively as if a 'social contract' existed between members; that is, they must negotiate as a unit to achieve a balance with collective awareness and coordination skills, and share a common view about how to approach their work as a board. On some boards, the collective ownership of an alternative viewpoint put forward by a director was achieved by the others adopting that challenge as their own, supporting them by probing, clarifying and confirming questions delivered in a way that showed their respect for others' challenges. There was evidence that a board's collective influence became fragmented when NEDs did not own such challenges as a legitimate part of board processes or the true nature of board work. Directors also reported that a resistant CEO who saw a board working in unison was more likely to take a challenge seriously. Some directors reported that, when personal challenges were not skilfully executed, they were perceived as a personal attack or a challenge to a person's professional expertise or experience. In cases like this, directors would attempt to distance themselves from the challenge or engage with the challenge in a way that helped soften the perceived sharpness of the challenge especially when there was social equilibrium in the boardroom.

However, while a collective will (likened here to a social contract) was important, so was the need to draw distance from a group and remain independent minded through such processes. As noted in Chapter 2, this is one of several paradoxes identified by researchers as implicit in board work (Demb & Neubauer 1992; Hooghiemstra & van Manen 2004; Roberts, McNulty & Stiles 2005; Sundaramurthy & Lewis 2003; Thuraisingham 2018; Van Ees, Gabrielsson & Huse 2009). These tensions can pull NED behaviour in different directions. The findings of the author's study showed that the perceived need for NEDs to feel collective ownership for the process might mask the pressure to conform, which can be achieved subtly through a form of social sanctioning often invisible to those external to a group. To put this another way, control in the processes of exercising accountability in a corporate governance sense can be viewed as a social phenomenon in which members perceived as having higher power may seek to prevent deviance from established collective norms (Thuraisingham 2018). This was particularly evident in decisions in which the consensus of a full board was required, as is the case of an acquisition. Directors reconciled these social pressures through the social competencies they demonstrated, as described in Chapter 4.

Powerful subgroups can persist. For example, the author's study revealed that individuals or subgroups perceived (by the narrating NED) as having higher power were reported to have more stable identities and board personas that were less susceptible to the social influence attempts of others. They were also perceived as being less likely to demonstrate empathetic concern for another's views. This finding supports the theory of perspective taking, tested empirically by Galinsky et al. (2006), which showed an inverse relationship between power and perspective taking. Views became resistant to change and were polarised, including, in one case, an entirely split board in which consensus was impossible to achieve. However, in most cases, the effect was more subtle; compliance with a subgroup view was ensured through a form of social sanctioning. This further supports the tenets of social distance theory (Magee & Smith 2013) when applied to a board context. It also supports the similarity–attraction theory tested in a board context in relation to the desired characteristics applied in the selection of a new CEO by a board (Zajac & Westphal 1996). Further, it suggests that 'people like me' is often the lens through which compatibility in values and beliefs is decided, resulting all too often in a binary response: they do or do not think like me. When there was a strong shared identity in a group, and when powerful subgroups were not reported to exist, NEDs recounted an open, robust and trust-driven dynamic, and open debate on difficult issues. However, directors reported that this shared mindset was only effective up to a point, after which it had the potential to be affected by groupthink. Board leadership (discussed in Chapter 5) was an important moderator of this delicate balance; in particular, a chair's role in creating psychological safety was pivotal when power was unevenly distributed across a board.

The social effects of power and identity described in this chapter and the director attributes relevant to the processes of influence described in the next chapter determine the unique culture of every board. While it may be difficult to describe the intangible differences between boards that NEDs (who hold multiple directorships) report that they experience, they are often able to intuit such differences. A typology of board cultures driven by the effects of

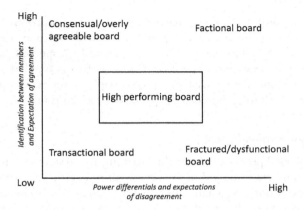

Figure 3.3 The typology of board cultures driven by the effects of identity and power.
Source: Thuraisingham (2018).

identity and power derived from the author's research is shown in Figure 3.3. The typology shows that high performing boards result when the social effects of identity and power are in equilibrium. While typologies run the risk of over-simplifying what occurs in reality, they are useful in helping boards better understand the differences they can often sense.

The cultures depicted in Figure 3.3 can be described in the following ways:

High-performing board

Despite high commitment and engagement of all members in the processes of governing, divergent views are encouraged and characterised by open, lively value-adding inquiry, brave questions and robust analysis of alternatives; 'gritty' conversations are common, anchored by a shared clarity about board's purpose. Personal agendas are rare and members openly respect/value each other's experience and knowledge, however different from own.

Factional board

Characterised by powerful factions, where decision-making is determined by delineation of board member allegiances/personal ties; decision-making is often a contest to see which faction will win out; behind the scenes lobbying, private co-option and agenda control are common. Influence is in the hands of few seeking to mediate the minority view, often described as 'cliquish', 'efficient' 'majority vote'

Consensual board

Most members will value board harmony and will avoid robustly challenging each other's views; group acceptance is valued and may result in self-censuring concern. Dominant views are generally respected, assumptions underlying those views left unquestioned and conflict is avoided—unanimity is often an illusion; these boards more often opt for the 'safe' option or the status quo, referred to as 'agreeable', 'friendly', 'harmonious'.

Fractured/dysfunctional board

Where the normal processes of decision-making are chaotic and dysfunctional and where members disregard or are openly disrespectful of each other's perspectives or positions. The chair is usually regarded as 'absent' in action, sometimes participating in or condoning power plays: It is often a matter of time before they break apart because there is little agreement on fundamental issues.

Transactional board

The board resembles a group of individual members rather than a team. Sense of membership is absent, and the board goes through the motions in ensuring compliance matters are met as a minimum; Members may feel de-authorised and may not feel they have a voice or choose not to use their voice. These boards fail to have any influence.

Board cultures are multilayered and complex and are an important consideration in exercising 'soft governance' a term referred to in previous chapters. Consensual boards can masquerade as highly functioning and efficient boards but they are not so. Similarly, factional boards can masquerade as highly functioning because decisions are carried quickly often by a powerful clique, leaving those not in the clique to feel they have not been fully heard. Importantly, the appointment or departure of one or more NEDs can change the culture of a board. For example, a high-performing board can, through the poor hiring decisions, morph into a factional board, just as some great hiring decisions can turn a consensual board into a high-performing one. Chairs and chairs of nomination committees therefore need to be alert to the direction of travel of a culture and be aware of the impact that hiring decisions can have on board cultures.

In order to better understand and improve the culture of the board, it is useful for NEDs and especially the chair to reflect on two questions about the dynamics on their boards:

1   How strongly do members of the board group identify with each other and what is the direction of that shared identity? Is it centered around a robustly debated and shared view of what is in the best interests of the company and what the board is there to do, or is it centered around

ensuring harmony and preserving loyalty in the group and limiting divergent viewpoints and the contention of issues and ideas?

2   Is there an even distribution of power across the members as evidenced by board capital relativities? Are power differentials on this board large enough to create 'constellations of power' along 'like-me' and 'not-like-me' distinctions that may sway the dynamic in ways that are not helpful either in leveraging the collective experience of the board or ensuring the integrity of decision-making processes?

In summary, individuals and groups are affected by the social reality in which they find themselves. It is clear from the foregoingthat unless this largely hidden social reality is fully understood, despite best intentions, the effectiveness of an NED's influence attempts may not be fully realised. That is, the presence or actions of others (real, implied or imagined) can influence an individual's feelings, thoughts or behaviours. When there is substantial identification between members, shared views of the world emerge and expectations of agreement are greater. When there is lower identification between members, multiple views of the world emerge and expectations of disagreement are greater.

The invisible social reality in which the processes of influence occur can be compared to the water in which a fish swims. A fish is unable to perceive water, seemingly unconscious of its existence, despite being essential to its life. Knowledge of the importance of the water only comes when a fish is removed from this environment. In the case of boards, while the psychosocial infrastructure is impossible to see, it is the vehicle through which influence is enacted. Directors' knowledge of the workings of this infrastructure is essential, as is their skilful exercise of social competencies and associated behaviours if they are to remain influential in decision-making in and around a boardroom. The typology provided in this chapter demonstrates how social factors such as power and identity can have pervasive effects on the influencing climate in and around the boardroom, potentially compromising decisions and the effectiveness of the board.

Group effects: the big bad five

When reflecting on the culture of their boards, NEDs might want to consider some of the group effects that can come to define a board culture. They may also ask themselves if such behavioural risks exist on their boards and what as a collective group they need to do to address these or prevent them from emerging on their boards in the first place.

Researchers have studied and reported on 'group effects' within teams, including TMTs, for some time. However, few have examined these effects in the context of boards and as we know boards differ from TMTs in a number of salient ways as described in the introduction to this book. Table 3.1

Table 3.1 How the social effects of board membership can affect decision-making

Phenomenon	Description	Effects on decision-making
Groupthink	When individuals get together in a group they think and act in ways that they may not have done independently on their own on account of the pressure to conform to the thinking of the group. Members value harmony and consensus over accurate analysis and critical evaluation	Members refraining from expressing doubts, judgments and disagreements defaulting to the consensus view in order to gain approval or acceptance by the group
Pluralistic ignorance	A phenomenon in which most board members disagree with a position, assumption or belief but infer, albeit incorrectly, that most other board members accept it and thus they accept it. It typically occurs when the norms are older than all members of the board group or when one NED or a small group is dominant and encourages conformance with the norm, and fails to explicitly check for the veracity of each other's positions, beliefs or assumptions	Decisions are made without ensuring that there is full alignment of the group on the underlying assumptions
Social loafing	An NED who exerts less effort both in quality and quantity than they would if they were not operating in the group context. It may not imply diminished personal accountability but simply a lower exerting of effort on the assumption that others would pick up the 'slack'. This phenomena is generally more noticeable on larger boards and may sometimes be referred to as the passenger or bystander effect	Failure to contribute to robust dialogue on a given issue, unless drawn in, and even then contribution is generally observed by others to be superficial. Not scrutinising committee papers on the assumption that committee members would have done the 'heavy lifting'
Social distancing	A relatively informal kind of social control that is usually subtle and designed to prevent deviant behaviours. It may result in the exclusion of one or more NEDs who may be viewed as a threat to the dominant position of a powerful person or subgroup. Behaviour is usually in the form of subtle ostracism and informal exclusion to some degree from board interactions and associations	Neglecting to ask for one's opinions or advice on an issue; failure to extend invitation to attend important conversations that may take place in between board meetings; failing to validate comments during discussion; failing to recognise contribution into the group; paying less attention to the remarks of some over the remarks of others; failing to maintain eye contact when the person is speaking; and cutting them off in mid-sentence
Social sanctioning	A form of informal control that is less subtle and more punitive in its effects; it is designed not only to deter the contribution of another but also to pressure them into conforming to a particular position held by a powerful person or persons who hold the balance of power on a board	Swift and dismissive closing down of divergence, disagreement or contention with the effect of silencing legitimate doubt and constructive dissent

Source: Thuraisingham (2018).

describes some of the invisible 'group effects' that were reflected in the lived experiences of NEDs participating in the author's study, and summarises their possible effects on the integrity of strategic decisions made by boards, as well as effectiveness of boards more generally.

Chapter 4 provides prescriptions for how independent mindedness can be maintained and the integrity of the decision-making process preserved despite these invisible forces.

In conclusion

As noted, an NED's relative board capital (a combination of experience, reputations, connections and networks) forms the basis of an invisible social hierarchy that determines how NEDs respond to influence attempts and how social support for the influence attempts of others was granted or withheld.

Decision-making behaviours are influenced as much by a social context as by the cognitive aspects of a decision at hand. In particular, the social context determines an NED's preparedness to mount influence attempts and the strength with which such attempts are mounted. The resulting behavioural variations in an NED's use of influence are critical in that it ultimately shapes the character of the board.

Boards rarely speak openly about this hidden hierarchy; however, the recounting by NEDs involved in the author's study of their own and other' decision-making behaviours showed varying levels of awareness of it (Thuraisingham 2018).

As described in this chapter, a hidden hierarchy, based on the informal and subjective ranking of board capital, acts as an internalised guide and leads to a power dynamic and behavioural efforts to 'be heard', some of which, this study showed, may create a political undertone. When identification and power effects are not in equilibrium, some directors may be heard over others, some may speak up more than others, some may underspeak and some may choose to attach more importance to more confident and strident views. When this occurs, independent mindedness—the very role entrusted to NEDs—is lost and decision-making processes are compromised, which, in turn, affects the board's effectiveness as the peak decision-making group.

Additionally, each board seemed to have a set of behavioural norms that evolved through the working history of the group—behavioural norms that the group came to advocate and exemplify as 'what is acceptable around here'. These norms acted as a constraint on 'deviant' behaviour. A director's desire to fit in and retain the respect of their peers acted as a constraint on deviance, ensuring that efforts to establish one's own legitimacy to influence must conform to what is generally accepted by the board.

While real influence is achieved through the director's use of their own board capital, once a director joins a board, a hidden hierarchy of social structure and associated social effects influences how or why they may, or may not,

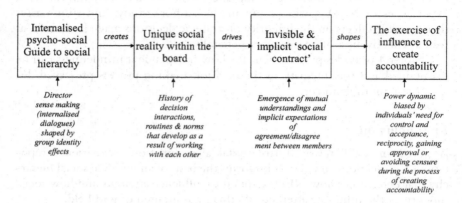

Figure 3.4 Accountability as a contextual and relational phenomenon.
Source: Thuraisingham (2018).

choose to use their influence. Until this hidden hierarchy is acknowledged, its effects fully understood and steps taken to create a more 'level playing field' in the capacity and skill to influence, efforts of boards to strengthen decision-making processes and effectiveness may fail.

This psychosocial hierarchy, invisible to those in the boardroom, has a salient link to the processes by which high performance is achieved. Figure 3.4 summarises these relationships and suggests that, to truly understand what goes on in and around the boardroom, a psychosocial approach needs to be adopted.

Actionable strategies

Desired outcome	Strategies the board may take collectively	Strategies the individual director may take
Independent mindedness	Agree on an approach to conducting regular board effectiveness reviews that focusses not only on board process but also on decision-making behaviours; use the outcomes of these reviews to test/reflect on how the board behaved in the context of a specific big decision it had to make to get a more granular collective understanding of the decision-making behaviour of the group	When a view is taken (by you or a peer NED), ask what the counterview may be and be prepared to ponder and debate that counterview openly; seek out NEDs who you admire because of the way they demonstrate independent mindedness, discuss and learn from their approaches; be prepared to role model these behaviours and call out when you feel these are not being demonstrated in decision-making

Desired outcome	Strategies the board may take collectively	Strategies the individual director may take
A single, shared view of the work of the board	Use board effectiveness reviews to reflect on role alignment in particular agreement on the board's role in strategy; the chair should facilitate conversations with NEDs when it emerges that there is not a complete alignment among NEDs	When you sense there may be some misalignment between your and others' views, seek out a mentor to explore perceived differences and a way to resolve them

References

Cialdini, R & Goldstein, N 2004, 'Social influence: compliance and conformity', *Annual Review Psychology*, vol. 55, pp. 591–621.

Demb, A & Neubauer, FF 1992, 'The corporate board: confronting the paradoxes', *Long Range Planning*, vol. 25, no. 3, pp. 9–20.

Galinsky, AD, Magee, J, Inesi, M & Gruenfeld, DH 2006, 'Power and perspectives not taken', *Psychological Science*, vol. 17, no. 12, pp. 1068–1074.

Hillman, A, Nicholson, G & Shropshire, C 2008, 'Directors' multiple identities, identification and board monitoring and resource provision', *Organisation Science*, vol. 19, no. 3, pp. 441–456.

Hooghiemstra, R & van Manen, J 2004, 'The independence paradox: im(possibilities) facing non-executive directors in the Netherlands', *Corporate Governance, An International Review*, vol. 12, no. 3, pp. 314–324.

Latané, B 1996, 'Dynamic social impact: the creation of culture by communication', *Journal of Communication*, vol. 46, pp. 13–25.

Magee, JC & Smith, PK 2013, 'The social distance theory of power', *Personality and Social Psychology Review*, vol. 17, no. 2, pp. 158–186.

Oakes, PJ, Turner, JC & Haslam, SA 1991, 'Perceiving people as group members: the role of fit in the salience of social categorizations', *British Journal of Social Psychology*, vol. 30, pp. 125–144.

Onorato, RS & Turner, JC 2004, 'Fluidity in the self-concept: the shift from personal to social identity', *European Journal of Social Psychology*, vol. 34, pp. 257–278.

Pick, K 2007, 'Around the boardroom table: interactional aspects of governance', PhD thesis, Harvard University, Cambridge, MA.

Roberts, R, McNulty, T & Stiles, S 2005, 'Beyond agency conceptions of the work of the non-executive director: creating accountability in the boardroom', *British Journal of Management*, vol. 16, pp. 5–26.

Simoes, A, Kakabadse, A & Ramos, M 2013, 'Behind the boardroom's door: the role and contribution of corporate boards', *Journal of Global Business Administration*, vol. 5, no. 1, pp. 627–650.

Sundaramurthy, C & Lewis, M 2003, 'Control and collaboration: paradoxes of governance', *Academy of Management Review*, vol. 28, no. 3, pp. 397–415.

Thuraisingham, SM 2018, 'Exploring the social factors that influence the decision making behaviours of non-executive directors in Australian public companies', PhD thesis, RMIT University, Melbourne.

Van Ees, H, Gabrielsson, J & Huse, M 2009, 'Towards a behavioural theory of boards and corporate governance', *Corporate Governance: An International Review*, vol. 17, no. 3, pp. 307–319.

Zajac, EJ & Westphal, JD 1996, 'Director reputation, CEO-board power, and the dynamics of board interlocks', *Administrative Science Quarterly*, vol. 41, no. 3, pp. 507–529.

4   Essential NED skills for strengthening strategic influence

This chapter in summary

The process of gaining and growing one's influence has to be continually negotiated and renegotiated through dialogue that demonstrates directors' finely tuned social astuteness. The mere possession of board capital is not sufficient; it is the skill with which board capital is used that determines how influential directors become in the board group. Based on research into what successful directors actually do to resolve role and task tensions, as opposed to what they should do, this chapter details the four social competencies that influential directors demonstrate to mobilise their board capital to resolve task and role tensions. The research also reveals three underlying director dispositions necessary for playing an influential role on a board.

The micro-judgements NEDs made about the social competence and propensities of their peers determined how skilful they judged others to be in navigating the hidden hierarchy and this determined their response to the influencing efforts of others. These perceptions were in no way static; instead, they were subject to continually negotiated and renegotiated relations through the directors' discursive practices accompanying each influence attempt.

The chapter proposes strategies for how influence is gained through questioning and contention; shared through feedback and learning; asserted through purposeful use of relevance and expertise; and supported through initiating, engaging with and owning challenge as a necessary part of healthy board processes. Despite the important role they play, social competencies and dispositional attributes are rarely considered in the selection of new directors or the development of existing directors. The chapter concludes with a handy framework to guide what boards need to look for in hiring new directors and developing existing ones.

This chapter includes a second letter to the nominations committee; it suggests that relational and dispositional attributes (the means by which board capital is mobilised effectively) must be taken into account to achieve the right board mix. The letter challenges the frequently heard label 'right fit' that may be used to hire directors who will not 'rock the boat'. The notion of fit may adversely affect the contention of ideas and diversity of perspectives and viewpoints so essential for a healthy decision-making dynamic, resulting in an overly agreeable boardroom. Strategies are offered to the committee for getting the right board mix to allow constructive contention to thrive, rather than hiring more of the same to fit in with what you already have.

Transformative decisions have the potential to profoundly change the strategic direction of a business. By their very nature, strategic decisions contain significant complexity and ambiguity; therefore, they are open to multiple interpretations by decision-makers, each with their own diverse career experiences and cognitive histories. This can contribute to the inherent task and role tensions that decision-makers have to contend with when they work together as a group on such decisions.

The uncertainty that often surrounds large strategic decisions comes in two forms:

1   substantive uncertainty, which results from an objective lack of data about some aspect of the decision problem.
2   procedural uncertainty, which results from incomplete knowledge or understanding of the decision-makers.

The more uncertainty that surrounds the decision, the more important the knowledge of the decision-maker becomes. Given the information asymmetry that boards are subject to, this is a major task-related tension. How NEDs get the knowledge they require to address the perceived uncertainty through robust and persistent probing and challenging while keeping boardroom relationships in tact is critical. Directors show variation in how they go about navigating and resolving task tensions. These variations, as revealed in director-recounted experiences, support the author's experience in working with boards and top teams.

However, task uncertainties amplify the need for NED effectiveness beyond the cognitive talents they bring. Personalities and traits also play a role. The author's study shows that NEDs mount influence attempts according to their dispositions, which, in turn, shapes the style and behavioural approach they adopt. Psychological aspects of NEDs, such as motivational needs, personality type, propensities or social competence, have rarely been studied in relation to boards (Bailey & Peck 2013). These aspects are salient to board decision-making culture and processes. NED dispositions bring a productive balance to the dilemmas faced in being open to the influence of others, while simultaneously retaining independent mindedness. Their dispositions determine their tendencies or propensities to act in certain ways, and these are often observable to others.

Dispositions and associated propensities are driven by motives and needs (McClelland 1985; Schutz 1958). The stories NEDs told in the author's study showed that they observed the propensities of their peers on a board and that these observations affected the use they made of the contribution of other NEDs during the decision discourse. For example, Director A, who valued the propensity to be independent minded, recounted how they drew another NED into a conversation in an attempt to demonstrate and model the importance of independent mindedness.

This chapter describes how both relational skills and dispositional attributes mobilise a director's possessed power (described as 'board capital' in Chapter 2) into real influence. With regard to relational skills, the author's study revealed four social competencies are described in this chapter: social perception, impression management, articulacy and adaptability. The study also revealed that NEDs made inferences about the influencer's dispositions—particularly, their propensity to be influenced, or to influence, when working with others. These inferences a director made about the influencer's propensities reflected three themes: the propensity to act and reflect with others, propensity to practice detachment and distance while involved, and propensity to concede to or resist social pressure.

Clearly, these findings are relevant to those responsible for director selection and development. Board nomination committees need to recognise that board capital is only valuable if it is accompanied by social competencies and socially alert dispositions; yet, these are not consistently selected for.

In summary, director work is not merely an expression of agency but also an effect of social factors such as identity and power. The complex interplay between an influencer (in this case an NED) and an inner context creates a 'social reality' unique to every board. This social reality—in effect, a psychosocial infrastructure shaped by identity and power effects—is invisible to those in a boardroom, but is critical in determining how influence is exercised (Thuraisingham 2018).

Behavioural variations in NED use of board capital for influence

As noted, an NED's board capital derived from their cognitive history did not completely determine their power to influence. The sense NEDs made of the 'social reality' they encountered on the board and the choices they made (consciously or otherwise) to use their board capital determined how influential they become. This section describes how NEDs, in a variety of different ways, went about trying to influence the strategic direction of the company in the various stages of a strategy-shaping process, as described in Chapter 1. Task and role tensions were recalled by narrating directors during such interpersonal interactions while shaping strategy. The first part of this section describes relational themes found in NED narratives concerning their decision-making experiences. The second relates to the dispositional themes reflected in the NED narratives. The term 'relational theme' refers to interpersonal behaviour that emerged between NEDs when dealing with task tensions; 'dispositional theme' refers to the underlying propensities evident when NEDs were confronted with role tensions. There was significant complexity and uncertainty among the 15 NEDs contemplating acquisitions in new markets in the author's study; therefore, conflicting views were likely to emerge, particularly between TMTs and NEDs. This is particularly noticeable in situations in which management fails to fully acknowledge, recognise or actively utilise the depth and breadth of knowledge, expertise and networks that NEDs cumulatively provide. Participating NEDs also recounted conflicting perspectives and differences among their NED board peers—a consequence of cognitive or ideological differences within a board group.

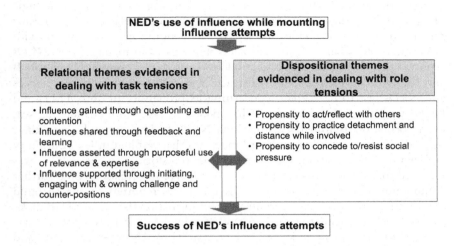

Figure 4.1 NEDs' use of influence: relational and dispositional themes found in the study of NED influence attempts.

Source: Thuraisingham (2018).

All 15 decision narratives evidenced competing or paradoxical demands that NEDs needed to resolve by influencing others and remaining open to the influence of others—that is, by supporting or challenging a proposal. Both task and role tensions emerged in this process, the former depicted by four relational themes and the latter by three dispositional themes. These themes are discussed in 'Relational themes' and 'Dispositional themes', and are summarised in Figure 4.1.

Before discussing these themes, a key issue needs to be acknowledged. As is evidenced in Chapter 3, despite NEDs having the power to influence discussion and debate, it is clear that they did not always choose to exercise it (consciously or otherwise). Consequently, a number of questions need to be addressed: How are divergent views and associated tensions resolved? Are there variations in how some directors managed these tensions? How do power differentials affect the actual enactment of influence attempts and what explanations might there be for behavioural variation?

Relational themes

The existence of cognitively diverse views forced NEDs to entertain alternative perspectives and courses of action and to engage in careful examination of identified alternatives. This was evidenced by contentions contained in director-recounted experiences. It was reported that this debate required NEDs to simultaneously challenge assumptions made and to argue for alternatives without fearing loss of acceptance or damaging existing board relationships.

In the face of the uncertainty and complexity associated with transformative decisions, NEDs were required to uncompromisingly and unapologetically seek out the answers they needed to satisfy themselves on the strategic logic of a proposal. In the minds of several NEDs, this logic related to both return on capital and management capacity, as new acquisitions can compete with domestic business and require considerable focus from management. NEDs reported that this aspect was often underestimated. For example, Directors B and I noted that 'management overreach' was common in their experiences and NEDs had to be vigilant concerning its propensity in both TMTs and NEDs with limited experience. What made this task more challenging was the information asymmetry with which NEDs had to contend, given their limited involvement between board meetings that resulted in less continuity and depth of information. Concerning large transformative decisions, it was reported that levels of uncertainty and incomplete information could further compound information asymmetry issues. NEDs reported having to build trust with management to ascertain all the information they required to make sound decisions during the entire period of a 'live' deal. NEDs reported variations in the levels of trust they experienced on a board between executive and non-executive members, the chair and each other.

Anxiety was heightened when it related to what was perceived as a ground-breaking transaction that did not conform to the normal investment metrics used by a company. Typically, participating NEDs reported that, at the early stages, some peer NEDs were in favour of a deal, others were not and some were neutral. For those reporting their position as sceptical at this early stage, there was a level of anxiety about the likelihood of others being captured by the 'deal fever' often associated with high-profile acquisitions. Those reporting that they felt positively disposed to such a deal pending further debate, expressed concern that some peer NEDs were too conservative and risk-averse. These themes further support the evidence that director work is filled with cognitive paradoxes and group-related tensions that need resolution.

The rest of this section describes four relational themes that reflect the 'social competence' required to successfully mount influence attempts, as reported by NEDs while enacting their strategy-shaping accountabilities. These influence attempts solved the twin challenges of needing to reduce the perceived uncertainty associated with a deal decision and, simultaneously, demonstrating trust in the judgements and expertise of others.

Theme 1: how influence was gained through questioning and contention

NEDs reported acute interest in whether assumptions stacked up in the first place. This was achieved through questioning and contention. As Director I reported, what was perceived to be in contention and how it was questioned were both important:

> The things that were of most interest to me [were] whether we hadn't allowed hubris to overtake us in terms of what we thought the forward trajectory of the target business would be. That we did not necessarily

assume that our sales projections were going to come to fruition and not recognise that more supply will be coming into the market and the owners of that supply may be as successful as we would be in forming those relationships ... [I]t is a problem when directors become too in love with the ethos ... [T]hey have to be able to detach themselves from sacred cows ... and be prepared to challenge and be challenged.

Directors indicated that a tactic they often used during a debate was to ascertain for themselves how much contention there was among a management team. This evidence was often used as a litmus test for how well reasoned a proposal was in the first place. As Directors L and I observed:

> I was concerned also about the misalignment amongst [sic] management in their conversations with us. It concerned me ... [A]re you guys on the same page?... Do you all agree the price is right? Are you all supportive of doing this? I wanted to know that there was good contention within the management team around price. So, I said, 'convince me that you are getting counter views and challenge from the finance people to make sure we do not overpay'. It took me a while to expose the process [and] later ... it was characterised by weakness and left people feeling uncomfortable about where we landed on price.
>
> (Director L)

> If management does not bring to us [in addition to what they propose] what they reject, then you are not having as robust a discussion as you should. It's like the John West analogy [referring to a tuna cannery's quality claim] ... [W]hat fish did they reject? It's a discipline that some boards get into and others don't.
>
> (Director I)

Most NEDs participating in this study attached considerable danger or risk to hubris and the pervasive power of 'deal fever', which can overcome management as well as a board. Emotional states (such as hubris) associated with different parties involved in takeovers have long been investigated by researchers (Chatterjee & Hambrick 2007; Malmendier & Tate 2005). Generally associated with arrogance, vanity and self-importance, hubristic behaviour often leads to an exaggerated sense of one's accomplishments and capabilities. For example, Director A stated that the tactic of role-playing a fictitious deal scenario in a target country could be useful both as practice and as a means of securing pre-agreements about decision protocols, including 'go-no-go' parameters. He suggested that the tactic could also reduce the danger of losing perspective in the middle of a large deal when emotions were usually high and objectivity could be lost due to overconfidence.

In relation to the style of questioning, participating NEDs varied in their approach to working through what they perceived as task tensions. Some suggested that an NED's persistent questioning could be perceived as either helpful or a nuisance, depending on their delivery. The persistence required to face a resistant CEO was another theme some NEDs reported. For example, Director A stated:

> The going-in position of management had been that the target had a very strong management team. I did not think that necessarily … I had concerns from experience. I was concerned about the expertise in the finance and risk areas and felt we needed to put our key people into those key roles. There was a need to integrate the supply chain and also [sic] fully integrate the staff into the organisation (culturally). I had two to three goes with the CEO before the penny dropped for the CEO on this issue.

Director K described the need for incisiveness and directness in questions, and wariness about repeated and previous failed attempts in a target market:

> This board, in particular, is very wary of 'this time it's different' statements because this is a biggest cop-out for managements as well as boards. You actually have to go back and say [sic], 'how is it different, why it's different' … [It is] all too easy to say 'this time it's different' … This is really about challenging assertions that management are making and exploring those. Also, [it is] about testing the credibility of their assertions … and determining if they are extracting the right lessons from past experiences the company has had in China.

The style of questioning was also key. Director E described one ex-director's 'acerbic punch in the nose style'. While acknowledging that, as the chair of an audit committee and impatient with their CEO's lack of swift responses to his audit concerns, the director had asked some great questions, in the process he 'blew up all the relationships around him'. This particular director would accept feedback from NEDs in closed sessions and improve for two to three meetings; however, his acerbic style would then reappear. Director E (who served on a nominations committee) recounted that although the board appreciated the director's insightful questions, it briefed a recruitment consultant to find a director with a similar depth of audit knowledge, but with a more constructive style. This reveals that an NED's ability to read social cues is an important aspect of questioning style.

Some NEDs reported that the style of questioning could, at times, result in a board judging an executive too harshly; it seems there is a very fine line that may be crossed by an interrogative board in the questioning style they adopt. For example, Director L, as chair of a human resources (HR) and remuneration committee, reported:

> It emerged over a board dinner that some NEDs doubted the sponsoring executive's capabilities. I tried to temper this view by saying she comes

from a different world ... let her management decide her development. We have to be careful we are not judging her too quickly because she is different. I think of myself as a coach on these HR issues.

In summary, the contention and skilled questioning revealed NEDs' skills and competence in accurately perceiving what was going on in and around a boardroom to reveal more of what must be known to move forward. The tone or style of questioning was critical to ensure trust was preserved. This demonstrated the significant amount of self-control required for an NED to not leap in and take over a debate.

Theme 2: how influence was shared through feedback, learning and adaptation

A second relational theme reported by participating NEDs was how others reacted to their contribution, which could either drive learning and adaptation or narrow what was perceived as permittable at board meetings. When some NEDs spoke and their contribution was poorly received, this response fed back into their self-construal. NEDs made various interpretations of this response. Some concluded that others did not value or understand their contribution. Others reappraised what they brought to a board or reappraised the relevance of their perspective on some issues. Such reappraisals, according to the literature on identity (Hillman, Nicholson & Shropshire 2008; Lawler et al. 2002; Nadler 2004), are continual and modify the dynamic of individual and group behaviour, which, in turn, influences a board dynamic's level of engagement or passivity. This was evidenced by the narratives of all NEDs in this study. Power and identity effects appeared to determine who learned what from whom.

NEDs learned by observing their peers, even when they had significant prior board experience. For example, Director N asked, 'why did I not think of that question?', referring to a peer's question. Director N had observed that the peer spoke very little, but when he did, his questions were consistently impressive and, in this instance, reflected a unique way of reframing an issue or concern and opening up the conversation.

Others adapted their thinking through the course of a discussion without expressing their views, even though their perspectives had changed because of the well-reasoned arguments they had heard. For example, Director P reported his learning from the experiences and attitudes of others:

I expect as a lawyer you are taught to surface and identify risks ... [Y]ou can't eliminate risk, but you can optimise it ... but there were some directors more optimistic than me, especially those with a financial services background. I learned to adapt my approach over time [on this board] ... to appreciate the upside as much as the downside.

While some experienced NEDs showed an openness to learning, board tenure differentials also acted as a means of learning. NEDs new to board life, adjusting to the transition from an executive to a non-executive role, were generally viewed by their peers as being on a learning curve and expectations of their contribution to strategy were not high. Importantly, NEDs who were new to board life, or early in their first term at the time of the transaction under study, were hesitant in their contributions.

In the case of NEDs new to a board or new to directing and on a learning curve, some of their behaviours were telling. For example, NEDs with longer tenure reported that newly appointed NEDs looked for ways to make an immediate contribution to debates and justify their appointment. This need, at times, resulted in raising what were perceived as irrelevant, peripheral or nitpicking questions. Conversely, other new NEDs admitted to reticence and to hanging back deliberately to grasp a decision-making dynamic—particularly how divergent or dissenting views were reacted to by a chair and the extent to which these views were encouraged. As Directors P and G reported:

> While banking is at one level a simple business, at another level it is complex, and I found it very difficult to understand. I looked around the table and formed an assessment about the directors in terms of reliability, competence and judgement and listened especially to those who had more experience in that sector than I had.
>
> (Director P)

> I was new and sitting back learning about the competence of the individuals. I did not have the confidence to say this [referring to a challenge about who would be the better owner of the business] at the time. It took me two to three meetings to notice individuals whose opinion you should pay attention to.
>
> (Director G)

This was further evidence of directors learning from others and consciously applying self-control to manage the perception of other directors with more seniority (in tenure terms) than their own. Director K described the way that NEDs shared their influence by playing 'bad cop, good cop' to get a result when faced with a CEO they perceived as resistant or as recalcitrant.

Long tenure was accompanied by familiarity, shared understanding and higher levels of group learning. However, there were also some challenges perceived to be associated with long tenure, such as strategic persistence and lower tolerance for risk. As Director I observed:

> The reason why after 10 years it is probably time you go … by then you have seen enough and made so many decisions, you get invested in the trajectory and lose a bit of independence of thought … It is the classic

dilemma because you are on the board because you have the expertise ... and have enough information in order to do the oversight ... [but] you can't oversight something you don't understand.

Clearly, more learning occurred in some board contexts than others. Likewise, an experience of shared power on one board did not mean it was transferable to another. Director B reported that their experience of a banking board was distinctly different from a resources company board; they found that the resources sector was not always as open to strategic logic sourced from other sectors and this, in their view, was a lost opportunity. According to Director B, the resources sector tended to value long tenure in that sector over lessons derived from other sectors. This experience reflects how the influence of an NED can differ from board to board because of the extent to which some board groups perceive and value 'outsider' cognitions. This experience was a common theme. The evidence in response to the interviewer's question, 'are there some boards that engage you more than others and why', suggests that, in the experience of participating NEDs, some board groups were more receptive to 'outsider' perspectives. These findings confirm the theory of perspective taking, tested empirically by Galinsky et al. (2006), which showed an inverse relation between power and perspective taking. Perspective taking, in this context, refers to the propensity to step outside one's own experience and imagine the emotions, perceptions and motivations of another—the antithesis of the self-interested behaviour often displayed by the powerful (Galinsky et al. 2006).

Some NEDs perceived some of their peers on their last term as resisting learning and adapting. These longer-serving NEDs were more concerned about jeopardising their legacy; therefore, they adopted a 'safer path' by discouraging what they perceived as a high-risk acquisition with a long-term payoff. As Director A reported:

I think there were a couple of board members who from the start were not sold on the idea ... because they may have been thinking about their own reputational risk in a 'not on my watch' kind of way ... not willing to invest for the long term or accept taking a short-term hit. They may have had deep reservations that remained unspoken. When concerns or fundamental objections are not drawn out early and remain unspoken, they can come back again later in the process in a different guise, as I suspect it did in this example.

This finding supports Finkelstein and Hambrick's (1996) study, which showed a positive relation between team tenure and strategic persistence. By contrast, Golden and Zajac (2001) found a curvilinear relationship—that is, tenure had a positive relation only to a certain point, beyond which it had an adverse effect, thus creating a greater attachment to current strategies. The finding also supports the work of Scheepers, Ellemers and Sassenberg (2013), who found group status (in-group or out-group alignment) mattered in the promotion or prevention of choices in group decision-making. Groups that were deemed to have more status would seek to preserve the status quo. This study shows that some of this effect can be sought covertly.

In summary, learning to share power, learning from each other and adapting one's approach was critical in contributing to effective NED decision-making. These NED behaviours, associated with openness to learning from other NEDs perceived to have more experience, were accompanied by a desire to be perceived as open, balanced and considered in their approach during decision-making processes.

Theme 3: how influence was asserted through skilled articulation of relevance and expertise

NEDs found that judgements concerning the relevance of a contributor's experience and standing, determined how much attention was paid to their comments or questions. This third relational theme was qualified by a salient warning from some NEDs about the dangers of experience and how it could blind, especially when faced with a business environment characterised by less certainty and more disruption. An NED's embeddedness in the NED community appeared to influence the personal standing attributed to them. This manifested in how others showed respect for their perspectives and, in some cases—but not all—ascribed significantly greater weight to their contributions relative to others; consequently, this strengthened their relative influence over the direction of a debate. For example, with 11 years of experience as an NED and responsible for the Asian division of a global business, Director H reported feeling confident about his challenges to a debate. He believed he had the respect of others around the table because of his long CEO experience in emerging markets. More particularly, he reported his success in clearly articulating to other board members the notion of growth optionality in the target market, convincing them to not get too hung-up on the price of the target entity and consider the value of the growth option in that market.

Experienced directors often volunteered or were asked to play informal roles in a debate, as described by Director E:

> A year ago, when we were doing the transformation, this part of the business was on the sale list, and now we wanted to bulk on it, it did not make sense ... But the CEO was now a convert to it, and I always worried about converts ... [H]ad he got deal fever from spending too much time with the investment bankers? ... [Y]ou pay a large amount of money to engage an investment bank, which is on a success fee and of course they will tell you why this is a good idea. The logic of taking out a competitor just because someone else may buy it did not stack up! I wanted to make sure we kept an eye on the 'no case' case ... I was

sceptical from the start, so, the chair asked me to be the black hat … I did not need convincing!

However, several NEDs reported an interesting nuance about subject matter experience. A common theme was the observation typified by senior directors (Directors O and H) that less experienced NEDs often assumed that they had to have expertise in a subject to make a good contribution:

> It is often thought that you have to have expertise in a particular subject to make a good decision. You need to know what questions to ask, and this comes from well-rounded commercial experience … [I]t's the totality of that experience and how you use it that matters.
>
> (Director O)

> He [referring to the chair] does not go to the subject-matter experts around the board table to ask them what they would do in this instance … he does not turn to the directors with marketing experience and ask what do you think of this marketing campaign. Otherwise, the board is getting dragged into being the expert, and it is not.
>
> (Director H)

In several cases, NEDs reported that the unique body of expertise they possessed was not present on the board on which they had been invited to serve. This included international, M&A and start-up experience. This finding was not unexpected because the scenario selected for this study was a major transformative decision. For example, Director C observed:

> This was one of the reasons they were attracted to me, and I was attracted to this particular company. They were looking at doing significant expansion in Asia they had had a few stop-start attempts. This is where my experience lies … in this particular part of North Asia.

As noted in Chapter 2, the degree to which an NED felt their experience was unique to that board was an important validation for their construal of their place or role within that group (Hillman, Nicholson & Shropshire 2008; Thuraisingham 2018). For example, Director L—previously CEO of a major company in the technology sector and well known in that sector—joined a board in which his experience (in his self-conception) was unique because he was the only person with a technology background. Therefore, this director perceived that he should be recognised as the 'go-to' person on that board for advice and opinion on technology-related matters. This self-perception, in turn, affected the role (active or otherwise) Director L played. His subjective sense of power and personal confidence in the relevant expertise area was evident in the decision story he relived.

However, this approach was not always viewed positively by other participating NEDs. Some raised the danger associated with board thinking being abdicated to NEDs perceived as subject experts. They suggested that over-reliance on some NEDs, including committee chairs had, on occasion, resulted in the unintended consequence of typecasting directors into narrow and rigid roles by their peers. It also resulted in misplaced trust in one person's advice that affected boardroom opinion disproportionately—for example, a board being captured by an expert's own cognitive biases. Three NEDs suggested that, as a rule, the deep domain expertise of an NED was most relevant in committee work, not board work in which broader business and commercial experience were more relevant.

In summary, the assertion of influence through the skilled articulation of relevance and expertise relies on an NED's ability to assemble and frame their arguments and to state the merits of their position eloquently. Drawing on their past experiences, without being biased by it was deemed as key. Further, it appears that while subject matter experts were important, participating NEDs did not consider such expertise to be influential if the commercial relevance to the discussion at hand was not demonstrated clearly.

Theme 4: how influence was supported through the challenge process

A final relational theme centered around the method of the challenge process. The way that focussed and persistent questioning was successfully received in a boardroom relied, to some extent, on how NEDs worked collectively to support the NED posing a challenge question. NEDs did this by adding a comment of their own to questions posed, asking a clarifying question of a director to make a point clearer to management or making a helpful restatement. When an individual NED decided to take on a decision challenge, it could involve a critique of management and result in a defensive response. NEDs also reported being prepared to own a peer–director critique by asking questions to clarify a challenge to a CEO and signal support for a question. Presenting a 'united front' in this way resulted in a CEO taking a challenger's question more seriously. As Directors B, K and I, respectively, reported:

> He referenced that offline conversation we had had at the coffee break [during which he had sought reassurance from me about a technology platform issue in which he had no prior experience], back into the boardroom and said I had helped him think through his reservations. He said to the board he was still nervous and why, which then allowed the others to join in and ask for additional information to be provided to address his residual concerns.
>
> (Director B)

Certainly styles on this board are different. I tend to play the role quite often [sic] of getting beyond conflict. Sometimes I found it very valuable outside the boardroom to go to the person and ask what is really troubling you [about the valuation of this deal].

(Director K)

Someone will say something, and a director will ask a question about it, not to offer a different view but to clarify the point and to better explain [sic] what the person was putting in the room ... and this is helpful for others of us too.

(Director I)

Participating NEDs showed support and trust during a decision-making process, which was distinct from collective ownership at the end of that process when consensus was required. Collective ownership of the process itself played a role in signalling to NEDs that there was both permission and space for contention and challenge, and that the processes of challenge were an equally owned and shared responsibility of every NED, despite their power status. These findings appear to suggest that the strength of collective ownership of the challenge process depended on the strength of group identification.

Several NEDs spoke about the protocol of providing notice of a challenge to a CEO or chair (or both), which, hence, provided an opportunity to deal with a challenge before a meeting. As Director H observed:

One of the conventions [on this board] is that you don't open the discussion with dissension ... [I]t comes later ... an unwritten rule ... [A]lso if directors have studied the paper and have issues they will raise it beforehand either with the chair or CEO: 'heads up, this is an issue that is troubling me'.

In summary, the four relational themes demonstrate the behaviors that NEDs employ (consciously or otherwise) to mobilise the board capital they possess. However, this power is only mobilised by the behaviours NEDs demonstrate when interacting with others. These findings lay the groundwork for a social competence framework, discussed in 'Framework of social competence required for director effectiveness'.

When task tensions were resolved effectively, NEDs reported facing tough conversations with courage, conviction, persistence and determination, while showing respect for and trust in others' judgements and ideological differences. The more deal-anxiety experienced and the greater likelihood of divergent views, the more inquiry skills were used (coupled with preparedness) to learn from the experiences of others. NEDs also invested the time required to reach across cognitive or ideological differences and satisfactorily address divergent views while simultaneously being mindful of the need for efficiency, given most transformative decisions (such as acquisition deals) have immovable timelines. The ability to read social cues that may convey hubristic sentiment and sense the level of management contention prior to a proposal coming to a board was also important in how questions were posed. For this kind of contention to occur, the existence of intra-boardroom trust was pivotal, as was a chair's encouragement of contention and the creation of an environment in which all NEDs felt they had a voice in debate, even if there was no agreement. Essentially, these relational skills neutralised any potential adverse effects of power differentials.

However, these relational skills are only one part of the explanation of differences in NED behaviour concerning task tensions. The skilful behaviours that NEDs employed, as described in this section, are, in turn, determined by underlying NED dispositions that also shaped their attitudes to the role they play in and around the boardroom. 'Dispositional themes' describes NEDs' underlying propensities or traits and their relevance in resolving the role tensions that NEDs experienced.

Dispositional themes

The second tension evidenced from the 15 cases studied related to an NED's role. As an independent director who represents the interests of shareholders, an NED is, when necessary, expected to demonstrate independent thinking (Berghe & Baelden 2005; Huse & Rindova 2001; Johnson, Schnatterly & Hill 2013; Stiles & Taylor 2001). To work effectively with others in a board group in a unified way they need to show a propensity to identify strongly with a board; however, as independent directors, they must feel comfortable to stand alone in their views, if required. In respect of a major strategic decision on which much is at stake, this capacity for independence manifests as an NED's ability to strike a balance between their propensity to influence others versus their propensity to be influenced by others. Both are critical for director effectiveness.

Therefore, NED motives were a relevant consideration in studying how directors managed this balance. As discussed in Chapter 2, NEDs demonstrated certain motivations in their narratives, particularly when responding to questions posed by the researcher at the start of the semi-structured interviews: 'how did you come to be on this board?' and 'what attracted you to join this board?' Since needs and propensities predict and shape behaviour (McClelland 1987; Schutz 1958), the responses to these questions revealed a variety of underlying motivations as described in Chapter 2.

Further, research suggests that, in discharging director accountabilities, there are dangers of over-identification with a board group and that this may result in silencing one's own doubts in order to be accepted (Fritsche et al. 2013; Turner 1987, 2005). Conversely, a lack of identification with a board group may generate interpersonal friction and disunity, resulting in suspicion and low trust levels impacting the collective ownership of the challenge process as described in 'Theme 4: how influence was supported through the challenge process'. NED propensities could explain how these tensions arise. These propensities—disposing NEDs towards certain recognisable behavioural strategies and responses observed by others—reflected a variety of underlying traits. As Director H explained:

> There are people who are the devil's advocates, some the cheer squad, conciliators [who bridge differences] ... some are chatterboxes, and others are more reserved ... and all of those different styles in a team are evident here. I think most people are predominately one thing or the other ... no one is one third, one third, one third, if you know what I mean ... [M]ost people are temperamentally predisposed one way or another.

The author's study found three recurring dispositional themes in the data that may explain how behavioural strategies and responses of participating NEDs were used to resolve role tensions. The rest of this section describes these themes.

Theme 1: acting and reflecting during discourse with others

An NED's propensity to initiate action or show bias to act (as opposed to engaging in quiet or passive reflection) when working with others on issues of high-level complexity was a double-edged sword. NEDs perceived by others as having a strong bias for action tended to control conversations rather than let them emerge. Other NEDs were described as being more considered and reflective in their responses to complexity, more willing to allow a conversation to emerge without needing to control it, synthesising the contribution of others and adapting and responding as they went.

Participating NEDs suggested that the need to opine on every issue could be a distraction in a boardroom and observed the tendency of some of their peers to act in this way. Some speculated that this reflected a desire to 'show they have read all the board papers' or a tendency to construe themselves as experts on every topic, regardless of complexity. The capability of directors for self-reflection emerged as an important theme and was perceived by narrating NEDs as helpful when balanced. For example, Director I explained:

> There is definitely one director who feels the need to make a comment on virtually everything that is raised on this board, which is not the way this board operates, which is tedious ... and likes to intellectualise things ... and I don't find that particularly helpful.

Others were described as quieter, keen to keep their options open (especially when things were a close run) and not wanting to commit too early to one side or the other. One director observed that 'pacing' in a conversation was a skill because 'you may not want to be the first person to say yes every time or the last person to say yes every time'. Conversely, some NEDs spoke about the lack of contribution by some peers, suggesting that they were either intimidated or overwhelmed by the context or simply on a board because they needed to fund their post-executive life.

Director motivation has been examined closely by Guerrero and Sequin (2012) who suggested that the extent to which a director was self-oriented or showed pro-organisation orientation was the key determinant of contribution— that is, one's commitment to the goals and benefit of an organisation versus self-orientation. The author's study showed that personality-related factors also played an important role. A director's contribution appeared to be a complex manifestation of orientation, personality traits and learning habits. Director G described this phenomenon as follows:

> I guess it is that some [NEDs] are more reserved, diffident in their views. I remember X [refers to his mentor who has now retired from board life and was on the same bank board] used to say, 'I might be stupid but can you run that past me again' ... which then tended to get more conversation going. I know from experience that is not uncommon for directors to sit there without saying anything even if they don't understand the issues ... reluctant to admit that they don't know or understand. Part of the ego thing. Most directors are very experienced, and they have got there because of their experience. So, it is hard to admit you don't know ... not wanting to look stupid or appearing like a hot rod. Or, in some cases having been part of the school of hard knocks, you learn not to declare your hand too early and are more guarded.

In their decision stories, NEDs suggested that a fine balance between acting and reflecting was required to optimise their ability to learn from others and adapt their approach. While these were individual dispositions, some directors spoke about them in a collective sense. For example, Director L suggested that the ability to reflect collectively as a board group (with and without management) would become increasingly important as companies looked to acquire adjacent but related businesses about which they had little knowledge. This was the case with his decision story, which related to the acquisition of an offshore entity in an emerging technology:

> We had maybe half a dozen or more clunky, unproductive and frustrating discussions. First with management in the room and then without, discussing why we seemed to be collectively having a problem with this

proposal ... [W]e were having difficulty getting clarity over what the business was, why it was strategic and why we should pay this money for it.

(Director L)

Several NEDs also spoke about the need for boards and management to adopt an emergent style (i.e., not seek to control conversations too tightly), especially when contemplating a complex international growth strategy: a fluid, conversational style—dynamic, ongoing and not just 'deal driven' (i.e., reacting opportunistically when a good deal comes along). A recurring theme in the narratives was the acknowledgment by NEDs that, as an environment became more uncertain, questions of strategy also became more uncertain. In such an environment, board conversations needed to change; people needed to have the opportunity and permission to be frank about their uncertainty and levels of comfort. This suggests that fact-based, logical arguments are not the only skill required; a disposition to deal effectively with ambiguity and uncertainty is also required.

These findings provide support for a good balance between the propensity to act and reflect by both an individual NED and a board when working through complex decision challenges characterised by uncertainty. They also provide support for the seminal learning theories of Argyris and Schön (1978), which give prominence to the process of reflection as the key to how people learn. It suggests that more learning may occur in boardrooms if more time and space is created for reflection, something a chair can facilitate and nurture as explored in more detail in Chapter 5.

Theme 2: practising detachment and distance while involved

As distinct from the propensity to act or reflect with others, when dealing with high levels of complexity the propensity to detach oneself from a situation was a common theme. Constructive detachment from a situation or group is difficult, especially when you are clearly a member (Latané 1981; Oakes, Turner & Haslam 1991; Simon & Oakes 2006). Some NEDs reported the ability to be part of this process while staying above it, while others observed peers who had varying abilities to perform this skill.

This disposition was reflected by an NED's expressed commitment to a decision process but detachment from a decision outcome. Director C was the only person (board and management) with deep experience in the target geography. Although new to a board, she was placed in the role of directing. She explained:

I had to try and be very even-handed and put in a sense my pro-X view [referring to the target country] aside ... [and] consciously step back from that [her optimism about X] ... I had to be very careful that I was being very objective and consciously work out the risk, really understand the risk–reward analysis and at what point we will [sic] not proceed.

In describing the attributes of change leaders, Heifetz and Linsky (2002) draw on the metaphor of a dance floor and a balcony to explain the different picture one would get if one was looking down from the balcony, seeing patterns unseen from the perspective of the dance floor.

Likewise, it could be suggested that NEDs may only gain both a clearer view of the 'social reality' of a boardroom and some perspective by distancing themselves from the fray. However, to affect what is happening, one must return to the 'dance floor'. Hence, one needs to be among the dancers while simultaneously being on the 'balcony'. Staying with the Heifetz and Linsky (2002) metaphor, NEDs implied that affective contributions to board decisions resulted from the propensity to go back and forth between the two, using one to leverage the other. Director A explained this disposition as follows:

> I think one needs to be careful as a NED that one is not captured by the process if, for example, there is too much informal front-end work with the management team (on the deal) then you end up being in a position where you are advocating the deal rather than drawing distance from it in order to provide the required oversight.

The decision stories also reflected examples of NEDs, including chairs, over-identifying with a decision and channelling their contribution to fit with a conclusion they desired. As Director H reported:

> Some chairs have made up their mind already and see their job as getting everyone to reach that decision. A good chair gets the directors to reach the decisions themselves and does not play tricks to get you there.

Effectiveness in navigating this tension required NEDs to exercise a constructive level of 'social distance'; motivated by the desire to be respected rather than liked, confident of the value they brought to debates and prepared to engage with the value that others brought. Director H reported that management had been known to 'play games' and that NEDs needed to be mindful of this:

> Some management spends a lot of time 'marinating' the board so that when the decision comes around the board directors are all soft and tender and say yes immediately ... [T]his was a very fraught area. Of course, management has to do some socialising of ideas to get [d]irectors up to speed and tease out concerns but this can sometimes go too far ... when

they pick off directors they think would be most supportive [of the proposal] and whom they marinate first.

As noted in Chapter 3, social distancing investigated by Westphal and Khanna (2003) is a means of social control, which included keeping less powerful board members in line. Where power differentials are large— that is, where significant differences exist in the origins of power, as described earlier in this chapter—Westphal and Khanna found evidence of subtle control to 'guide' the decision process towards an outcome. In the author's study, this was reflected in Director D's observation that a major part of a decision was made beforehand by the chair and deputy chair (on the basis of their relatively long experience in the mining and resources sector) and 'choreographed into the room'. The negative effect such political manoeuvrings have on director accountability and governance is clear and is supported by previous studies (Bailey & Peck 2013). The propensity of an NED to stay in the fray while simultaneously staying above it and intuit what may be happening is important for retaining objectivity and independent mindedness, especially when faced with powerful and influential experts or by overconfident decision-makers.

Theme 3: conceding to and resisting social pressure from the influence attempts of others

The dominant logic in corporate governance is that NEDs who are held accountable for their judgements will resist agency pressures (Roberts 1991; Stiles & Taylor 2001). However, this view ignores the social reality of groups. Social influences acting on groups have a long history of research (Cialdini & Goldstein 2004). According to social impact theory, how we respond to influence attempts by others is dependent on who the influencers are, how many there are and the immediacy of their effect (Latané 1981).

The propensity for an NED to be attracted to 'people like me', how they respond to influence attempts by others they see as similar or dissimilar and the cognitive processing they engage in when their views deviate from the norm are described in previous chapters. Almost all of the NEDs participating in the author's study cited the attraction of working with particular board members, including high-profile names, as their motivation for joining a board. Some of the judgements made by participating NEDs about 'peer compatibility' can be explained by a range of social influence theories reviewed by Cialdini and Goldstein (2004).

The admiration that NEDs expressed for peers on a board (discussed in Chapters 2 and 3) is relevant because of its potential to make them more positively disposed to certain decision processes and less questioning (Lorsch & MacIver 1989). Conversely, Forbes and Milliken (1999) suggested that there must be a minimum level of interpersonal attraction for board members to have mutual trust regarding judgements and expertise. For example, Director J was impressed by the quality of their board: 'The people on the board were highly respected for their achievements [the director proceeded to name them], and it also had several members of the board who were from overseas, and this attracted me'.

By contrast, three directors spoke openly of their disappointment after joining their boards, as their initial external impressions did not completely match their subsequent experience. This suggests that dispositional factors can make social influence more complex than some previous theories have suggested. That is, members of a group, such as a board, will make careful and conscious reassessments of their prior judgements to determine how their contributions might fit a group. This conscious process was evident when NEDs described their early experiences with new boards. For example, Director C reported:

> When you are first appointed to a board, you don't participate fully until you have worked out the personalities ... [Y]ou have to take a back seat and observe ... work out what particular topics interests particular directors, how the chair related to the directors, whether they are strict timekeepers, inclusive and allow everyone to speak.

The data showed the existence of dynamic and fundamental patterns in which majority ideas were dispersed and diffused such that some subgroups in a majority (the in-group) got bigger while others in a minority (the out-group) got smaller. This is evidenced in Director P's observations:

> I found it [referring to the financial services sector] difficult to understand ... I looked around the table and formed an assessment about the directors in terms of reliability, competence and judgement and listened to those who had more experience in this sector than I had.

These influences confirm the tenets of dynamic social impact theory (Latané 1981, 1996), which holds that groups working together over time produce subtle shifts in power relationships between subgroups. Further, data from the author's study showed that, once members had established themselves, their response to influence attempts (by others) was motivated by affiliation and the maintenance of a positive self-concept. This is consistent with recent research that shows that the activation of social effects is subtle, indirect, heuristically based and often unconscious (Thuraisingham 2018).

The social categorisation theory (David & Turner 1996), which describes 'in-group' and 'out-group' effects to determine the receptiveness to influence attempts by majorities or minorities is relevant here. According to this theory, when a target receives an influence attempt from an in-group minority, they are more likely to become pressured to conform. Conversely, when an out-group minority attempts to send an influence attempt, the pressure to change opinions in the direction of an advocated position is minimal. This suggests that the 'people like me' construct has a pervasive effect on how influence attempts are responded to in a board-group setting. Therefore, the influence effect is dependent on whether a message source is an in-group or out-group. Here, it is significant that Director O recalled that the credibility of a position depends on who is making the point.

Director O also reported that, although he strongly disagreed with a chair's view that a board continue to entertain an acquisition proposal, he made a judgement not to raise his continuing concerns directly with the chair. Instead, he deferred to more senior colleagues, reflecting a process by which he was undertaking a conscious rational process shaped by what he perceived to be the strength of shared identity in the group:

> I guess I felt this was a responsibility for the more senior directors (than me) who had a closer relationship with the chair and had worked with the chair for a longer period of time to have that one-on-one conversation with him.

> (Director O)

Finally, most NEDs described raising concerns during a decision process and felt their concerns were addressed along the way. None reported that their concerns remained unresolved to the point that they were noted in the minutes (a formal protocol on most boards). They suggested that, although this was allowed in formal protocol, this request was likely to have unintended effects on boardroom harmony. It would also be perceived by peers as a self-serving attempt by an NED to, as Director N put it, 'cover their backside'.

Only one NED described a scenario in which he had a different view from the start of the process and it was only after several meetings that another NED began to accept his view. Up to that point, the dissenting NED went along with the majority view, raising his concerns, but not strongly. Other NEDs, while not attributing such dissent to themselves, described their experiences of other sole dissenters on their boards. It was easier for an NED to stand their ground on an issue if there was at least one other NED in a group that agreed. As described by social impact theory (Latané 1981, 1996), and supported by the author's study, clearly there is strength in numbers.

Lending further weight to the importance of numbers, high-power directors (i.e., those perceived to have longer and more established cognitive histories) commanded greater attention: 'when they spoke others listened', one NED reported. This is a form of social control. However, in some cases, experience was discounted when a director did not have tenure. High-power NEDs who had joined a board recently were less able to exert influence on the direction of a debate, as evidenced by Director N. Despite having considerable experience as a CEO on global acquisitions and divestments before joining a board, Director N's self-construal of his newness played a part in his reluctance to challenge decisions robustly. He recounted his hesitation during a debate a few months after he joined a board: 'Fellow directors all seemed reasonably relaxed about it, and you start to think that maybe I am wrong and I don't feel that confident that I have some divine inspiration that they don't have'.

Framework of social competence required for director effectiveness

As evidenced in the foregoing, there is wide variation in the nature and sources of NED influence and the skill with which it was mobilised, ultimately determining how NEDs enacted their strategy-shaping accountabilities.

The social competencies implicit in the relational and dispositional themes reported in the author's study included well-developed skills in questioning and dissenting constructively. They also involved openness to learning and feedback, alertness to emerging thinking, articulating the relevance of one's experience eloquently, owning and engaging constructively with the challenges and counter-positions of peers, the propensity to reflect and practice detachment while staying involved, and resisting social pressure while being prepared to concede a point or argument in the face of a strong rationale.

This section, summarises what causes a distinctive board culture to emerge and persist, proposes and examines the social competencies that NEDs need to acquire and demonstrate to thrive in the culture of a board (Thuraisingham 2018).

The relational and dispositional themes and the role they played in how NEDs influenced strategy reflected a variety of skills and behaviours that NEDs demonstrated. The framework capturing these social competencies is shown in Table 4.1. For example, in exercising influence through questioning and contention (one of the four relational themes), directors demonstrated the ability to sense that something needed more explanation and then engage in persistent but respectful questioning when required—a honed situational sensing that required the accurate reading of social cues. Similarly, in exercising the propensity to resist social pressure (one of the three dispositional themes), NEDs demonstrated alertness in the face of strong views of persuasive advocates. In this way, each of the four relational themes and three dispositional themes could be broken down into behavioural indicators, as shown in Table 4.1.

Table 4.1 Emerging framework defining the social competence required to exercising boardroom influence

Behavioural indicators	Definition (of propensity/ proficiency)	Social competence clusters
• Ability to read social cues by sensing others' internal states including unspoken concerns, meanings, intentions and motivations • Intuitively sensing when something does not feel right and requires more exploration • Knowing incisively what is relevant and what questions need to be asked to obtain this knowledge • Checking regularly for (one's own and other's) understanding or appreciation of complexities • Sensing tensions that require diffusing constructively to move things forward • Vigilance in the face of strong views or positions by persuasive experts or advocates	Propensity to accurately perceive the motives, traits and intentions of others; read social cues accurately; gauge their needs and emotions; and act with honed and well-timed questioning using a style/tone that will preserve trust	Situational sensing (social perception)
• Desire to be seen as supportive (of a deal), as well as simultaneously challenging it • Desire to promote oneself as balanced in judgement and considered in approach • Desire to make a material contribution to a debate rather than opining on every issue to demonstrate relevance • Consciously avoiding 'offline huddles' that may be misconstrued as political or lacking transparency • Attentive use of language to convey openness and confidence to others including management • Attentiveness to the timing and pacing of one's own contribution for maximum influential effect	Propensity (consciously or unconsciously) to engage with counter-positions constructively to convey the impression of considered, balanced and wise judgements and interventions	Impression management
• Persistent, purposeful but respectful questioning of peer and management intentions and assumptions • Respectful engagement with others' underlying beliefs and values for the position they take • Build on the contributions of other NEDs—synthesising and extending the strategic contributions others make • Preparedness to stand alone on a strongly held position, issue of principle or value. • Presenting well-researched and well-rounded arguments coherently	Propensity to express views, opinions and ideas clearly to generate enthusiasm in others to gain their support including the purposeful use of relevance and expertise to position and land arguments well	Articulacy

(Continued)

Behavioural indicators	Definition (of propensity/ proficiency)	Social competence clusters
• Being alert to emergent thinking—quickly sensing shifts in the unfolding discussion and emerging perspectives • Being alert to how one's own experience may bias a position; willingness to compensate for that bias • Routinely and deliberatively exploring what others see to calibrate, learn and adapt • Candidly admitting to lack of knowledge or insight about a subject and an openness to learn • Preparedness to collectively own and engage constructively with challenges by others • Willingness to allow conversations to emerge rather than feeling a need to control them	Propensity to adapt to and learn from a wide range of new social situations including feeling comfortable with people who are different, including adjusting one's behaviour when required, able to talk to anyone about anything	Social adaptability

Source: Thuraisingham (2018).

As shown in Table 4.1, the behavioural indicators can be clustered into four 'social competence' groups: situational sensing, impression management, articulacy and social adaptability. Social competence enables an influencer to understand what others want and how they perceive things, which, in turn, enables them to select an appropriate influence strategy to use. The social competence that an NED had was in effect a leveler in as much as it compensated for an NED having relatively less board capital than their peers but nevertheless able to exercise influence successfully through these skills and dispositions. Significantly, the clusters appeared to map across to the well-cited Baron and Markman (2003) study, which was based on entrepreneurs in the high-tech sector. This 2003 study confirmed the seminal, extensively cited five factor personality model originally put forward by Barrick and Mount (1991).

In conclusion

In conclusion, when identity and power effects are not in equilibrium, the processes of accountability may be compromised. Understanding the subtle working of emotions in board processes and the propensities required to engage frequently in reflection, becoming mindful and alert to important social cues, regularly taking a 'balcony view', being alert to subtle forms of social control, being vigilant about 'groupthink' and being comfortable with uncertainty and emergence are all crucial for NED effectiveness.

As the economic, business and social environment becomes more unpredictable, NEDs acknowledge the need to become comfortable with more emergent forms of strategic decisioning (Thuraisingham 2018). This includes a preparedness to value frankness about the uncertainty they experience, engage in disruptive thinking and collectively acknowledge associated discomfort. Importantly, there are implications for the criteria by which NEDs are selected and developed. The criteria should include adaptive and agile thinkers who are comfortable with emergence and the use of intuition; multi-dimensional thinkers less binary in their approaches; those comfortable with ambiguity; and those who demonstrate an ability to engage skilfully in collective reflection.

In summary, commercial and functional knowledge and expertise is insufficient. NEDs require social competence and certain dispositions to skilfully mitigate the incipient effects of identity politics and strengthen their boardroom influence.

The social competencies that directors require to become influential, described in this chapter, together with the dispositions described in this chapter, go some way to assist current boards in a practical sense with the selection and socialisation of new directors. More broadly, developing social competence also holds implications for how board cultures might be strengthened, and board renewal approached.

Actionable strategies

Desired impact	Strategies the board may take collectively	Strategies the individual director may take
Future focussed skills	Review the board's skills matrix, taking a broader view in relation to board capital; consider how fit for future the current board capital is and what mix would place the board in the best position to navigate the future, focusing beyond commercial or functional expertise; consider also the social competencies that are required to develop a strategically active board and where the gaps may be and how these may be addressed	Reflect on a more holistic set of social competencies required to strengthen your influence, beyond the board capital you bring; in particular, reflect on how you might be travelling on deploying a skilled combination of behaviours when managing the dilemmas of directing. Informed *and* Heedful, Challenging *and* Supportive, Detached *and* Involved

(*Continued*)

Desired impact	Strategies the board may take collectively	Strategies the individual director may take
A healthy board dynamic	At regular intervals, use the closed sessions to take a quick pulse check of the ways of working; at least once a year in between formal externally conducted reviews, discuss practices and disciplines that the board as a collective will need to start-stop-continue to ensure a high-performing board culture	Seek out specific feedback from trusted others about your propensity to influence others as well as your propensity to be influenced by others; ask yourself how open you have been about concerns and doubts you may have and reflect on what may be standing in the way of that openness; be prepared to call out behaviour you feel may be counterproductive to a high-performing culture; actively encourage and mentor your quieter colleagues to step into the dialogue
Renewal of the board	Consider if you have an agreed approach to board renewal before renewal is required or forced on the board by external stakeholders	Continually consider the value of the personal contribution you are making and ask if this is you at your best and commit the time to continuous learning and self-improvement efforts

Letter to the nominations committee

To: The Nominations Committee

From: BoardQ Advisory

Re: Board Culture

Recently, the decision culture of boards has come under intense scrutiny. Regulators have questioned massive write-downs due to expensive acquisitions, badly timed forays into adjacent markets, a string of failed consolidations or the failure to swiftly dispose of a doomed business. Capital/Debt management strategies, the approval of executive incentives for lacklustre company performance, difficult to defend safety compromises and the failure to respond quickly enough to new entrants have also raised questions about how boards make decisions.

Some advisors and consultants will tell you that you need to ensure decision rights are clear or build new decision protocols or adopt better governance tools/processes or ensure that the board has more and better information. Others will tell you that you need to ensure you have industry experience on your board or that you need more functional expertise or offshore experience. Others will tell you that motives of directors must be evaluated carefully at the point of hiring to ensure that the directorship is not being pursued as a life style choice. All these are good nudges and are necessary areas of focus. However, they do not guarantee that the decision culture will change. This is because board culture is both the effect and consequence of its 'social reality', which is a complex and informal mix of expectations (stated and unstated), norms, routines and habits that have built up and persist over a history of interactions between board members and is self-regulating in the sense that divergent views can be 'brought into line' often subtly. This may prevent disagreeable questions from being asked. Therefore, in the context of these group membership effects, it is important to ask: how can these adverse effects be contained in a way that ensures that decision-makers feel psychologically safe to express dissenting views? The biggest casualty of not attending to the psychological safety on any board is its collective knowledge and intellect—a key reason for the board to exist in the first place.

Psychological safety is vital to any healthy decision dynamic, but it is fragile. It is not present when the benefits of staying silent far outweigh the benefits of speaking out. It is present when members believe that they will not be shamed for asking 'stupid' or disagreeable questions, speaking their minds on something that is troubling them (but does not seem to be troubling anyone else), and voicing a position or opinion that is divergent from the group norm or from broad conventions or even from a small but persuasive minority. Ultimately, it is a moral courage. It is possible to develop this on your board.

There are a number of collaborative practices that we believe are key to ensuring a healthy decision dynamic and creating a safe environment for each member of your board group. We offer these suggestions to you to consider:

- Develop, as a board group, the conscious skill of separating the idea from the person to ensure that the idea is the only thing being debated or challenged—not the person with the idea; resist seeing contention as disloyalty to the group.
- Own and support each other's challenges (i.e. adopting the challenges of peers as one's own through probing, clarifying confirming questions delivered in a way that shows respect for others' challenges).
- Engage in generative dialogue in which there are no 'winners' or 'losers' and in which different points of view can be held without having to protect, defend or even agree. Generative dialogue is an acquired skill and often triggered by turning the problem statement into a question, one that starts with 'how might', 'in what ways' or 'what might be all the ways'.
- Engage with and reward the exploration of issues and allow the time for such exploration, acknowledging that some people may need more time for their views to form and emerge rather than be managed or constrained by a time regimented agenda.

- When a dominant discourse is playing out, step back as a board and collectively ask what might be the minor discourse that is not having voice. While breaking a dominant discourse in a formalised agenda-driven setting is challenging, the chair can make such 'process interruptions' an accepted practice.
- When presenting a viewpoint, the board member is required to also present at least one counterargument.
- Ensure that, as chair, your views are always left until there has been a frank and open exchange of ideas so that there is no undue influence on other members. When summing up the views of others, this summation is tested with the group for its accuracy before moving to provide the chair view.
- Adopt the principles of Toyota's 'five whys'—an iterative interrogative assumption/belief testing technique used to explore, as a group, a given problem/challenge to arrive at the root cause or work up from first principles.
- Reflect together, from time to time, on things that matter and use as reminders:
  - What can we count on each other for?
  - What is the collective purpose that unites us as a group?
  - What is the reputation we collectively aspire to have?
- What do we need to do differently to achieve that reputation and fulfil our purpose?
- Provide new directors with developmental support in building mental toughness. Mental toughness determines how people respond to challenge, stress and pressure and is closely related to resilience, grit and moral courage. There are tactics that can strengthen one's confidence and resilience to stand alone or speak truth to power.
- Rather than a perfunctory box-ticking exercise, approach the formal externally conducted board review as a transformative learning exercise.

References

Argyris, C & Schön, DA 1978, *Organizational learning: a theory of action perspective*, Addison-Wesley, Reading, MA.

Bailey, B & Peck, S 2013, 'Boardroom strategic decision making style: understanding the antecedents', *Corporate Governance: An International Review*, vol. 21, no. 2, pp. 131–146.

Baron, RA & Markman, GD 2003, 'Beyond social capital: the role of entrepreneurs' social competence in their financial success', *Journal of Business Venturing*, vol. 18, no. 1, pp. 41–60.

Barrick, MR & Mount, MK 1991, 'The big five personality dimensions and job performance: a meta-analysis', *Personnel Psychology*, vol. 44, no. 1, pp. 1–26.

Berghe, VD & Baelden, T 2005, 'The complex relations between directors' independence and board effectiveness', *Corporate Governance*, vol. 5, no 5, pp. 58–83.

Cialdini, R & Goldstein, N 2004, 'Social influence: compliance and conformity', *Annual Review Psychology*, vol. 55, pp. 591–621.

Chatterjee, A & Hambrick, DC 2007, 'It's all about me: narcissistic chief executive officers and their effects on company strategy and performance', *Administrative Science Quarterly*, vol. 52, pp. 351–386.

David, B & Turner, JC 1996, 'Studies in self-categorization and minority conversion: is being a member of the out-group an advantage?', *British Journal of Social Psychology*, vol. 35, no. 1, pp. 179–199.

Finkelstein, S & Hambrick, D 1996, *Strategic leadership: top executives and their effects on organisation*, West Publishing Company, Minneapolis, MN.

Forbes, DP & Milliken, FJ 1999, 'Cognition and corporate governance: understanding boards of directors as strategic decision-making groups', *The Academy of Management Review*, vol. 24, no. 3, pp. 489–505.

Fritsche, I, Jonas, E, Ablasser, C, Kuban, J, Aamnger, AM & Scultz, M 2013, 'The power of we: evidence for group based control', *Journal of Experimental Social Psychology*, vol. 49, pp. 19–32.

Galinsky, AD, Magee, J, Inesi, M & Gruenfeld, DH 2006, 'Power and perspectives not taken', *Psychological Science*, vol. 17, no. 12, pp. 1068–1074.

Golden, B & Zajac, E 2001, 'When will board influence strategy? Inclination × power = strategic change', *Strategic Management Journal*, vol. 22, no. 12, pp. 1087–1111.

Guerrero, S & Sequin, M 2012, 'Motivational drivers of non-executive drivers: corporation and engagement in board roles', *Journal of Managerial Issues*, vol. 24, no. 1, pp. 61–77.

Heifetz, RA & Linsky, M 2002, *Leadership on the line: staying alive through the dangers of leading*, Harvard Business School Press, Boston, MA.

Hillman, A, Nicholson, G & Shropshire, C 2008, 'Directors' multiple identities, identification and board monitoring and resource provision', *Organisation Science*, vol. 19, no. 3, pp. 441–456.

Huse, M & Rindova, V 2001, 'Stakeholder expectations of corporate boards', *Journal of Management and Governance*, vol. 5, pp. 153–178.

Johnson, SG, Schnatterly, K. & Hill, AD 2013, 'Board composition beyond independence: social capital, human capital and demographics', *Journal of Management*, vol. 39, no. 1, pp. 232–262.

Latané, B 1981, 'The psychology of social impact', *American Psychologist*, vol. 36, no. 4, pp. 343–356.

Latané, B 1996, 'Dynamic social impact: the creation of culture by communication', *Journal of Communication*, vol. 46, pp. 13–25.

Lawler, EE, Finegold, DL, Benson, GS & Conger, JA 2002, 'Corporate boards: key to effectiveness', *Organisational Dynamics*, vol. 30, no. 4, pp. 310–324.

Lorsch, JW & MacIver, E 1989, *Pawns or potentates: the reality of America's corporate boards*, Harvard Business School Press, Boston, MA.

Malmendier, U & Tate, G 2005, 'CEO overconfidence & corporate investment', *Journal of Finance*, vol. 60, pp. 2261–2700.

McClelland, DC 1985, 'How motives, skills, and values determine what people do', *American Psychologist*, vol. 40, pp. 812–825.

McClelland, D 1987, *Human motivation*, Cambridge University Press, Cambridge.

Nadler, D 2004, 'Building better boards', *Harvard Business Review*, vol. 82, no. 5, pp. 102–111.

Oakes, PJ, Turner, JC & Haslam, SA 1991, 'Perceiving people as group members: the role of fit in the salience of social categorizations', *British Journal of Social Psychology*, vol. 30, pp. 125–144.

Roberts, J 1991, 'The possibilities of accountabilities', *Accounting, Organizations and Society*, vol. 16, no. 4, pp. 355–368.

Scheepers, D, Ellemers, N & Sassenberg, K 2013, 'Power in group contexts: the influence of group status on promotion and prevention decision making', *British Journal of Social Psychology*, vol. 52, pp. 238–254.

Schutz, WC 1958, *FIRO-B: a three dimensional theory of interpersonal behavior*, Holt, Rinehart & Winston, New York.

Simon, B & Oakes, P 2006, 'Beyond dependence: an identity approach to social power and domination', *Human Relations*, vol. 59, no. 1, pp. 105–139.

Stiles, P & Taylor, B 2001, *Boards at work: how directors view their roles and accountabilities*, Oxford University Press, Oxford.

Thuraisingham, SM 2018, 'Exploring the social factors that influence the decision making behaviours of non-executive directors in Australian public companies', PhD thesis, RMIT University, Melbourne.

Turner, JC 1987, 'A self-categorization theory', in JC Turner, MA Hogg, PJ Oakes, SD, Reicher & MS Wetherell (eds), *Rediscovering the social group: a self-categorization theory*, Blackwell, Oxford, pp. 42–67.

Turner, JC 2005, 'Explaining the nature of power: a three-process theory', *European Journal of Social Psychology*, vol. 35, pp. 1–22.

Westphal, JD & Khanna, P 2003, 'Keeping directors in line: social distancing as a social mechanics in the corporate elite', *Administrative Science Quarterly*, vol. 48, no. 3, pp. 361–398.

5 Rethinking the leadership of the board

This chapter in summary

As the first among equals, the role of the chair is a complex one. Chairs tend to be strong personalities but they have to use that strength as a force for good: allowing robust debate to thrive; letting a debate run its course but making well-timed calls about when to coral the debate in, creating tactical interventions to generate the deeper reflection necessary with big, high-stakes decisions; and creating the psychological safety required for directors to feel secure enough to disagree with the chair and with each other. Given the pivotal role that norms and routines play in shaping interactions and dialogue between directors, the chair also plays a subtle role in proactively managing boardroom norms and routines (discussed in Chapter 2 as part of the informal processes of accountability).

This chapter explores the eight essential attributes that a board chair should have to unlock the potential and collective influence of the board group in deciding on strategic change. The chapter also challenges the limitations of leadership being viewed as concentrated in a single role and discusses the model of distributed leadership and the role that all directors play in the collective leadership of the organisation. The chapter also explores the relationship between the board chair and committee chairs and the responsibility that directors have for ensuring that they do not over-rely on the committee chairs doing the heavy lifting. It also explores actions that the chair can take in the face of a resistant CEO who is not open to engaging with the perspectives of more experienced others.

A high-performing board, as is the case with any top team, is greater than the sum of its parts, although a number of boards may fail this acid test. The chair plays a pivotal role in ensuring that this test is passed. The chapter provides strategies for how a chair could reform the board evaluation/review process from a perfunctory box-ticking exercise into a transformative learning experience. The evaluation/review process is discussed in more detail in Chapter 7.

All leadership is contextual. The kind of leadership a board needs is dependent on both internal and external issues. While there are several external issues that may require a distinctive type of board leadership, such as the stage in the company life cycle, the configuration of the company's shareholding and pace of sector regulation, this chapter is primarily focussed on the inner context and its implications for board leadership.

Leadership and its social context

The author studied the board group as a 'social system' to illuminate the processes by which individual directors influenced each other. As noted in previous chapters, position, power and status matter in how relationships form and operate, and how stated and unstated goals influence group behaviour and group cohesion. Through this prism of how influence is exercised in and around the boardroom, the author observed the real-life complexities of how board leadership was actually practised. It provided strong evidence for the understanding of leadership as a social phenomenon, rather than a role that is assigned.

These inner context issues are unique in the context of the board chair in which the incumbent is an elected peer—elected by board members who are as highly experienced, educated and accomplished as the chair. Further, in contrast to the CEO's authority over management, the chair has no formal authority over NEDs on their board. These factors make the style of leadership and the influence a chair might exercise on the group different when compared with other leadership roles. In such a context, in which there is no significant power distance between the chair and board, research has shown that relationships and influence are challenging. In the literature, 'power distance' is used synonymously with the size of power differentials (Magee & Smith 2013) created by differences in structure, prestige, ownership and expertise (Finkelstein 1992). The role of the independent director is enshrined in independent mindedness, especially the willingness to stand alone on an issue if need be. This means that a chair, as first among equals, has to strike a fine balance between asserting their preferred approach (or direction) and ensuring that they are not unwittingly forcing a 'false consensus' to emerge on a decision.

Given the distinctive features of a board, leadership is best achieved by recognising that it is a socially accomplished phenomenon in which every member (in a given group) engages in a fluid and mutual influence process in which responsibility for influence is shared and distributed among members. The primary consideration of a group such as a board is to make collective sense of the challenges; mobilise, direct and align management to face difficult and complex challenges; and continue to collectively work to create the conditions for effective group functioning.

A leader who finds themselves in such a dynamic process becomes less important than what is needed for this social system to function through the micro-behaviours of directors influencing the direction, alignment and commitment of the collective. As these changes happen, the distinction between who is a leader and who is a follower becomes less clear or relevant; everyone will be both at different times. Directors who view their boards as high-performing experience board leadership in this way. It is evident from the author's experience and research into boards that each chair takes up their role in distinctive ways, and not all chairs recognise the complexities of leadership as a phenomenon rather than a role that is assigned.

Seen in this way, rather than focus on the leader or their role, it makes more sense to focus on leadership as a dynamic, interactive influence process among individuals in a group for which the objective is to lead one another to the achievement of group or organisational goals or both (Pearce & Conger 2003). One of the reasons why this notion of shared leadership is not more widely practiced is the previous executive experience of NEDs—in essence, a case of habit, skill or both. NEDs are the product of their experiences in which the century old top-down unitary ideology of heroic, hierarchical leadership has permeated narratives about the leader. Through their executive careers, directors would have been exposed to, and experienced, such traditional notions of the leader in the organisations in which they worked. When they joined a board, despite recognising the distinctions between a board and a team, as part of a habitual response, they may have viewed the chair role through that same lens—seeing the chair as being accountable for much more than they are. This often manifests in the tendency some NEDs have to hang back and wait for the chair to take the lead on issues, even when they themselves may be best placed to take the lead. Chairs are a product of similar experiences and may take up their roles in similar ways, seeking to 'manage' the NEDs in a traditional hierarchical sense. The author's experience with boards has shown that 'command and control' tendencies continue to be exhibited by some chairs.

Suggesting that leadership is a shared process is not the same as suggesting that a nominated chair does not have unique and specific duties to perform and coordinate. For example, they typically lead the process to develop the board agenda, communicate with directors in between meetings, oversee the creation of the board papers/packs to be presented at board meetings, and become the face of the company with investors, analysts and media. They are also tasked with initiating board effectiveness reviews. However, the real challenge confronting the chair is how they facilitate and participate in the process of leadership, which this chapter focusses on.

What leadership can the chair expect from members of the board group?

There are several behaviours that are critical in strengthening the practice of shared leadership and are not solely the responsibility of the chair. According to the author's research, there are six things a chair can expect from board members, without which their chairing role can achieve very little.

First, effective engagement

Directors need to engage proactively but thoughtfully, be honest and open with their views while showing curiosity and openness to the perspectives of others, displaying tenacity, resilience and tough mindedness in the face of pressure to conform. These micro-behaviours that directors demonstrate in their interpersonal interactions are driven by the character-based strengths of all good leaders, such as wisdom, humility, courage, tenacity and openness. These traits can be observed in various ways. For example, wisdom can be observed in the quality of judgements; courage can be observed in one's tenacity and resilience; humility can be observed in the degree of curiosity shown and seeking out of learning opportunities; humanity can be observed in empathetic responses, listening and inclusion. These cannot be developed as a consequence of board interactions; instead, they are character strengths that directors will need to be selected for. Regardless of how skilled a chair is, if directors do not come to the board with these leadership qualities, a chair is likely to be impeded from delivering fully on the purpose of a board.

Second, equal participation

Directors are expected to proactively and confidently express their views in board discussions and decision-making, although this is influenced by personality factors. Directors vary in their confidence levels as well as their cognitive habits; some habitually do their thinking 'inside their heads' (generally the habit of introverts) or 'outside their heads' (i.e., they like to think with others, which is generally the habit of extroverts). Additionally, to appear to be wise, calm and considered by directors more senior than them, a director may also choose to say less than they would ordinarily. A chair can adopt a number of tactics to increase participation; however, directors—through personality, habit or to impress management—make free and informed choices about if, when and how they wish to participate and lead on issues.

Third, mutual respect

As directors do not have any formal authority over one another, their credibility in this process lies in the eyes of the beholder (i.e., one or more directors must recognise the professional value they bring to the group). Therefore, the existence of mutual respect is critical for a board to function well and the process of leadership to work optimally. Directors are rarely openly disrespectful towards one another. The consequences of doing so may be catastrophic for their careers in such a close-knit pool of elite professionals. However, respect or the lack of it can be expressed in many subtle forms that may not cause offence but still amounts to a discounting of the experience of another. A director's propensity for perspective taking is driven by 'like me'/'not like me' categorisations that individual directors make (explored extensively in Chapters 2 and 3).

In turn, a director's propensity for perspective taking is a reflection of the level of respect that thrives on a board. A chair can address this at the margins, but not entirely.

Fourth, collective support

The author's research also revealed an interesting behavioural pattern in relation to how challenge was reacted to and supported. The way that focussed, persistent questioning was successfully received in the boardroom relied, to some extent, on how NEDs worked collectively to support the NED posing the challenge question (rather than leaving him or her to challenge alone). NEDs did this by adding a comment of their own to the question posed, asking a clarifying question of the director to make the point clearer to management or helpfully restating it. In doing so, they signalled collective support for the question, thereby presenting a 'united front', which could result in the CEO taking the challenger's question more seriously.

Fifth, no surprises

Most boards have a process for raising significant concerns with the chair offline so that they can be effectively addressed either before or during the board meeting. However, unless they have a good relationship with the chair (e.g., through their experience on other boards), directors may not use this process for fear that such a step may be misconstrued by the chair. They may also fear putting other directors, who are not involved in an offline discussion, at a disadvantage. The author's study found that some directors with pre-existing links and relationships with one another (such as current or past membership of another board) may be more comfortable to test or calibrate their concerns with those directors rather than with the chair. Therefore, they may not raise the issue with the chair until they get to the committee or board meeting. Although governance by ambush is not acceptable, it is often difficult for a chair to control because of pre-existing relationships between NEDs.

Sixth, external relations

Board members are expected to play an active advocacy role on behalf of the company. While the chair will generally retain overall ownership of communications with the media, investors or analysts, and regulators, there is a fine balance in this. Some chairs will organise for the board to meet formally (as distinct from a cocktail party or lunch) once every six months with large institutional shareholders and proxy advisors, with a formal discussion agenda in mind. A chair who shields board members from all external contact will not convey confidence to the market of the wisdom or depth of board talent that sits around the table or expose potential successors for leadership roles (board or committee) to key stakeholders. However, the level and type of exposure needs careful consideration in order that in-board tensions do not result.

In summary, there are a number of behaviours that chairs can legitimately expect of the directors on their board. Unless these expectations are explicitly articulated by the chair and met, the work of the chair will be challenging to achieve. A key question remains: how must the chair behave to ensure that the right conditions are created for the group such that members can take up the collective responsibility required to make sense of the complexities, clarify direction, establish alignment and garner commitment? We now turn to the role that chairs play in answering this question.

The role of the chair in unlocking collective capability and performance

This notion of shared leadership does not mean a 'weaker' or 'softer' style of leadership; instead, it recognises that distinctions have to be made in the unique skill sets required of the board chair as 'first among equals'. The role of the chair is to bring the collective capacity and capability of the board group to bear on the strategic direction and performance of the organisation. This is achieved through a collective process that the chair is part of and contributes to shaping. Chairs can shape, steward and facilitate this process but not manage or control it. Some NEDs in the author's study characterised this as a style of 'leading from behind' rather than 'leading from the front'.

In the author's study, the stories NEDs recounted of their experiences of board leadership varied extensively. At one end of the spectrum, chairs anxiously imposed close control of the debate to ensure cohesion was achieved at all costs, implicitly conveying that a lack of agreement in some way denoted group failure or was evidence of disloyalty to the group. At the other end were strong enablers and facilitators who treated conflict as a normal part of group processes, building into the role of leadership less anxiety about the presence of conflict. To create this kind of balance, chairs have to walk a narrow tightrope. It is useful for them to consider the 'discussion space' as one that is owned by the group, not the chair alone.

The study found eight themes characterising the contribution an effective chair can make to the processes of leadership: deep knowledge of member talents, ability to spot, coach and moderate director influencing personas and styles of NEDs, impartial and faithful representation, well-timed judgement calls, skills in reflective observation, effective process management, creating tactical interventions and nurturing psychological safety. None of these themes were exclusively the domain of the chair for the very reason that leadership in the board context is a process, not an assigned role. Hence, the eight themes apply equally to all members of the board, reinforcing the collective nature of board leadership:

I think positioned as I am with four boards, one of the things that is quite critical to effective board operation is the behaviour of the chair—typically they tend to be strong personalities—but have to use that as a force for good ... Some chairs are too ready to jump in and say what they think—they need to let the debate run and also coral it in when they need to .... Keeping the debate even handed—letting everyone say what is they can usefully say—without beating it to death ... it is the skill of facilitation that not all of them have.

(Director A)

This board has a very strong chairman—very consultative—very good at making sure everyone has a say and keeps the debate going. He makes sure no one talks more than others. We have one director who does sometimes go on labouring the point—he (the chair) will say 'I think we understand that point, but it's really important we move on'.

(Director C)

Deep knowledge of and insight into member talents

Given the complex and ambiguous environment boards operate in, no single board member is likely to possess the full complement of information and knowledge necessary to achieve desired goals, including the chair. Therefore, the success of the group is highly dependent on the unique skills, knowledge and backgrounds of all its members. To unlock collective leadership, a chair has to know the talents of the group intimately. Some NEDs in the author's study, particularly on bigger boards, reported that the wealth of experience that NEDs brought was not known or leveraged well enough:

In large part they were unfamiliar with my experience ... During the interviewing process only the chair and two others on the nominations committee were really aware (even when I think of the most recent hire to the board). They were then introduced to the others at the first board meeting but there was no process (formally in the introductions) where I had to talk about my experience and articulate what I would bring distinctively to this board. Perhaps there should be such a process involving the whole board which is a briefing that covers, first his/her experience and second, what they can uniquely add. In my case while functionally my experience was primarily in finance and risk, I had experience with M&A economics and extensive engagement with investors and the market.

(Director A)

NEDs observed that effective chairs were proactive and did not wait for directors to insert themselves in the discussion, instead inviting views, because they had a deep knowledge of what each director brought to the table:

He is also good at saying 'Director X, I know you have experience in this would there be anything you like to add—or Director Y, is there anything you can add to this debate'. He will actually facilitate that rather than waiting … if he feels he wants directors to specifically talk about something he knows they have experience in he will ask them … some chairs don't do that.

(Director C)

While chairs may have an intimate knowledge of the talents of their group, they may adopt a 'hub and spoke' style of facilitating director contribution. For example, some chairs showed a tendency to call on those who had particular expertise to comment only on areas of discussion that were relevant to that body of expertise. As a result, directors may stay in areas with which they are familiar and within which they feel comfortable, risking the consequence of becoming typecast by other group members into specific roles. This is an issue that effective chairs are alert to and address early, knowing that when it occurs, an 'archipelago' style of board is created comprising individual islands of expertise that prevent the group from being bigger than the sum total of its parts.

If we apply situation theory to board interactions, it is possible that individuals at particular points of a board's discussion who are endowed with the greatest potential to satisfy team needs will take up a leadership role. This was evident in the decision story told by Director C, on whom the chair relied heavily during the consideration of a major North Asian acquisition. None of the directors had had hands-on executive experience in that region or executive responsibility for that part of the world in their previous lives (except for Director C). She became the lead director for a significant period of time while the large transaction was live, with the chair trusting her judgement and valuing her expertise sufficiently to feel confident to step back during these discussions. A different chair may have approached this with a more traditional 'she has to earn her stripes first' mindset before allowing her to take the lead on the discussion.

Ability to spot, coach and moderate director influencing personas and styles of NEDs

The author's study, which was focussed on a large transformative decision with significant strategic change implications for the organisation, revealed several board personas. Some chairs appeared mindful of these styles and others less so.

Nine director personas were distilled from the study findings; these are described in the following. Directors adopted these situationally, when influencing matters relating to strategic change. Some directors adopted several personas during the extended decision story, and also reported personas they observed in their peers. Some directors reported that peers adopted a manifestly different influencing style on other boards on which they shared membership. Some personas were more appropriate for particular stages of a company's growth cycle.

The mediator: the director who habitually adopts a mediating and integrating role, acting as a go-between between two subgroups/individuals that disagree or have divergent views/mental models; tends to look for common ground and tries to make connections between divergent views on a given strategic position; will generally have a more reflective style, attentive to other's inputs, seeking to clarify underlying thinking and build on other views; is generally seen as collaborative and a team player; may, at times, lose their voice in their attempt to be a peacemaker.

The cheer leader: the director who over-identifies with the group and believes their role is to reinforce the attractiveness of the group; is selectively focussed on the positive qualities of the group—in terms of the group's views and actions; often opines positively and frequently on almost all issues. When confronted with an acquisition proposal by management, they may choose to focus on the upside de-emphasising downside risks and, providing unqualified support to the proposal. Their discernment skills may be underdeveloped or supressed in order to be accepted/liked by the group.

The pragmatist: the director who is likely to have a realistic sense of the demands and constraints of the current circumstances and is interested in what will work or seems practical; may focus on the practical implications of a potential acquisition on management attention/focus and not necessarily on the upside potential and possibilities; may not be energised by 'blue-sky' thinking, believing that operational considerations and practical applications are relatively more important.

The conserver: the director who prefers the known to the unknown; may find ambiguity in a proposal unsettling; may prefer a proposal that is more incremental than one involving transformative change; tends to opt for continuous improvement, seeking to minimise uncertainty and ambiguity; is generally perceived as risk-averse. On occasion, the conserver is referred to as the 'black hat' because they focus more on why a deal or proposed strategic change should not proceed.

The sage: the director who says very little but, when they do, their contribution is perceived as wise; does not derive their wisdom from tenure, age or years of experience in the task at hand, but instead shows practical wisdom (i.e., they instinctively know the right way to do things). When the sage asks a question, other directors wonder why they did not ask it themselves. As such, the sage plays an important role in the learning of others, especially when contemplating strategic change.

The technician: the director who is manifestly functional or specialist in their orientation; does not stray far from their functional discipline or specialisation, preferring to leave others they perceive as experts in given fields to discuss such issues; tends to view all aspects of the decision through the prism of their discipline. In this regard, they are thorough and detail minded; however, they confine their contributions to discussions they think they are most 'qualified' to comment on or influence.

The politician: the director who pays close attention to 'how the wind is blowing' before taking a position (i.e., takes a position that furthers their own interests or personal ambition rather than the best interests of the company or stakeholders). This may include furthering their influence and connections with powerful board members in the hope of becoming more powerful by association, and engaging in covert political tactics to shore up support for their own position. This persona is inherently political, which is not to be confused with the display of political astuteness or savvy.

The innovator: the director who shows a preference for a radical approach to strategic change; continually challenging existing norms and mental models; is comfortable proposing change that may disrupt the status quo because they believe that change is good for the organisation. They do not just ask 'why', but 'why not'. They are generally seen to be counterintuitive thinkers and idea generators and respected for their vision and big picture thinking and contribution.

The bomb thrower: the director who is often viewed as disruptive to the normal flow of a conversation and has an opinion on most issues; has little regard or patience for group norms or past precedence; has a confrontational, pugnacious and belligerent style of discourse because they believe there is far too much politeness in and around board tables; often has a relatively low tolerance for emergent reflective conversation; is perceived by peers as unpredictable and volatile in their reactions and responses. Due to their inability to understand the personal impact of their style, they often show surprise about the reactions they get from peers.

In summary, these nine personas and the subjective roles that they imply have implications for the way in which the processes of accountability for strategic change may be exercised. Chairs need to be aware of these varying styles and consider how they might proactively adapt their leadership approach in response. For their part, NEDs can use this taxonomy to reflect upon their own styles and consider how they might work with the many personas they encounter in the boardroom. Further, they can use the taxonomy to better understand how each persona may enable or inhibit the exercise of accountability during the process of contemplating, debating and deciding a strategic change. In terms of self-reflection, it may help directors to consider whether they themselves are overplaying a persona to the detriment not only of the decision process, but also the collegiality of the board group.

Impartial and faithful representation of views

The processes of collective leadership were also strengthened through a demonstration of impartiality—the skills associated with faithfully representing the views of the directors. This can be especially challenging for chairs who have already made up their mind or who have a preferred option in mind and may, consciously or subconsciously, have steered the conversation in that direction. There were several ways in which directors reported that chairs attempted to stay impartial. Mostly, these related to why they listened, not how they listened; impartial chairs listened to learn rather than judge. This kind of listening not only aided the chair in staying open and impartial until all the arguments had been presented, but also helped to shape the collective thinking of the group.

Active listening was key and constituted asking three types of (active listening) questions to ensure that views were being properly understood and represented: clarifying, confirming and probing. These were not only valuable for the chair's own understanding but also for the understanding of other directors who may have chosen to remain silent despite not fully comprehending where the discussion was heading. Clarifying questions generally start with *'so I fully understand the point you were making, can I clarify that?'*, confirming questions typically start with *'can I confirm what I thought I heard?'* and probing questions generally start with *'tell me more about that'* or *'can you share the thinking behind your view?'* While some NEDs may feel they have a sufficient grasp on an issue to make a judgement call, others may ask questions to gain a more thorough understanding of an issue. Such differences are important because responses to the questions of the latter may deepen the insights of the former. Thus, directors play as critical a role in driving this dynamic through the posing of simple active listening questions as the chair.

Worryingly, the author's research showed that sometimes an NED may privately question the representation of a consensual view but decide that the process is too far gone to reopen it:

> But if there is not a clear consensus the chair has to make a call ... there are times when I felt there were slightly more people the other way ... We are a consensus board ... we never vote on issues, usually because it is quite clear a majority of people feel this way ... and it is obvious where the consensus lies ... Very occasionally it (where the consensus lies) is not obvious or clear cut and the chair makes a call ... and perhaps then if on the losing side you might feel it was a tough call for the chair to make because it was not that clear cut.
>
> (Director N)

In this particular case, Director N was describing not challenging the chair's representation on where the consensus lay had devastating consequences for the company and its shareholders. Regardless of how late in debate, chairs have a responsibility to ensure that views are faithfully represented—even if it means reopening debate. This is not exclusively the responsibility of the chair; it is a collective responsibility.

Well-timed judgement calls

The author's research suggested that, to unlock collective leadership, chairs needed to apply their judgement 'in the moment' to determine when to rein a discussion in or encourage more divergent thinking, being careful not to give too much time to well-known biases or well-researched views.

NEDs reported that effective chairs needed to resist 'putting the stake in the ground' too early on a proposal, instead letting the debate run its course, as this allowed a diversity of opinion to emerge. They also needed to time their interventions carefully, trying not to 'guide-rail' the thinking. A good sense of timing was essential to achieve strong alignment. Some NEDs spoke of the effects of a weak alignment coming back to haunt the decision process at the end, sometimes in the form of the discussion being hijacked or derailed by directors who had not felt heard or understood along the way.

Some directors reported chairs with more tact than others in facilitating such contributions. For example, one director recounted a time when the chair suggested firmly, *'we have heard that three times, we don't need to hear that a fourth time'* or *'John you have made that point ... it's time to move on'*. While overworking a point wasted time, chairs needed to judge and manage director contributions so that NEDs did not feel cut-off or not heard.

Directors reported that individuals in the group, including the chair, had to be vigilant and spot 'management cheerleaders' and those who may become pervasive advocates of a deal. The chair (and/or other NEDs) needed to intervene so that other directors could contribute to, and balance, the debate.

Importantly, effective leadership requires NEDs, including chairs, to recognise that not all debates are of equal importance. For example, some disagreements can exist without compromising the decision outcome. Conversely, some disagreements can be fundamental. Making this call is not straightforward. It requires a deeper dialogue style than relying on surface beliefs or principles that may be compromised by deciding one way or another. A good chair judges this by asking themselves how deep the divergence of views goes: does it go to the heart of the beliefs and values that the organisation upholds in the communities it serves—the customers, investors and employees? Chairs could contribute to alignment through well-timed questions, such as *'what do we have to believe for this to hold true?'*, or questions that encouraged members to consider the first principles involved in a given decision. Again, this is not simply the responsibility of the chair. On high-performing boards, all NEDs share the task of asking better questions to ensure the consistent use of a moral/ethical compass.

Reflective observation

Effective reading of the dynamics relies on good observational skills. This appeared to be a consistent theme for strong collective leadership to thrive. Some chairs were perceived as doing this well and others less well. This included the ability to recognise situations in which a director had a view but, for whatever reason, was reluctant to share it:

> Peter [not real name], I can see you looking pensive, is there something on your mind?'
>
> (Director L)

Certainly styles on this board are different. I tend to play the role quite often of getting beyond the conflict. Sometimes I found it very valuable outside the boardroom to go to the person and ask what is really troubling you (about the valuation of this deal)'

(Director K)

The author's study showed that NEDs and chairs needed to engage in more than just active listening; they needed to engage in deep listening (i.e., listening not only to what is being said but also what is not being said). This skill involved careful observation of what was really going on with the debate, in particular, social cues. It related to sensing when a director had something to say, but was not saying it for whatever reason and finding ways to draw them into the conversation.

An effective chair ensured there was rich engagement of spoken and unspoken concerns early in the conversation. However, this was not always the experience of NEDs in the author's research and underscores the importance of the processes of collective leadership:

I raised it with the chair and said that there was a lot of anxiety that was not surfacing at the board meeting ... he was frankly more than negligent on this. He politely listened, agreed but did nothing about it.

(Director G)

This decision story ended with four directors with similar concerns getting together and, in the face of the chair's inertia, resolving to 'force the debate' at the next board meeting. This is an example of distributed leadership in practice. Although it does not reflect well on the chair, the final outcome was a good one, because the NEDs recognised their responsibility in collective leadership. However, another story of boardroom dynamics reflected quite the opposite. An NED who judged his chair as insufficiently sensitive to the unspoken concerns of a small group of long-tenured NEDs about a complex acquisition, recounted how, in his view, 12 months of the board's good work was swept aside for the wrong reasons:

I think there were a couple of board members who from the start were not sold on the idea. And it is possible that there was some exchange with the CEO ... they may have been thinking about their own reputational risk 'in a not on my watch' kind of way—not willing to invest for the long term or accept taking a short-term hit. A strategic move like this would not pay dividends for some time and perhaps they felt that there was too much risk to the near term result. They may have had deep reservations that remained unspoken. Perhaps in the end if we had more familiarity with the issues, we would have been less surprised (at the outcome) at the end. Also perhaps we could have had a more meaningful conversation about how committed we were to the long term ... When concerns or fundamental objections are not drawn out early and remain unspoken they can come back again later in the process in a different guise as I suspect it did in this example.

(Director A)

It could be argued that this example reflects a traditional perception of the role of the chair, in which directors rely on the chair to draw out concerns early in the process. However, in the shared leadership model, all directors are responsible for observing board dynamics and proactively engaging in drawing out peer concerns.

Effective process management

As timing is critical in large transformative deals, and most transactions have key 'drop dead' dates, NEDs in the author's study reported that it was important for chairs to be flexible about processes and allow additional time for debate to clarify the direction and scope of discussion. Instead, chairs had to keep revisiting previously agreed decision processes (e.g., relating to the review of internationalisation proposal) and flex timings to allow debate to run for longer or allow additional information to be presented or advisors more time to do their work. During the period of this study, the commodities market in Australia collapsed and this external factor required boards and chairs to adjust board processes to account for factors outside the organisation's control.

Effective process management also included skills in ending debate. The failure to create an end point through skilled framing and articulation left issues in limbo, potentially undermining other debates. This was evident in several of the decision stories that directors told. The following story shows how—despite clear warning signs in relation to changes in the speed of technology and consumer habits—indecision and procrastination on the part of the board resulted in the unintended destruction of value in the subsidiary:

> Even though there was scepticism amongst the board [referring to the strategy management was pursuing], it was never really properly addressed as an issue. However, fairly early on in my time there, it started to gather pace and it resulted in us having detailed discussions about what we should do ... and the alternatives really were to sell the business while it was still on a high and going well, or make a decision to change direction of the business and reinvest ... A lot of debate backwards and forwards ... a few more corridor conversations and then a bit later it actually got on the agenda ... The main thing that stuck in my mind was the procrastination—we would discuss it and then for one reason or another we would always defer the decision—'it's going OK we will discuss it again', 'it seems to be going OK, we don't have to decide today', 'let's think more about it and let's see how this goes and then we will discuss it again' ... I remember saying at the time—its fine but eventually if we

don't make a call it will be forced on us ... and that's exactly what happened ... A number of years later we were forced to divest this business but by then it had lost most of its value. It was a salutary lesson to all concerned.

(Director N)

Creating tactical interventions

In addition to the skills mentioned earlier, NEDs participating in the author's study recounted a range of tactics and skills they observed chairs demonstrating. Concerning very large transformative decisions, directors recounted two ways in which chairs supplemented their facilitation skills in the boardroom. First, a chair spoke individually to each NED offline to ensure there were no concerns or questions not being raised at the board. Second, a chair used closed sessions to bring concerns to the surface that may not have been apparent during the debate:

> Some directors, because of their personality, have a bigger voice and may be more articulate/less fearless and a debate can get off the rails as a result ... they become a pervasive advocate that can sway the whole conversation. That is why a good chair is important, as they can create the interventions for others to contribute.
>
> (Director A)

> This was the time when some directors raised any concerns or reservations they may have had [which they were uncomfortable raising while the CEO was present]. Even if they don't disagree with the CEO's proposal, they may wish to voice a particular emphasis'
>
> (Director A)

Another tactical intervention relied on the simple technique of stopping the discussion midstream and signalling a 'process check' to restate individual positions. A process check could be used to check for understanding or to explicitly identify areas of agreement and disagreement or simply to create more reflection. In some cases, this had the effect of signalling that progress has been made and restoring energy and focus, especially when the issues were complex, decisions multifaceted and discussions protracted. Process checks also created the opportunity to offer clear summaries or a restatement of first principles, such as 'go-no-go' principles in an acquisition discussion.

A board dinner (with or without the CEO present) was another tactic that some chairs employed. Several directors suggested that the conviviality of a dinner, held after the conclusion of a board meeting, often brought interesting observations or nuances to the surface not voiced at the board meeting. It is not uncommon for more expansive reflections to be compromised by a tightly managed board meeting agenda.

These reported tactics, practised by some but not all chairs, were critical in bringing unspoken concerns (especially early in a decision-making process) to the surface, and moderating the influence of pervasive advocates of a position that was not in the best interests of the process or outcome.

Nurturing psychological safety

The effects of psychological safety on the behaviour of a group has been well researched (Edmonson 1999). Psychological safety is a shared belief held by members of a group or team that they can practise interpersonal risk-taking safely. How members of a group treat each other in the conversational space and the sensitivity shown to the feelings of others matters. For example, cutting people off, not allowing someone to finish their point or ignoring or sidelining a person's contribution affects feelings of trust and interpersonal safety. In the main, its effect is fear, which results in overthinking, under speaking and group think.

If a powerful coalition of directors hijacks the direction of discussions, a lack of psychological safety can be the result. An effective chair will be alert to the chilling effect such groups can have on board debates, taking firm and decisive action to address such groupings and their effects.

NEDs reported that the boards they regarded as most effective were those in which a sense of psychological safety was created, such that NEDs were made to feel safe to disagree and challenge each other, including the chair. This was not simply the task of a chair but instead was implicit in the micro-behaviours of all directors, especially committee chairs and long-tenured and relatively more influential directors.

Psychological safety is fragile and vital to the success of any group. In situations in which members have interdependent roles, it is vital. When we feel psychologically safe, we are more likely to be open, candid, motivated, resilient and persistent. We are more likely to engage in solution-seeking behaviour and divergent thinking thrives. We are willing to be vulnerable in front of peers and acknowledge that we do not know things, as there is less blame for getting something wrong.

Tactics and techniques to strengthen board leadership as a shared practice

To summarise, the skills chairs require do not differ vastly from those required of NEDs because leadership is a group process. However, there are some in-meeting tactics and techniques that are helpful for chairs to use to unlock collective leadership. Chairs can also play a vital role in keeping feedback loops going between meetings. Despite the reluctance of some chairs to initiate informal feedback/coaching catch-ups with board peers (perhaps for fear of being seen to co-opt support for their perspectives), this is a vital part in contributing to the process of leadership.

We recommend that chairs plan to have at least six monthly if not quarterly informal catch-ups focussed on how the shared process is experienced by individual directors—asking for feedback and giving feedback that may help to strengthen the collective processes described in the foregoing. Closed meetings offer another opportunity to coach the group as a whole, focussing on which of these collective processes are working well and what needs improving. A range of other in-meeting tactics can also be applied. These are summarised in the following under three headings: chair strategies, NED strategies, and process changes to help shift the dynamic towards leveraging shared leadership more fully.

Chair strategies and tactics

- calling on a director who may have an interesting, even counterintuitive or contrary view, that may add value and fullness to deliberations. This process can be formalised by appointing a particular NED a discussion leader among the NEDs to lead the discussion on a topic/agenda item/decision
- orchestrating 'conversational turn-taking', usually in relation to a complex issue in which subtle but important nuances may be important. Some refer to this as polling, although polling has a more formal and less conversational feel
- designating a devil's advocate role particularly in the context of a major investment decision. It is particularly effective when a chair anticipates overwhelming agreement and brings into the discussion space an alternative view that opens up the dialogue and cultivates new possibilities and alternatives. A confident management team should welcome a board that challenges and adds value to an investment decision
- designating an NED to become the conduit for all requests for additional information or analysis so that NEDs feel confident they are not the only people in the room with the least information or knowledge
- investing in an on-boarding process for newly appointed NEDs that does not simply include a formal introduction to the board of their background and experience but also includes the opportunity for the new appointee to speak to what they feel they can personally bring to the board.

NED strategies and tactics

- active listening involving asking three types of questions: clarifying, confirming and probing. These questions are a useful way of capturing nuance and subtleties in a conversation not only for themselves but also to provide illumination for others. Importantly, they will ensure that chairs can test if they are faithfully representing the views of members
- process checks are important in protracted discussions in which there may be as much agreement as disagreement and in which there may be

value in teasing out the threads of consensus from the threads of contention. These are checks for shared understanding and offer the group clear summaries

- assumption/belief testing, especially when there are high-stakes decisions involved. This requires the group to go back to first principles. The most effective way of leading into such a discussion is to ask 'what do we have to believe for this to hold true'
- building a more emergent style of engaging to open up discussion. It is important to ask open-ended questions such as 'what do you see that I am not seeing', 'is this issue part of a bigger systems issue we need to acknowledge', 'are there some questions we are not asking', 'what issues do we feel remain as contentious or unresolved', 'what experiences have you had that might further illuminate this issue', 'is there something that is absorbing all our attention that may be better directed elsewhere' and 'what assumptions have we made that may not hold in this particular circumstance'
- role modelling actions that reflect the practice of shared leadership, reinforcing and rewarding the behaviours of members that drive healthy contention while forging collective alignment. These may be as simple as role modelling the use of open-ended questions or as sophisticated as showing openness by being prepared to argue against one's own long-held position. It may also include praising NEDs who inquire into the views of the less vocal directors.

Process changes

- holding pre-meetings designed to foreshadow, frame or anticipate concerns. Pre-meetings, if framed and handled well, are a useful tactic. However, if managed badly, they can come across as unhelpful political ploys to build support for a proposal ahead of the board meeting—a 'softening up' of directors assumed to have strong contrary positions on an issue
- closed sessions can be used at the end of every meeting as a powerful 'in the moment' check on how the process of leadership is working. They may also be useful in bringing unspoken concerns to the surface that did not emerge during the board meeting. Closed sessions provide a reflective space in which broader changes can be discussed to strengthen board effectiveness
- strengthening the externally run board effectiveness review to include an assessment of how the notion of shared leadership is being enacted by the board collectively. Instead of any report resulting from the review being an aggregation of individual NED effectiveness, it should seek to explore how the board is fulfilling its obligations in practising shared leadership.

In conclusion

Board leadership is a dynamic, shared practice in which a mutual influence process at the collective level is continually being negotiated by members of the group. There are formal and informal interactional aspects in which different directors may need to step forward and provide leadership for the board at different times. As group members interact with each other, dynamic constructs such as trust, cohesion and commitment determine the quality of group dynamics, which are constantly being negotiated. In enabling this process (rather than hindering it), an effective chair brings humility, intuition, courage and influence, and a leadership style that is inclusive; however, such qualities are rarely among the hiring criteria for a chair role. Chairs are more often than not hired for their standing in the community, reputations or for their sector experience.

The chair's alertness to identity politics, the role of social factors and the emergence of subgroups and their effects on board dynamics are essential. A chair needs to create psychological safety, nurturing a safe environment in which power differentials do not thwart the openness of dialogue and debate, and create the space for contention to thrive alongside consensus (Thuraisingham 2018). While coaching directors about the need to collectively own the decision-making process, including the challenges of others, chairs need to ensure that this is not done at the expense of the dissenting voice. Chairs may wish to consider whether they are doing enough to affirm the identities of those who may be perceived as having less power. They may also consider how to better prepare for big decisions. Such preparation may involve reflecting on subgroup views that may form or emerge along certain cognitive or ideological fault lines, social factors that may be at play during the process and the multiple personas that may exist on a board. By being alert to these factors, chairs may become more mindful about potential shifts in the balance of power during discussions.

However, the chair's leadership is not the sole determinant of success. Leadership is not simply concentrated in the chair, but is distributed across committee chairs and among those with expertise related to the decision. The most effective boards were those in which leadership was a collective process and leadership was shown by all directors in the actions they took to influence each other in the boardroom, believing that accountability did not reside in one role—the chair—but could only be achieved through a shared sense of accountability, led by a skilful chair.

It is time for a rethink of the qualities currently used to determine succession into the chair role. The chair creates conditions for members to make independent and informed choices about the direction they will take in a given discussion. They do this as a discussion leader through the inclusive and intentional use of time and space, asking not telling; they are a provider of structure and a keeper of the process, while never losing sight of the big picture of ensuring the whole is greater than the sum of its parts.

References

Edmonson, A 1999, 'Psychological safety and learning behavior in work teams', *Administrative Science Quarterly*, vol. 44, no. 2, pp. 350–383.

Finkelstein, S 1992, 'Power in top management teams: dimensions, measurement and validation', *Academy of Management Journal*, vol. 35, no. 3, pp. 505–538.

Magee, JC & Smith, PK 2013, 'The social distance theory of power', *Personality and Social Psychology Review*, vol. 17, no. 2, pp. 158–186.

Thuraisingham, SM 2018, 'Exploring the social factors that influence the decision making behaviours of non-executive directors in Australian public companies', PhD thesis, RMIT University, Melbourne.

Part II

NEDs play an important role—they link the company to the outside world. Notably, they reassure the corporate establishment comprising shareholders and other stakeholders regarding the probity and competence of a board through acting as a powerful linking resource. Therefore, it is important to know what enables this linking role to be exercised effectively and, conversely, what impedes it.

Part II looks closely at the expectations external stakeholders have of the boards' accountabilities. Building on Part I, it extends the plan for creating a more strategically active board. This is followed by a detailed description of how to undertake robust board evaluation/effectiveness reviews, highlighting the limitations of current approaches. It concludes with two chapters that consider the expectations of investors and implications for boards, and how governance is evolving in the face of rapid technology, regulatory and societal changes, and what this means for boards today.

Part II

6 Developing a strategically active board

This chapter in summary

This chapter opens with the context that organisations find themselves in today in which strategies, business models and assumptions are being upended by new entrants and greater consumer power, underscoring the need for boards to become more involved in strategy.

Building on the opportunities to shape strategy described in Chapter 1, this chapter examines the range of practices that boards currently engage in, ranging from simply approving strategy to shaping the content and conduct of strategy. There are life cycle reasons for why these variations occur from one board to the next, such as boards needing to involve themselves more when the company is under financial stress. However, Part 1 showed that, often, strategy shaping depends on the confidence and capabilities of NEDs in navigating the power dynamic in the boardroom.

First, the chapter considers the case for change and how rapidly changing expectations of corporations requires boards to consider the role they play in creative disruption of strategy and the role modelling of this skill in their interactions with management. Second, the chapter describes the challenge of shaking off legacy thinking. Finally, it considers what a strategically active board may look and feel like and suggests four common characteristics, providing predictive power in distinguishing effective boards from ineffective ones: diversity in sources from which board capital is derived, CEOs who demonstrate perspective-taking behaviour, chairs skilled at managing agreement as well as disagreement and directors who show as much humility as courage—humility to know they may be wrong and need to be open to the perspectives of others and courage to stand by their convictions in the face of social pressure to conform with 'groupthink'.

The chapter provides some tools for boards and NEDs to reflect on how strategically active they have been, and explores practical ways in which NEDs may strengthen their involvement in strategy and become more strategically influential as a group. It doing so, it challenges the rational models used today to explain strategic decision-making, which largely ignore the social and relational dynamics that result when individuals interact in groups to make strategic decisions. The chapter also identifies some of the pitfalls in the approach taken by current board effectiveness reviews and suggests some improvements.

It is because [of] boards' failure to create tomorrow's firm out of today's that so many famous names in industry continue to disappear.

Sir John Harvey-Jones, Chairman, Imperial Chemical
Industries (ICI), 1982–1987

For boards to play a more strategically active role, there must be clarity about the delineation of roles. The CEO is responsible for running the company and making operational decisions and it is important that the board does not undermine this authority by giving operational guidance or direction to management. However, the board must ensure it is doing everything it can to ensure the company performs and creates value.

An important distinction is often made between boards that demonstrate all the traits of strategic persistence and strategically active or change-driven boards. This is not a theoretical distinction; indeed, it is as pressing an issue today as it was some decades ago as reflected in the Harvey-Jones quote. In reflecting on their involvement in strategy, NEDs may have some concern about crossing the 'red line' and drifting into the domain of management, as noted. However, setting the strategic direction of the company is a core board responsibility and boards must have the capabilities and capacity not only to review and endorse strategy but to be in a position to co-create it with management. This expectation, that boards should place greater emphasis on the strategic development of the firm, is gaining strong support from directors themselves. The 2018 report of McKinsey & Company's global governance survey of 1,100 directors appears to show little change since their 2015 survey, with about 27% of time spent on strategy with 52% of directors indicating that they wanted to spend more time on strategy. When asked about potential business disruptions, such as digitization, geopolitical risks and cyber security, surprisingly few directors say these topics have found their way onto the board agenda.

This chapter lays out the case for change, arguing that boards will need to invest more time in thinking about how they might strengthen effectiveness. While the vast majority of FTSE 350 and ASX 100 firms undergo a board effectiveness review, there is no consistency or transparency around how well these reviews are undertaken. For example, in its 2016 annual report, Carillion, the UK construction giant who in 2018 collapsed, stated that their board evaluation had confirmed that the board, each of its committees and the directors continue to be highly effective. Part 1 of this book observed the overly narrow perspective taken to determining board composition. Board capital—the concept introduced and explored in detail in Chapter 2—as proxy for the cognitive diversity that boards so badly need and how that board capital is used in and around the boardroom, provides a most holistic approach to the appointment and evaluation of directors on boards. Board evaluations and effectiveness reviews must start to adopt this broader prism for reviewing both their composition and their ways of working. How a robust board effectiveness review may be developed and conducted is dealt with in Chapter 7. The

Financial Times argued that the collapse of Carillion 'underscores structural problems in how many UK companies are run and held accountable ... if we can manage to solve the issues with corporate governance, fewer companies are likely to go under' (Sadan 2018, p. 18). The article references work by major institutional investors, such as Legal & General Investment Management, who are pushing for changes to improve the system. Much of the focus is on board accountability, including making it compulsory for directors to disclose the names of firms they have previously been associated with, thereby ensuring that directors who have been on boards that have failed in their duties are transparent about that link. Of course, the majority of boards discharge their stewardship duties admirably and justifiably feel let down by the contagion damage flowing from high-profile collapses.

During times of extreme financial stress (such as is now confronting the Carillion's board), the board will typically get more involved and the delineation of roles may not be as evident. When the company is performing well, board involvement may not be deemed as necessary. However, the boards that take a more hands-off approach when things are going well do so at their peril. Even during times of outstanding performance, boards must continually challenge the assumptions underlying the strategy and help executives spot weaknesses. This is because a strategy may be failing long before there is obvious evidence that it is failing. Besides changes to strategy will take some time to demonstrate their value creating impact.

Given the degree of change facing most firms, and the real challenge of being strategically and operationally futureproof, strategically active boards must find ways to work closely with management to co-create strategy. They must also, independently of management, school themselves in knowledge of the sector, deeply understand the fundamentals of the sector and the competitive landscape facing it. This is a significant paradigm shift for some boards and may challenge many traditionally, and/or more conservatively, minded directors who believe strategy formulation is the domain of management.

Incumbency and the case for change

This section considers the case for change in the face of disruption of traditional business models, as this is arguably the key strategic issue facing most corporations and most sectors. However, the strategic and operational change driven by disruptive technology should not disguise other challenges, particularly those evident in the growing forces of globalisation and the increasing debates associated with the social purpose of corporations (which is covered more fully in Chapters 8 and 9).

Of course, industry and market change is not a new phenomenon as the quotation from the British industrialist Sir John Harvey-Jones at the beginning of this chapter reminds us. The difference today is the very real potential for revolutionary change to occur—as seems to happen every 100 years or so. Joseph Schumpeter's (1942) *creative destruction* thesis has never been so much a reality. New asset-light, technology-driven, business models that are now taking on long-established incumbents reflecting Schumpeter's 1942 prediction. Consumers have embraced start-ups like Netflix, Uber, Airbnb, Amazon, Facebook and other business models that are fundamentally changing competition. Airbnb already has more rooms around the world than established hotel chains like the Marriott, Hilton, Intercontinental and Westin, yet it does not own a single hotel. Uber now operates in over 70 countries and processes more rental car service transactions in a year than the aggregate of taxi service providers in matching Anglo-American markets, yet it does not own a single car. Netflix is on course to become a truly global entertainment company, threatening many domestic television networks. It now serves 125 million households, double the number it had in 2014 ('The tech giant' 2018). China now has similar disrupters such as Alibaba. These and other new business models and products have the potential to impact society in the same way that the Model T, Microsoft Word, Google, Amazon and Apple iPhone have done. Technology-driven change is transferring greater power to consumers through the internet and social media, globalisation has continued at pace and entry barriers have fallen; these changes have the potential to shift the balance of power away from large firms, reshaping industries and profoundly changing the nature of competition. The retail and financial services sectors already see these powerful forces at play through online shopping and the emergence of fintechs. Little is known about blockchain technology and how it may potentially alter the role of today's institutions. Food retailing businesses are also experiencing challenges in maintaining expensive high street supermarkets, as consumers drift in large numbers to online grocery shopping. Online grocery shopping, home delivery and click and collect in the UK is the fastest growing purchase channel, both in terms of value and growth, according to retail analysts IGD. The average value of weekly online sales in predominantly food stores has more than doubled between 2010 and 2016, with the UK forecast to become the second largest grocery market worldwide after China by 2020. With the introduction of 'pure play' and adoption by online retailers such as Ocado and AmazonFresh, and smaller more niche paddock-to-plate disrupters, traditional supply chains are being disintermediated. At the same time, societal habits and expectations are changing; this is particularly driven by millennials whose environmental concerns are influencing consumption behaviour ('Danone rethinks' 2018).

Of course, the problem is that, as a firm grows and becomes more complex in its composition the more difficult it is to properly manage and govern its activities; principal-agent problems become more apparent and diseconomies of scale set in with the management and governance costs of size surpassing scale benefits. This is a reality that many large financial services firms and industrial firms like General Electric (GE) are already facing. The many corporate governance challenges facing such firms is discussed in more detail in Chapter 8. Diseconomies of scale and organisational complexity can cause higher shareholder costs and present arguably insurmountable challenges for current corporate governance models.

In the Innovator's Dilemma, Harvard Business School's Strategy Professor Christensen (1997) cites the reason why great companies fail. He suggested that the reason why large firms face strategic, operational and cultural challenges is that they want to employ their resources in substantial markets that offer higher profits, play to their comparative advantage and allow them to employ economies of scale and scope. To expect these same firms to meaningfully nurture disruptive business models, thereby risking significant investment in uncertain outcomes, is akin to flapping one's arms with wings strapped to them and hoping to fly. Christensen argued that such expectations involve fighting fundamental tendencies about the way big organisations work and how their performance is evaluated. The track record of challenger incubators succeeding within large firms is nowhere near as successful as those same incubators performing outside the 'shackles' of the large firm. Being a fledgling business within a large firm can be a very lonely place when the initial enthusiasm wanes and other priorities, often reinforced by short-termism, cause capital to be prioritised on what counts today—namely, keeping the current business model competitive and short-term earnings in line with market expectations and preserving executive incentive arrangements.

Today, technology is enabling the disruption of many traditional business models, eroding many transaction costs and making it easier for smaller firms to challenge the dominance of big firms, often using a judo strategy (i.e., speed and agility to combat the size and strength of incumbents) (Yoffie & Kwak 2001). Boards and management in big, dominant firms can become complacent of the risk of new entrants, largely because of the emotional equity they have invested in their strategies. They can be dismissive and sometimes arrogant towards the many advantages that new, start-up firms have. It can be difficult for incumbents to conceive of how 'their' business of 100 years standing, with attendant economies of scale, can be 'beaten' by a new entrant, yet they also fear the Eastman Kodak destiny. Sometimes anticompetitive market structures can fuel complacency and arrogance, such as in the banking sector in Australia and the UK electricity generation market; as with the dominant players in smartphone and computer operating systems such as Apple, Google and Amazon. Attitudes and ways of working can become deeply entrenched in such companies as they come to believe their own success.

The curse of legacy thinking and conservatism

> This world demands the qualities of youth; not a time of life but a state of mind, a temper of the will, a quality of imagination, a predominance of courage over timidity, of the appetite for adventure over the life of ease.
> Robert F Kennedy (Stigter & Cooper 2018)

This section suggests that an affliction of legacy thinking lies at the heart of incumbency. Boards need to be realistic in acknowledging that new entrants may have significant advantages, which can be summarised as the absence of four legacies:

- technology
- infrastructure assets
- business processes
- management and board thinking.

In so many ways, the biggest risk facing many incumbents today is not legacy IT or infrastructure assets (though this is a big issue in banking and retailing), but legacy thinking. There are early warning signs of legacy thinking. People who have exercised power, enjoyed success and developed a reputation are not accustomed to being challenged; they often develop a sense that they are frequently right (a sense that has served them well in the past). Strong convictions are common among senior executives involved in sectors that have experienced unbroken double digit growth for the last two decades. NEDs, including chairs, may need to reflect more deeply on the reasons for the company's success or failure, attributing the former to their contribution and the latter to external factors.

The example of Scandinavian telecommunication equipment giant Nokia illustrates how 'success is toxic', to quote Nokia's chairman ('Telephone tower' 2018, p. 65). In 2007, Nokia accounted for 40 per cent of global handsets and had a market capitalisation of $290 billion. However, because of its complacency towards industry change, emerging competition from Asia and lax attitude towards software, its market capitalisation in 2018 averaged $33 billion. Other case studies, such as Borders, House of Fraser, General Motors, Marks & Spencer, Sony, Wells Fargo, Commonwealth Bank of Australia (CBA) and GE, provide further examples of the hypothesis that 'success is toxic' and illustrate why boards cannot be strategically passive, particularly if the firm is currently enjoying a position of strength. Corporate UK and Australia provide numerous examples of how once great businesses become susceptible to the 'success is toxic' disease and how the consequences can linger for years.

Former Australian treasurer, Peter Costello, commenting on his country's four major banks, which are among the most profitable in the world, stated:

> They are absolutely immune from market discipline, living in a highly profitable cocoon: they think all these high returns are from their own brilliance, but what they haven't understood is they have a unique and privileged regulatory system which has delivered this to them.
>
> (Creighton 2017, p. 26)

Special licence privileges or other forms of high industry entry barriers such as in the case of the Australian Banking industry can lull whole sectors into a feeling of safety, dulling their instincts for change. A sobering reflection is that, according to Accenture, just over half of the names of companies on the Fortune 500 have disappeared since the year 2000.

Rather than focussing on what it is today, strategic curiosity and courage are required to think about the future and what the financial profile of the firm might be. This may be a challenge for some board directors in part because of the emotional equity invested in the current strategy. Legacy thinking can be a powerful barrier to change and can downplay the risk of disruption. Evidence of legacy thinking can be found when firms are trapped in a product rather than a customer experience mindset. Industries such as hoteling, e-payments, entertainment and transportation are examples of incumbents imagining a world beyond a product mindset. The absence of this mindset is evident in the collapse of iconic firms such as Eastman Kodak; Toys R Us; film and video rental firm Blockbuster; book and music retailer Borders; electrical retailer Comet; and UK retail giant Woolworths, a staple of every UK high street until it went into administration in 2008.

A related theme is the *curse of conservatism* or risk aversion, particularly in regulated firms. In their book, *Boards that dare*, Stigter and Cooper (2018) called for courage. Courage is needed in good measure particularly in sectors such as commercial banking, telcos and retailing in which there is evidence that incumbents may be locked into a path-dependent future—that is, a future that is a continuation of the past while new technology-advantaged and agile challengers attack profit pools within the industry. The irony is that boards can find their agenda consumed by regulatory, compliance and security matters in which the emphasis is 'tick the box' compliance-oriented work, which research by McKinsey & Company suggests that can take around 70 per cent of board time (Casal & Caspar 2014). As a consequence, some boards may struggle to focus on strategy and/or culture that can be core to the firm's future success—the key to the firm being strategically and operationally futureproof. The strategic agenda can become a once or twice a year deep dive off-site, a skilful execution by management of a highly choreographed series of presentations in which information 'dumping' is the order of the day; however, this can leave many directors feeling that they are being 'managed' and their contribution is at best perfunctory.

As well as disruptive change, directors today know that the traditional role of the board and the way it engages with the firm's stakeholders is unlikely to satisfy the needs of the future, particularly with the rise of shareholder activism, anti-business populism and rising societal interest in the culture, conduct and purpose of business, as discussed in Chapters 8 and 9. Societal expectations of business, particularly 'big business', has changed following the global financial crisis. The rise in populism, which, aided by social media, has engendered negative portrayals of business on matters such as CEO remuneration. At a time like this there is also a greater need for firms to be clear on their *purpose* and the societal value they contribute beyond profits and dividends. This point is discussed further in Chapters 8 and 9. All of these are clear strategic choices that boards have to make about how they go about exercising their leadership.

NED exposure to disruptive forces and diverse thinking

An unavoidable reality is that the desire to create a more strategically active board is not always accompanied by the appetite, motivation, awareness, skills and capability to do so. The capacity of boards to lead the thinking (or challenge management) on innovation is constrained not just by crowded board agendas, but also, more significantly, by the board's own experience and insights into innovation and risk-taking. For example, few directors would appreciate the potential of Cloud-driven transformations, the scope for API's (application programming interface allowing secure connectivity with external data sources), the nature of the risks from cybersecurity or blockchain as an alternative to trust-based disintermediated relationships. Some directors may be left feeling that the pace of change driven by technology is like a runaway train, which has left many of them behind. Although something of a generalisation, it remains the case that many directors over the age of 50 may feel considerable anxiety about their lack of first-hand experience in providing the required oversight of the organisation's response to technology-driven disruption or the risk of cybersecurity. They may also not feel comfortable in reshaping a business model by allocating significant capital investment into uncertain project outcomes. These are competencies more closely associated with entrepreneurs, and a very shallow pool of intrapreneurs, rather than the technocratic and conventional nature of skills that dominate many boards (e.g., consultants, bankers, lawyers and accountants). It is worthwhile remembering that technology is simply an enabler, rather than itself the disruptor of business models. *Creative disruption* as a skill comes from boards that engage in diverse thinking. In turn, diversity of thinking comes from diverse backgrounds making it more likely that diverse backgrounds on a board will challenge traditional ways of doing things and find new approaches to old problems. Although diverse thinking is not always linked to diversity in age, education, gender, ethnicity, social–economic background, it is often correlated. The reference to age should be not be misunderstood; as Stigter and Cooper (2018, p. 120) have argued, the overriding quality is neoteny—that is, the retention of youthful qualities such as energy and an inquisitive, curious mind. These learning agile qualities can be found in certain people regardless of age and are important in a board seeking to ensure the firm is futureproof. The Robert F Kennedy quotation earlier in this chapter summarises this position well. A good measure of diverse board tenures as well as dispositions and interaction styles also contributes to diverse thinking, a point extensively discussed in Part 1 of this book.

As discussed in Chapter 2, sourcing directors from a narrow pool in what may be described as a cosy 'eco-system' has implications for how much strategic challenge and contention there may be. The bias towards appointing board advisors, consultants, lawyers and accountants without practical, multidisciplinary experience, may produce NEDs who are singularly focussed on their specific area of expertise thereby not bringing broader value to a discussion and as a result narrowing the quality of judgement. In Australia, research by Watermark has questioned the bias towards hiring lawyers and accountants on boards and showed that less than 20 per cent of the top 300 directors in Australia had direct industry experience, while close to 50 per cent had a legal or financial background (Evans et al. 2018). A leading newspaper captured this when it printed:

> Australia's boardrooms have a problem. Too many people who sit on them are not up to the job because they are drawn from narrow circles, or are more interested in building their own brand than their firm's.
>
> ('The questions' 2018, p. 26)

Functional bias is not the only challenge facing boards seeking to build their *creative disruption* muscle. For boards to play a more influential role in strategy and in particular engage more skilfully in *creative disruption*, they need to also take a hard look at the current mix of directors in relation to socio-economic background, ethnicity and gender. For example, a series of reports in the UK posed questions about various dimensions of diversity on boards, revealing the glacial speed with which the composition of boards in the UK are changing: the Tyson Report into the recruitment and development of NEDs in 2003, Lord Davies of Abersoch's report on gender balance in British boards in 2011 and Sir John Parker's report on ethnic diversity on UK boards in 2017. The fourth edition of the ASX Corporate Governance Principles and Recommendations for listed entities (now in its consultation phase) has proposed substantial changes. It proposes that the diversity objectives the board or a committee of the board sets should include appropriate and meaningful benchmarks that are able to be, and are, monitored and measured. This new guideline was motivated by the tendency for some boards to simply confirm that they had a diversity policy in place rather than showing how they were bringing about more meaningful change. It further proposes that these could involve, for example:

- achieving specific numerical targets for the proportion of women on its board, in senior executive roles and in its workforce generally within a specified timeframe; it has recommended 30 per cent as a benchmark listed companies should aspire to
- achieving specific numerical targets for female representation in key operational roles within a specified timeframe with the view to developing a diverse pipeline of talent that can be considered for future succession to senior executive roles; or
- achieving specific targets for the 'Gender Equality Indicators' in the Workplace Gender Equality Act.

Further it suggests and provides guidance for what should be contained in a diversity policy, making reference to other forms of diversity that ASX boards are encouraged to pay attention to. These benchmarking measures are in addition to the *'if not why not'* requirement for all listed companies in Australia to explain the differences in gender balance in the management pipeline, brought in January 2011. The fourth edition principles proposed require ASX companies to ensure more specificity in the strategies and actions they are taking, beyond simply confirming they now have a diversity policy communicated across the company.

From the dance floor to the balcony

Today, many directors have to grapple with the ever growing (and often mind-numbing) 'box-ticking' compliance related workload and the relentless pressure for short-term earnings growth. It is no surprise that boards can struggle to stay on top of the range of issues that they are expected to be across; however, this cannot be allowed to be an excuse for poor corporate governance. Such preoccupations may result in the tendency for directors to be stronger on compliance, delivering EPS growth, and weaker on resolving the challenges of strategy and culture.

In the face of this ever-expanding workload, it has become difficult for even the most diligent board members to absorb, digest and reflect on all the material they are sent. The reality is that the sheer burden of compliance-based paperwork and range of matters that can find their way onto a board agenda, leaves little time for the big strategic issues, materially hampering board effectiveness; many directors would agree that there is little time to 'get off the dance floor and onto the balcony' to consider the major strategic themes that may shape the future of the firm and that this weakens board relevance on strategy. As revealed in Part 1, how companies involve themselves in strategy can vary across a wide spectrum—at one end, board members actively co-creating the strategy with management and, at the other, simply endorsing and approving strategy presented to them. While some executives may welcome a strategically passive board such an approach only creates the potential for agency costs.

To ensure the balance is right between their monitoring and advisory roles, boards can apply a few tests. First asking themselves periodically what proportion of time they are spending on value creation-related conversations and what proportion they are spending on value preservation-related conversations. Second, in addition to time allocation considerations, boards may need to challenge their ways of working. For example, the traditional process of reviewing corporate strategy once a year may be outmoded in that in today's rapidly changing business environment, strategies may lose relevance almost as soon as they are developed. Boards need to adopt a more iterative process such that they schedule through the year well-chosen strategic topics that are reshaping the environment/sector. Such a process should also be accompanied by a more emergent style of thinking. They may also have regular deep dives on the competitive dynamics or on specific strategic options which also gives the board the chance to interact more broadly with the management team and to assess C-suite talent while doing so. Third they may want to ask if the appointment of directors actually reflect their strategic priorities. For example, if growth in China is a top priority, would the appointment of a former executive of a company who has successfully led growth initiatives there provide them a strategic edge? By ensuring deep skills on the audit committee and other committees and using these committees more effectively, the board can free up the time it needs as a group to partake in strategic matters. Provided of course that board members are not abdicating their legally mandated responsibilities to committees.

Monitoring and adapting strategy

While boards have a critical role to play in co-creating and shaping strategy, they also have a critical role in monitoring the strategy being executed. There is a big gap between the financial performance promised by strategies and what is actually realised by those strategies. The board has a critical role in this, alert to any course-correcting that is required and providing the counsel to management to work to close this gap.

As shown by the Mankins and Steele (2005) research summarised in Figure 6.1 companies on average delivered 63 per cent of the initial performance their strategies promised. What is worrying is that the causes of this strategy-to-performance gaps are sometimes invisible to top management. Management can then pull the wrong levers in their attempt to turn performance around:

- Pressing for better execution when they actually need a better strategy or
- Opting to change direction when they really should focus the organisation on execution

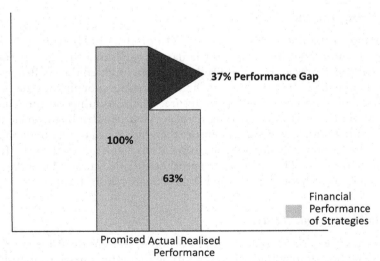

Source: Mankins & Steele HBR 2005 Turning Great Strategy into Great Performance research

Figure 6.1 The strategy-performance gap: the gap between the financial performance promised and realised.
Source: Mankins and Steele (2005).

The result is a lot of wasted energy, lost time and continued under-performance. Boards have to be alert to the levers being pulled: the execution lever, that is, pressing for better execution when they actually need a better strategy, or the strategy lever, that is, opting to change direction when they really should focus the organisation on execution.

The reasons for strategic failure may have to do with the strategy itself. The research showed that the failure of strategy may have to do with three symptoms:

Poor strategic insight driven by
  • Poor insight about own market position
  • Underestimating the competition/complexity
Lack of strategic clarity driven by
  • Lack of coherence and strategic logic
  • Lack of competitive distinctiveness
Failure to be strategically agile driven by
  • Locking on to a strategy when conditions have changed (all competitive advantage is predicated on a particular set of conditions that exists at a particular point in time and for particular reasons and assumptions made will need to be challenged)

In monitoring the successful execution of an agreed strategy, boards play a critical role in asking the questions that will reveal the symptoms and root causes for strategic failure and to ensure agility.

Preparing for the future: some tools

Referring to the themes from Carter and Lorsch's (2004) *Back to the drawing board*, and reminding us how little has changed, in a thoughtful *Harvard Business Review* article, Hill and Davis (2017) highlighted the challenges that many boards face. In particular, in both allocating enough time to understanding and then preparing for the future. The constraints on time and, in the case of many sectors, increasing regulatory burden that boards must manage, together with the pressure to ensure that short-term results are delivered, means that insufficient quality time is spent on factors critical to the future success of the firm. This is one of the great board dilemmas and is at the heart of the question explored in Chapter 9: 'Are boards fit for future?'

Developing strategic clarity

To address the serious strategic issues of today and ensure strategic clarity, NEDs and boards may find reflecting on the following questions useful:

1 How high a priority is business model innovation on the board agenda?
2 What would a different owner of the firm (e.g., a major competitor or private equity) do with the business if they acquired it?

3 How well equipped is the board in understanding the scope and scale of all forms of innovation including technology-driven innovation?

4 How much time is the board spending on technology-driven innovation and future market direction?

5 Does the firm's risk appetite and capital and operational expenditure align with its innovation agenda?

6 What strategic options should the firm be creating? Does it have a good handle on why the strategic options deployed by competitors (including new entrants) may be succeeding or failing?

7 What new capabilities must the firm develop to survive let alone to succeed and what *buy-build-borrow* plans does it have to ensure readiness?

8 How will the firm tell if its strategies are locked on a path-dependent course?

9 Does the firm have the talent to drive innovation and does the board have the expertise to help ensure that the firm is embracing risks associated with innovation?

10 What is the firm's reputation with analysts and customers on innovation?

11 Why are customers defecting, what do the reasons for defection tell the firm about how innovative it has been/can/should be?

12 What do customers do when not trading with the company? What unfulfilled needs of customers should the firm be addressing?

Defining strategic effectiveness

An indicator of strategic effectiveness is not in the number of board and sub-committee meetings that are held. To monitor strategic effectiveness various approaches can be taken. A tried and tested approach to conducting board effectiveness reviews is described in Chapter 7. In addition, there are other simple tools such as the simple scorecard shown in Table 6.1. This intuitively simple scorecard has a maximum score of 40 and a minimum score of eight. An overall score below 30 would warrant careful board scrutiny, as would any individual category score below 3 (see Hamel & Prahalad 1996). However, it is important to emphasise that such quantitatively neat tools are always subject to judgmental overlay from the board.

This framework contrasts with the approach of more traditional boards who typically become involved only at the end of the strategic planning process and usually hold a board meeting to review and then approve strategy. By contrast, a strategically active board will insist on being involved at the beginning of the planning process. It is critical to manage this carefully so as to prevent CEOs and management teams from becoming anxious and defensive. Some CEOs may view such engagement as the 'thin edge of the wedge' and feel that their authority is being undermined. Some CEOs simply do not like being told what to do when it comes to strategy; yet, the risk of management being trapped in a deeply ingrained paradigm of the industry is all too prevalent. Boards should always consider what a different owner of the firm (e.g., a major competitor or private equity) would do with the business if they acquired it.

Table 6.1 Scorecard for measuring strategic effectiveness

How does the company's point of view about the future stack up against that of competitors?						
Conventional and reactive	1	2	3	4	5	Distinctive and far-sighted
Which issue is absorbing more of management and board attention?						
Reengineering core processes	1	2	3	4	5	Regenerating core strategies
Within the industry, do competitors and customers view our firm as more of a rule-taker or a rule-maker?						
Mostly a rule-taker	1	2	3	4	5	Mostly a rule-maker
What are we better at, improving operational efficiency or creating fundamentally new value creating propositions and products?						
Operational efficiency	1	2	3	4	5	New business development
What percentage of our advantage-building efforts focus on catching up with competitors versus building advantages new to the industry?						
Mostly catching up to others	1	2	3	4	5	Mostly new to the industry
To what extent has our transformation agenda been set by competitors' actions versus being set by our own unique vision of the future?						
Largely driven by competitors	1	2	3	4	5	Largely driven by our vision
To what extent is the firm embracing digitalisation or reacting to it?						
Mostly reacting	1	2	3	4	5	Fully embracing
Among employees, what is the balance between anxiety and hope?						
Mostly anxiety	1	2	3	4	5	Mostly hope

Source: Adapted from Hamel and Prahalad (1996).

An alert board will want to see a range of strategic options framed around a detailed review of competitors and potential disruptors. They would also expect to see key external trends that may affect the business and a candid assessment of the capabilities that differentiate the firm, allowing for superior financial returns to be earned. How this is done is central to the strategic effectiveness and prospects of the firm outperforming its competitors in a sustainable way rather than simply moving with the herd, stuck comfortably in the middle.

Developing a distinctive and differentiated strategy can be complex. This complexity can be compounded in the eyes of the CEO during the formative stage. The more voices, expertise and opinions involved in the formulation of strategy the greater the pressure on the CEO, which may result in a defensive CEOs feeling that management is losing control.

The chair plays a critical role in establishing a culture in which the CEO sees early engagement with the board in the strategic process as both a positive and natural way in which the firm is managed—not a form of shadow management. Chapter 5 explores the broad skill sets a chair needs to fulfil this and the other roles they play. A progressive CEO will understand that having the board actively engaged in the strategic process is a good thing and not an undermining of its authority (Banta & Garrow 2017). The chair will also be sensitive to the short-term pressures facing the CEO, who often has a shorter time in the role that the chair and feels the pressure for immediate performance; the average chair will manage 2.5 CEO's while in office, highlighting the potential conflict of time horizons between chair and CEO. This problem is accentuated by the fact that major strategic investments can take time to deliver financial rewards.

In summary, to ensure a rigorous and structured approach to the strategic process, as suggested by the evaluation framework earlier, a board needs to assess its own effectiveness. In doing so there are three questions that may be useful for boards to ask of themselves:

- Does the board understand the industry's dynamics well enough?
- Has there been enough board and board-management debate on strategy?
- Is the board satisfied that all the strategic options have been considered: what options were discarded and why? Was there adequate contention at the management level?

Behaviours: distinguishing strategically effective boards from ineffective ones

Recent research has identified four characteristics of a strategically active board, providing predictive power in distinguishing effective and ineffective boards (Thuraisingham 2018). These characteristics reflect how some boards make a material contribution to the shape and direction of the company's strategic future. Strategically active boards have:

- cognitively diverse, experienced and well-networked NEDs with lively discursive and inquiry skills and who are comfortable with robust contention and skilled in constructive dissent
- NEDs who operate collectively as a group with a single view about how the work of the board is to be approached and collectively own the process of arriving at the decision (not just owning the decision at the end of the process) to avoid fragmenting the collective influence of the board
- an alert and intuitive chair skilled in facilitation who creates a discursive space for reflection to occur and constructive dissent to thrive and is alert to unspoken concerns on the way to building a clear consensus
- boardroom norms and routines that have less procedural rigidity, allowing for open, emergent thinking and collective reflection, and in which good agenda management is as important as the quality of debate.

How do boards ensure they are effective in exercising their strategic role? First, effective boards have a deep understanding and feel for the industry that the firm operates in and are committed to continual improvement; such boards think deeply about how they carry out their role and the way that the organisation engages with stakeholders, including customers and employees. They ensure that they have a finger on the pulse of organisational culture through credible feedback loops that reliably inform the board about the quality of the employee and customer experience. In the case of employee feedback loops they should augment what might be gleaned from, for example, company run employee engagement surveys. These feedback loops are critical to identifying leading indicators of future problems, particularly how the culture of the business is reflected in behaviour and its reputation with stakeholders.

Second, boards need to review how they are spending their time on a quarterly basis. It is important to reflect on whether the board is spending the bulk of its time on the status quo (value preservation) or on the future of the business (value creation)? According to McKinsey & Company, most boards spend around 70 per cent of their time on matters such as reporting, budgeting and compliance (Casal & Caspar 2014). This use of time carries a high opportunity cost (in a strategic sense); addressing this must be a priority for a chairperson committed to having a board focussed on futureproofing the firm.

While time allocation is an important first step, it does not necessarily mean that better outcomes are achieved. It signals the importance that boards place on its involvement in strategy and may also contribute to improving the prospect of better strategy outcomes. However, how that time is used is critical and is dependent on the skill of both the chair (as explored in Chapter 5) and the directors to engage in deeper and richer discussion and debate (as explored in Chapter 4).

Finally, strategy is both a science and a craft with intuition playing a key role. The quality of strategic dialogue can be aided by a range of tools and frameworks (such as Michael Porter's five forces and value chain, GE-McKinsey's nine-box matrix and the Boston Consulting Group (BCG) growth-share matrix); however, there is much to suggest that great strategies come from *strategic intuition* or *strategic sensing*, as Stigter and Cooper (2018) described. According to them, strategic intuition is central to innovative thinking, which, of course, can be counterintuitive to the way boards traditionally think. Yet, great breakthroughs are normally associated with entrepreneurs who sense an opportunity and seek to prosecute it, relying more on intuition than science—on their instinct that there is a market opportunity (this is borne out by the evidence from the directors studied in Part 1). They may then back up their instinct with science, such as market research and financial modelling, but their appetite for risk, their natural instincts and ability to see the big picture (to think big) are what sets them apart. These attributes are not common in a traditional boardroom; yet, these are the very attributes that many boards badly need if they are to take the lead on strategic change. How to solve this dilemma should be a priority for many boards.

There are several possible approaches, some more obvious and easier to pursue such as the appointment of senior strategy director with deep industry knowledge to act as the lead voice and thought leader on futureproofing the firm in a strategic sense. Another approach would be to establish a small, dedicated, independent team to support the board in evaluating strategy, the strategic options open to the company and the financial and other implications associated with decisions. Naturally, how such a team was established would be important so as to avoid creating tensions with the CEO and management team. A traditional approach would be for the chair and the board to access senior advisors. These are a valuable resource; however, such an approach can have its limitations, especially if the advisors assume a 'special relationship' with the chair, as this could leave NEDs feeling on the outer of strategic discussions. Advisors may also, on occasion, have little reputational 'skin in the game' beyond M&A-related advice. Needless to say, in very special situations, such as M&A, the involvement of trusted external advisors is critical.

In conclusion

Boards that simply review and then approve strategy are failing a core duty of governing, which requires active involvement in establishing the firm's strategy and a core measure of its stewardship. This core demand can often be in conflict with the limitations of a time and compliance-related agenda, leaving little breathing space for meaningful engagement in strategy formulation. Yet, today, arguably more than ever, boards must also make sure that the firm is strategically and operationally futureproof and this requires a board that is more engaged in the strategic and operational readiness of the firm. This can make a CEO and management team feel that a line is being crossed and that a board is intruding in matters that are the domain of management. To overcome this, boards need to convey a clear message to management about the board's role and accountability for strategy and agree on clear rules of engagement. Positioning of the message is critical to ensure that management no longer sees strategic engagement in terms of calendar events but as a strategy formulation journey that the board and management are equal partners in.

Boards and their directors need to reflect on the gap between how they actually spend their time and how they would like to spend their time. Boivie, Bednar and Andrus (2016) captured how most directors would like to spend their time:

> Spending the bulk of the board's time and intelligence focusing on strategy: growing the business, anticipating and working with disruptive technology (as opposed to reacting after being negatively impacted by it), understanding the competitive landscape, and identifying contacts to form strategic alliances or expand into emerging markets.

A board's review of its strategic effectiveness must place greater emphasis on the readiness of the current board to lead the firm into a disruptive future in which individual courage on the part of directors will be important. A number of frameworks and ideas have been proposed in this chapter to help boards consider if it is focussed on the right things and if it has the capabilities required to strategically futureproof the firm? This core question remains open, highlighting the importance of board renewal, engagement with investors, corporate culture, social licence, diverse thinking and the digital economy—all of which are issues that the remaining chapters address.

It is an urgent imperative for boards to let go of an outdated and deeply ingrained mental model of corporate governance and what it means to be a director. In the absence of political intervention through new legislation, activist investors can fill a governance void that some boards have allowed to happen, particularly when it comes to their role in determining strategy. Chapter 8 explores the rise of shareholder activism in this regard.

References

'Danone rethinks the idea of the firm' 2018, *The Economist*, 9 August, p. 57.

'Telephone tower v rubber boots' 2018, *The Economist*, 10 March, p. 65.

'The questions that hang over our boardrooms' 2018, *Australian Financial Review*, 18 May, p. 26.

'The tech giant everyone is watching' 2018, *The Economist*, 30 June, p. 9.

Banta, K & Garrow, SD 2017, 'How CEOs can work with an active board', *Harvard Business Review*, 8 August, pp. 74–79.

Boivie, S, Bednar, M & Andrus, J 2016, 'Boards aren't the right way to monitor companies', *Harvard Business Review*, 10 May. https://hbr.org/2016/05/boards-arent-the-right-way-to-monitor-companies.

Casal, C & Caspar, C 2014, 'Building a forward looking board', *McKinsey Quarterly*, February. www.mckinsey.com/business-functions/strategy-and-corporate-finance/our-insights/building-a-forward-looking-board.

Christensen, CM 1997, *The innovators dilemma: when new technologies cause great firms to fail*, Harvard Business Review Press, Boston, MA.

Creighton, A 2017, 'Peter Costello's blast at the banks: bring in some competition', *The Australian*, 19 August, p. 26.

Evans, S, Durkin, P, Thompson, B & LaFrenz, C 2018, 'Too many lawyers, accountants 'surfing' boards', *Australian Financial Review*, 18 May, p. 15.

Hamel, G & Prahalad, CK 1996, *Competing for the future*, Harvard Business Press, Boston, MA.

Hill, LA & Davis, G 2017, 'The board's new innovation imperative', *Harvard Business Review*, November–December, pp. 103–109.

Mankins, M & Steele, R, 'Turning great strategy into great performance', *Harvard Business Review*, July 2005.

Sadan, S 2018, 'Carillion's collapse exposes deep corporate governance failings', *Financial Times*, 14 February, p. 18.

Stigter, M & Cooper, G 2018, *Boards that dare—how to future proof today's corporate boards*, Bloomsbury Business, London.

Thuraisingham, SM 2018, 'Exploring the social factors that influence the decision making behaviours of non-executive directors in Australian public companies', PhD thesis, RMIT University, Melbourne.

Yoffie, DB & Kwak, M 2001, 'How to compete like a judo strategist', *Working Knowledge*, 16 July. https://hbswk.hbs.edu/item/how-to-compete-like-a-judo-strategist.

7   The BoardQ approach to board effectiveness, development and renewal

This chapter in summary

This chapter describes BoardQ's proprietary and holistic approach to undertaking a board effectiveness review, taking into account the research and the challenges explored in preceding chapters. BoardQ is a board advisory practice founded by the author. The intellectual property (IP) outlined in this chapter is a drawn from the combination of her extensive board and top team effectiveness experience and more recently, her doctoral-level research.

In the UK, the Corporate Governance Code requires FTSE 350 companies to undertake an external evaluation of their board's effectiveness every three years. A similar guideline exists in Australia that requires boards to subject themselves to an external review at least once every three years. Some boards are now engaged in undertaking reviews more frequently than the three-year stipulation. However, these reviews are rarely done well and often treated as 'tick the box' exercises from which little or no real value is derived in strengthening the board's effectiveness and accountability. There are several limitations that the proposed approach addresses. These include:

- the tendency for reviews to not start from what 'good' looks like. Ensuring a clear collective aspiration of a 'fit for future' board acts as an anchor for the review and builds collective ownership for the review journey
- failure to develop a shared view of the role and work of the board as a critical foundation for attitudes to the exercise of director accountabilities (i.e., the failure to properly test the extent of convergence about the board's role as stewards)
- the tendency to show a clear bias for evaluating process (hard governance aspects), and de-emphasising the quality of interpersonal relationships and board life more generally (soft governance aspects)
- failure at the end of a review to have a skilfully facilitated discussion on what the board resolves to change in ways of working.

The chapter proposes a comprehensive approach to address some of these limitations in strengthening effectiveness and accountability.

The purpose of undertaking a board effectiveness review is to develop a high-performing board on two dimensions: first, a board that provides the stewardship the company needs to reach its full potential; second, a board that operates as a strategic decision-making group, embodying accepted principles of good governance. As noted, the very existence of a board as an institution is rooted in the wise belief that the effective oversight of an organisation exceeds the capabilities of any one individual and that collective knowledge and deliberation are better suited to this task; this then assumes that how directors work with each other matters greatly.

The intended outcome of a review is to provide the chair with a road map of specific actions to take to enable the board to achieve its full potential in both its advisory and oversight accountabilities and to ensure that the collective wisdom of the board is greater than the sum of its parts. The road map should also provide advice on aspects of board composition and mix that will equip the board in the face of rapidly evolving economic, commercial, geopolitical, sector and technological changes.

BoardQ's staged approach to achieve board effectiveness, development and renewal, ensures that the work is board owned and uniquely tailored to the purpose, mission and strategy of the organisation. The approach is bespoke in that the stages can be implemented in full or in part to suit the specific life cycle related needs of the board. The approach is broadly described as follows.

Stage 1: discovery phase

Review work is not context free. Therefore, the objective of this short and concise phase is to better understand key contextual issues. It will involve a conversation with the chair, key committee chairs and, where possible, NEDs with a range of different board tenures. Of importance will be the discovery of any previous reviews that may have been undertaken, including a discussion of the value they added and challenges, if any, associated with implementing the findings or following-up actions.

As many variations as there are with organisations, there are with boards. Some organisations are mature and well established and have a structured approach to management, leadership and governance. Others may be less mature in their governance practices; they may be newly formed companies or start-ups and have a way to go with maturing. Some organisations may, according to the nature of the sector they are in, have a 15-year strategic horizon while others have a 15-month strategic horizon. Similarly, some boards may be well established in terms of membership with little or no recent change in membership while others may have been recently put together because of changes in equity or ownership (such as M&A, delisting or corporate or sector turmoil). How a board functions can reflect all of these board membership complexities.

Another critical aspect of this discovery phase is to determine how the board perceives its role. This study uses the 3 Es—empower, enable, ensure—to assess the strength of role sentiment on the board, as this ultimately influences the way in which accountabilities are actually exercised.

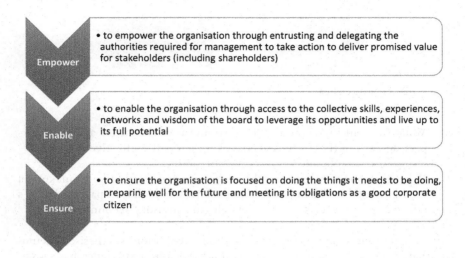

Figure 7.1 The 3 E board role framework.

A shared view of the role and work of the board is a good place to start this review (Figure 7.1).

Any divergence in view of the role and work of the board is best surfaced at this discovery stage, as it determines the shape and, importantly, the success of the remaining stages.

Stage 2: co-creating the board aspiration and building ownership for change

Effective boards look forward rather than backwards and have a clear view of what good looks like. The core objective of the second stage is to facilitate a director-driven determination of board aspiration (i.e., deciding the board you aspire to be, given the company's strategic ambition and goals). This critical step ensures that the aspirational gap (between where the board believes it is operating today and where it feels it needs to be operating into the future) is co-created collectively by the board. This collectively identified gap then acts as an important grounding conversation in preparation for Stage 3 (Figure 7.2).

When a board develops collective clarity and a shared understanding of areas for improvement and why such improvement matters, it develops collective ownership for the required change. This ensures that it is able to move forward in lock step, focus its improvement efforts and consider solutions to strengthen board effectiveness.

To affect this, the BoardQ principal will meet with every board member in a face-to-face session for approximately an hour each. During this time, two questions are posed about the workings of the board as a collective entity:

Figure 7.2 Aspirational gap.

- What (in your view) are the three strengths of this board and what impact do each of these strengths have on the board's effectiveness in exercising its oversight and advisory accountabilities?
- What (in your view) are the three changes you would like to make as a board and, if those changes were made, how would they impact the board's effectiveness in exercising its oversight and advisory accountabilities?

Director responses are collated and, without attribution, synthesised themes are shared in a presentation to the board (as a group). Experience has shown that the quality of this BoardQ facilitated conversation generates a shared view of the gap between where the board is now and where it aspires to be. This stage also builds collective ownership for the outcomes of Stages 3 and 4.

Stage 3: strengthening board effectiveness

This stage is intended to get a more in-depth view of current effectiveness as experienced by individual board members. Board processes are only as effective as the quality of relationships between directors (Figure 7.3).

We conduct this in two sequential steps:

A   a 'process'-focused online board effectiveness tool, emphasising the processes that are key to effectiveness
B   a 'relationship'-focused face-to-face peer feedback process using four broad developmental (relational) themes to reflect the quality of board life.

This two-step process results in a concrete and detailed action plan to strengthen effectiveness. Depending on the level of trust enjoyed between board members and the maturity of the board, these two steps may be timed in quick succession or disaggregated and phased over a period of time. Steps A and B are described in the following.

Step A: process effectiveness: composition, structure and workings (using an online tool)

Directors are asked, via an online diagnostic, to rate key processes and how well they are working. This online diagnostic takes approximately 15–20

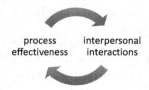

Figure 7.3 Relationship between effectiveness and interpersonal interactions.

minutes to complete. Key processes may include the level of role clarity evidenced in board charters, constitutions and/or mandates; the degree to which there are clearly defined meeting protocols; and the robustness of the processes associated with assessing the CEO's contribution, including how collaboratively these are developed, how coherently they are defined and the extent to which communication is transparent to all.

Step A generates a picture of what the board sees as the gaps in current process effectiveness and desired process effectiveness. There are three items relating to process effectiveness:

Composition

- nomination process—director evaluation, selection and on-boarding processes
- the process for achieving a diverse board mix (all forms of diversity, including diversity in life experience)
- capacity—how well the board is resourced to meet its committed charter
- board terms and the process by which these are managed for continuity as well as renewal.

Structure

- duties and responsibilities—clarity of charters, constitutions and mandates
- committees—clarity in purpose, scope and reporting
- annual calendar of key events (capturing all the key responsibilities the board has to enact in a given year)
- meeting protocols (including accurate compilation of meeting decisions, closed sessions, pre-meeting interactions and offline discussion protocols).

Workings

- use of time/agenda management
- attendance and effort norms
- quality of board papers and information flow for the required oversight (including the systematic and proactive reporting and management of predictable risks)

- use of advisors—process by which external input is accessed and leveraged including managing potential conflicts of interest
- decision-making protocols
- involvement in shaping strategy, including off-site structure
- board meeting effectiveness (including use of closed/'in-camera' sessions, now increasingly being used by boards as part of a continuous ongoing improvement strategy)
- committee and main board hand offs and interactions
- performance evaluation processes—board as a whole, committees and CEO
- CEO succession and appointment processes.

A report containing a summary of these themes is generated (aggregated responses with no attribution) and combined with outputs from Step B.

Step B: peer feedback on quality of board life (face to face meetings)

This step is a peer feedback process designed to generate a deeper understanding of board life and is undertaken by the BoardQ principal one on one and face to face. It is underpinned by four clusters that reflect the critical aspects of board life. These are:

- knowledge of key areas
- understanding of role
- quality of input
- contributions to interactions.

The BoardQ principal will organise face-to-face interviews with each director during which these four relationship themes are explored. Given the critical impact that the chair–CEO dynamic can have on board's overall effectiveness in exercising its accountabilities, a similar face-to-face interview will be held with the CEO.

While some directors may voice reservations about commenting on each other's effectiveness, it needs to be emphasised that these four items are focussed on continuous improvement in the processes of governance. In other words, the focus is on when contributions are effective and how contributions may be improved, rather than eliciting critiques of individuals as such. For example:

- *Knowledge of key areas* includes knowledge and understanding in areas such as strategy, finance, risk, sector, commercials and so on.
- *Understanding of role* includes themes such as relationships with management and knowledge of the role (e.g., the governing/managing of boundaries and the quality of preparation for meetings).
- *Quality of input* includes the extent to which input provided in board discussions and debates reflect the attributes of insight, curiosity, logic, persuasion, courage and humility.

- *Contributions to interactions* includes themes relating to how constructive contributions are to discussion and debate, the extent to which directors engage in quality listening and how the contribution of others is proactively engaged with.

At the end of this stage, and once individual debrief reports have been compiled, each director will have a confidential one on one debrief and coaching session with the BoardQ principal, who is a trained feedback coach, to explore the identified development priorities.

These director-level debriefs will be followed by a BoardQ facilitated conversation with the board as a group, focussing on developing an agreed action plan for strengthening effectiveness. In addition to the action plan to improve effectiveness, this step has often resulted in a board development and education plan that includes governance refreshers and learning sessions targeting specific areas of identified need.

Stage 4: determining a 'fit for future' board composition and succession and renewal plan

Stage 4 is conducted in two sequential steps designed to ensure that board composition is best positioned to provide the required stewardship into the future. The first step is a review of board composition, and the second is a renewal plan that builds on that review. The sponsor of work on this stage is typically the board chair and/or chair of the nominations committee.

This stage is intended to be forward looking and to help boards contemplate the 'fit for future' composition they will need. That is to say, while the composition of a board provides strategic continuity, at the same time planned renewal may also be required to navigate new emerging realities. Although there is no regulatory stipulation around tenure, there is an expectation in corporate governance circles that boards can self-regulate well and that directors will self-select out if they feel they are no longer contributing at the level they feel they should. Additionally, there is an expectation on chairs that they are able to manage the process of renewal by having open and respectful conversations with directors about the contribution they are making and improvements that can be made.

Strategic persistence is a problem that many boards contend with. This is because they have not developed a way of looking into the future and predicting the required skills and experience. In particular, identifying those that may be critical now but unlikely to be critical for the future, and, conversely, those that may not have been critical previously but are emerging as critical for the future.

While there is an expectation that self-selection will deliver the best composition, this is not possible without some form of transparent process, which this final stage focusses on. The output of this stage is a succession and renewal plan designed to strengthen board composition through the best mix of skills and experience. It takes into account the company's strategy as well as emerging economic, political and social realities that may affect the business environment and competitive landscape. It is one thing for a board's composition to fit with what the company is doing now but another to fit with where the company may be heading in five or more years' time.

BoardQ's approach is distinctive. Most boards attempt to achieve a fit for future composition through developing a skill review aided by a skills matrix. We argue that the approach as it is currently applied is too broad and generic to be useful. A better approach is to use the concept of board capital (as described in Chapter 2) as representing the directors' potential to contribute in a wider sense. The concept extends beyond a simple consideration of business or functional experience, because these are an imprecise proxy for the contribution or value directors bring to a board. Yet, as has been shown in Part 1, in particular Chapters 2 and 3, that the possession of board capital itself, does not imply its use nor does it guarantee an influential and strategically active board. Instead, board capital is mobilised through a set of social skills (described in Chapter 4) specifically relevant to how influence is actually exercised in small groups of peers. These are distinct from the non-specific communication skills and interpersonal skills commonly used in developing board skill matrices today.

By whatever means, once a board has identified gaps in what it may need in the near or longer term to strengthen its composition, it is important to work closely with the chair to develop a plan to bring the required board capital to the board. Boards may respond to the identified needs and gaps in a variety of ways:

- future appointment of directors
- development of existing directors
- extending committee membership to include experts
- retaining or engaging of independent advisors with the requisite expertise or ad hoc consulting as and when required
- creation of an advisory board.

The board chair is provided with a report with recommendations to assist them to determine how best to address the identified gaps. BoardQ provides advice to the chair on where and how the required board capital may be acquired or accessed, challenging the narrow gene pools from which directors are sometimes selected.

The outputs of a well-managed succession and renewal plan may require an 18–24 month (or more) time frame to implement. Advice is offered to the board chair (typically the key sponsor of this phase) on the appropriate phasing and pace to ensure a smooth transition.

In conclusion

If reviews are designed to be conducted once every three years, they need to be well thought through and planned. The tendency to use online surveys by external parties will not provide the quality insight required to strengthen the board's effectiveness. Aspects of the BoardQ approach can be used as a pulse check in between the three-year cycles, making this methodology a flexible and adaptive one.

8 What we expect from boards as investors

This chapter in summary

This chapter has two parts. The first part considers the full spectrum of investor engagement and shareholder ideology, contrasting the value actively engaged investors can bring at one end and noisy hostile investors at the other, and suggests the factors that have given rise to greater levels of shareholder activism.

The chapter also examines the importance of organisational purpose, society's growing expectations of what companies should stand for, how they should be evaluated and the challenge this can create for boards.

The second part of this chapter is a letter from a major investor to the board; it discusses the desire for greater accountability from boards and the challenges facing investors wishing to bring about change in a thoughtful and planned way. Emphasis is placed on strategies that boards can consider in fostering more productive relationships with investors: clear-eyed advice to boards on how they should engage with investors; how best to explain the company plans to protect and grow their investment; how to build greater alignment around objectives and ensure a meeting of minds on a range of governance issues.

Shareholder engagement is a way that investors seek to influence a company's behaviour by exercising their rights as partial owners. The scale of activism has most notably grown since the global financial crisis (GFC). An increasing number of activists are moving away from the more conventional 'behind closed doors' pressure on boards reflecting a greater propensity to go public and communicate directly with other shareholders, often via media channels, which adds pressure to the target company and its board. Of course, activism does not come in one size or form. There are different types of activists and different activist agendas. Some are motivated by the economic performance of the company while others are motivated by wider societal interests, such as climate change, broader environmental concerns and gender diversity. Further, activism is not restricted to equity investors. Fixed income investors are starting to make ESG (environmental, social and governance) issues part of their investment criteria, acknowledging that poor governance can lead to increased credit risk (Mooney 2018), something that bank lenders have long understood. Today investors expect to stay engaged by moving closer to their boards and building a better, more balanced, understanding of short-and long-term results. This is something that John Kay advocated in his 2012 UK government sponsored report into equity markets and long-term decision-making (Kay 2012).

In many ways, the term 'activist' is an unfortunate one, as it implies hostility and unwelcome interference. Activists are sometimes sensationally portrayed especially in media as the 'villains' of capitalism. It is a pejorative and unhelpful term that does not accurately describe reality. For example, some would say that Warren Buffet, who runs Berkshire Hathaway, is an activist when it comes to how companies he has invested in allocate their capital. Few would describe Warren Buffet as a villain. In this chapter, we use the less emotive term 'engaged investors' acknowledging that there is a wide variation in how they choose to engage. At times we use the term activist as it is commonly understood to refer to frustrated investors who often have good reason to challenge the boards of the companies they invest in because they don't feel heard.

The growth of activism and rise of activists

In the context of boards, activism as we know it emerged in the 1980s when companies such as RJR Nabisco, AIG and Heinz were subject to attention from the predecessors of DE Shaw & Co., Elliot Management, Train Partners, ValueAct and Jaan Partners. In Australia in the 1980s, activism was also apparent through high-profile investors such as Sir Ron Brierley. At that time, as is often the case today, the most common requests were for asset disposals, sale of the entire company, management restructure, board seats and capital restructure. Critics of activists argue that they reinforce short-termism and pay excessive attention to financial metrics rather than long-term wealth creation strategies. In extreme cases, some activist groups, or special interest groups, can bully organisations into actions that can potentially destroy long-term value. While this is true of some activists, such as some notable cases of hedge funds, it is not true of all activists. Many activist investors operate as patient, private equity investors might, fully grasping the complexities the company faces. Therefore, it is inaccurate to think of activists as a homogenous group.

Typically, engaged, active investors follow a three-step process. First, as in the case of Nestle, activists make a public announcement of their stake and the strategies that they want the target company to undertake. In most cases, the target firm will dismiss this initial request. Second, the activist becomes more confrontational, embarking on a bigger media campaign, and working through proxy companies in order to seek to win support from other investors and to pressure the target into acknowledging their issues. This stage often results in meetings between the chair and the lead activist. Third, activists look to the Annual General Meeting (AGM) and launch a 'proxy fight' in which other investors can lend their support.

Traditionally, high-profile shareholder activism has been associated with a powerful shareholder buying a 1–5 per cent stake in a company and seeking changes in board and/or management composition, normally because of periods of relative underperformance. For example, Edward Bramson's Sherborne fund acquired a 5.4 per cent stake in Barclays in 2018 with the aim of forcing a rethink on the bank's investment banking business; a similar situation occurred when New York–based Elliot Management campaigned to drive board changes at BHP in 2017. At Barclays, Bramson publicly laid out his agenda, which included a review of capital allocation, quality of earning, cost structure and the appointment of a new chair ('Activist investor' 2018). Activists often target businesses that are underperforming when measured against their industry peers. Sometimes, because of the complicated, conglomerate nature of the company's activities, activists argue that conglomerates underperform against specialists (e.g., German steel-to-submarines manufacturer Thyssen Krupp; Dutch paint maker, Akzo Nobel; and Swiss conglomerate ABB). Activists have also targeted underperforming global icons such as GE, Nestle, DowDuPont and Procter & Gamble. The truth is that no public company is immune from the gaze of an activist. These are noisy investors who can sometimes take to public media channels to highlight the issues and the solutions they seek to prosecute. They can occasionally demand a board seat, as was the case at GE. They can also cause the board to reflect on current strategies and consider options that were not part of earlier thinking. As one senior director told the *Financial Times*: 'When you have an activist shareholder, you have to think like an activist. You have to be bold' (Jenkins, Arnold & Binham 2018). The motives behind activism across Anglo-American markets are summarised in Figure 8.1 the 'other' category sweeping up in it performance including asset stewardship, balance sheet and governance issues.

Not all shareholder activism is hostile

Conventional asset managers, such as pension funds, have become increasingly 'active' after decades of being criticised for being 'absentee owners'. This does not mean that they behave in the same manner as noisy activists. Rather, these low-key activists tend to operate out of the public domain and through meetings with management and the board, sometimes using the services of proxy advisors. They tend to prioritise their efforts, focussing on executive remuneration, board renewal, underperforming divisions and ESG responsibilities. Their preference is to nudge change rather than follow the more publicly aggressive tactics of noisy activists, who often seek public spats to bring attention to their actions, thereby adding to the pressure on a target board. The more traditional institutional investors can, if they feel that their nudge tactics are not working, enter the public domain, and they are increasingly doing this. The most common method of expressing their displeasure is to register their voting preferences at the AGM. BT, WPP, John Menzies and Direct Line are examples of UK companies that had their proposed executive arrangements voted down by shareholders ('John Menzies' 2018). Following

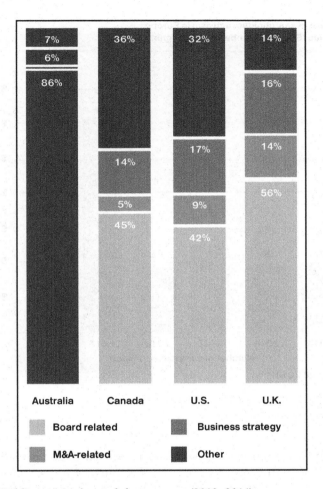

Figure 8.1 Public activist demands by category (2013–2016).
Source: Activist Insight Data.

a prolonged period of poor share price performance at BT, institutional investors called for the company to be broken up ('BT investors' 2018).

Activism once largely confined to domestic investors has also become increasingly global, with a significant increase in activity in Europe, as illustrated in Figure 8.2.

Following the GFC, the Australian government took steps to address the growing concerns about high levels of executive pay often not linked to performance. This centred in particular around termination payments (for unsuccessful CEOs who were being moved on before their contracts finished) amid market concerns about unmet expectations of return on equity. There

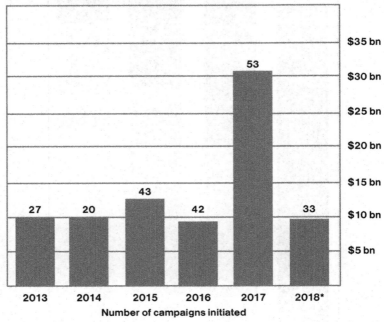

The rise of shareholders activism in Europe
By value ($bn) and number of campaigns

*First half 2018

Figure 8.2 Rise of shareholder activism in Europe.
Source: Lazard, Activist Insight FactSet: FT.

was also growing expectation of greater regulation of companies to reduce the risks of investing. In July 2011 the *Two Strikes Rule* was introduced in Australia following extensive consultation. Over 170 submissions from peak shareholder associations, companies, proxy advisors, governance consulting firms, remuneration advisors, legal firms, unions and academics were considered in order to give shareholders more influence in relation to executive remuneration. A company receives its 'first strike' if 25 per cent or more of the eligible votes cast are against a resolution to adopt the company's remuneration report. The company will then have to respond in its next remuneration report with what action it has taken and if no action is taken, stating the reasons for this. A company will receive its second strike if a resolution to adopt the remuneration report for the following year receives another 'no' vote of 25 per cent or more of the votes cast. If this occurs, a resolution that a special spill meeting be held must be proposed at the AGM where the second strike is received. Companies that receive a first strike will no doubt also wish to address shareholder concerns in explanatory material provided to shareholders with, or in advance of, the notice of the next AGM. A major concern with the two strikes rule is that because a 'no' vote is triggered by 25 per cent of the votes actually cast, a small percentage of disgruntled shareholders who choose to vote can determine the result. It is imperative therefore to proactively engage with all major shareholders well before such conflicts arise. The UK is not immune to shareholder revolts on pay. In the 2018 AGM season in the UK there were an unprecedented number of shareholder rebellions relating to executive pay. Any dissent in excess of 20 per cent in the UK is regarded as a significant shareholder protest and must be attended to. UK's Financial Reporting Council is reviewing executive bonus structures to promote long-term decision-making.

Despite the clear trend in the growth of activism globally as shown in Figure 8.3, few boards like being told what to do and can dig into entrenched positions, viewing the activists with disdain even when such a posture sets the relationship up for clashes in viewpoints. Boards that see activists as an issue that needs to be managed are potentially falling into a dangerous trap. Astute boards do not view activists with disdain. Instead they view them as signalling the need for greater more proactive shareholder engagement. They carefully read the signals that activists send. Matters such as executive remuneration are often the 'canary in the coal mine'. Frequently, the underlying message is a loss of confidence in the strategy that management is pursuing and, sometimes, by association, the board. Further, boards should recognise that there is no necessary correlation between the ownership stake held by an activist and outcomes. A 1 per cent stake can yield as much influence as a 5 per cent stake if other investors follow the lead of the activist.

While shareholders can be viewed as disciplinarians who right the wrongs of failing directors, a small subset of activists, especially hedge funds, can be opportunists looking for quick trading returns. Activism can also lead to unproductive conflicts between equity and debt holders, as BHP Billiton argued in response to a campaign by Elliot Management for asset disposals

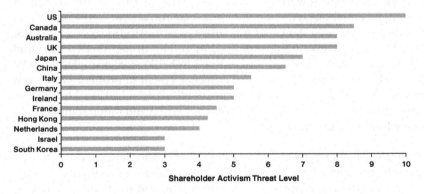

Figure 8.3 Ranking of shareholder activism threat level.
Source: FTI Consulting.

and a capital restructure including the payment of a special dividend. Activists in pursuit of quick profits are guilty of advocating and often successfully forcing through particular actions that result in destructive short-termism. In one recent case, activists believed that their presence on the share register, accompanied by a statement of intent, could spark a rise in the share price. Debt investors argued that such a move would increase the riskiness of the then US$24 billion of bonds the company had outstanding. An executive within the UK-based institutional investor, Standard Life, commented: 'We wouldn't be overly enthused with ongoing activist shareholder agitation, as these types of actions tend to benefit only one set of stakeholders—equity holders' ('BHP told' 2017).

Technology companies require three or four years to move a product, a fact that some short term-oriented hedge funds ignore. The threat of activism can be a disincentive for boards to take risks, which, given the imperative for companies to deal with disruption and demonstrate greater strategic courage (as discussed in Chapter 6), can be highly problematic.

In summary, rather than activists being forced to seek wide-scale board and management change as a last resort, activism should be viewed as a positive influence and a force for change. However, for activism to be a positive influence boards must be prepared to engage with shareholders differently, a theme revisited later in this chapter.

The rise of societal disquiet and the social licence

In addition to the rise of shareholder activism described in 'The growth of activism and rise of activists', a growing societal disquiet with how businesses operate gained momentum following the GFC. The dangers of having an overly weighted bias towards sustained shareholder value outcomes were starkly illustrated by events in the global banking industry during and after the GFC and underscored the need for a broader stakeholder view. Together with weak corporate governance, the corrupting nature in the design of short-term incentives heavily linked to financial outcomes was the major reason for the cultures that damaged numerous great institutions, such as RBS, HBOS, Deutsche Bank, Citigroup and, in recent times, Wells Fargo and the CBA. These scandals were not confined to banks; for example, the VW emissions cheating scandal, the material overstatement of profits at Tesco and the bribery and corruptions claims against Rolls-Royce had, at their source, a culture that valued and rewarded profits over ethics and moral standards. As Professor John Kay reminded us:

> People's behavior typically meets the expectations generated by the environment in which they operate. Incentives aren't an alternative to culture; incentives, appropriate or inappropriate, and trust and confidence, or its absence, are the product of the culture of financial organisations.
>
> (Kay 2012)

Kay highlighted how a single-minded focus on shareholder value can lead to decisions that emphasise financial considerations (and often, by association, short-termism) over long-term value creation. He drew attention to the differences between how ICI described its purpose in 1987 and 1994 (Kay 2012). Compare the following statements:

[1987] ICI aims to be the world's leading chemical company, serving customers internationally through innovative and responsible application of chemistry and related science. Through achievement of our aim, we will enhance the wealth and well-being of our shareholders, our employees, our customers and the communities which we serve and in which we operate.

[1994] Our objective is to maximise value for our shareholders by focusing on businesses where we have market leadership, a technological edge and a world competitive cost base.

It was not difficult to see how this shift in focus sowed the seeds of its slide into irrelevance. In 2007, ICI was acquired by Dutch company AkzoNobel and thus no longer exists as an independent company.

Accompanied by a robust debate over the last five years or so on the notion of social licence (a theme that first came to prominence almost 50 years ago), this disquiet has created an environment for greater political and regulatory intervention. It has been witnessed in the banking industry in the US, UK and Australia post-GFC and similar trends are evident in the energy markets.

Questions about social licence are, at their core, questions about the purpose of a company—the enduring statement of *why* a business exists. A clear statement of purpose should anchor all strategic decisions. In the 1990s, Harvard's Christopher Bartlett and the London Business School's Sumantra Ghoshal argued that companies needed to move away from an emphasis on strategy, structure and systems and empower their people through the development of an engaging corporate purpose. A single shared goal that encapsulates why a company exists gives direction and meaning to everything it does. Investors who recognise the impact stakeholder groups can have on the company's potential want purpose to be properly defined. A focus on shareholder value has the benefit of specificity, but it is an incomplete statement of legitimacy, let alone success. Yet, most executives and directors with business school or professional training will look to economic logic as the key driver of company performance. Given this paradigm, they come to look at purpose in the same way that many looked at CSR—often as a program of work rather than a way of leading. However, an authentic higher-order purpose can ignite latent enthusiasm and engagement within a company, as Bartlett and Ghoshal described.

The growing importance of purpose was succinctly captured by Black-Rock's CEO, Larry Fink, in his 2018 letter to the CEOs of the S&P 500:

Without a sense of purpose, no company, either public or private, can achieve its full potential. It will ultimately lose the licence to operate from key stakeholder. It will succumb to short-term pressures to distribute earnings, and, in the process, sacrifice investment in employee development, innovation, and capital expenditure that are necessary for long-term growth.

(George 2018)

The concept of shared value, popularised by Harvard's Michael Porter and Mark Kramer argued that the capitalist system is being questioned, largely because companies are trapped in a narrow sense of shareholder value as the primary goal. A shared value approach brings business and society together to generate economic value for society by addressing its challenges, reconnecting business success with social progress through a well-defined corporate purpose (Porter & Kramer 2011).

The challenge for well-intentioned companies such as those shown in *Table 8.1* is how to translate these ambitious purpose statements into business practices and communicate them widely as key decision-making tools. In this regard, Johnson & Johnson's famous credo, crafted in 1943 by its founder Robert Wood Johnson, a chair and member of the founding family, talks about stockholders making a fair return. The Johnson & Johnson credo still stands today; it persists as a decision-making tool when the company is faced with difficult choices. This notion of fairness and shared value is increasingly moving the conversation beyond ethics and legality into the realm of fairness for all stakeholders. John Lewis Partnership, a unique employee-owned retailer—one of the largest in the UK—is led by a constitution drafted in 1929 that has seven clear and enduring principles. It regularly outperforms its competitors on a broad set of measures and has, as its central purpose, 'the happiness of its partners through their worthwhile and satisfying employment in a successful business'. Similarly, the CEO of Danone, a large French food company, argued that the 'purpose of this company is not to create shareholder value, but instead to get healthy food to as many mouths as possible,

Table 8.1 Examples of companies that have a stated purpose beyond shareholder value

A purpose beyond shareholder value
ING: empowering people to stay a step ahead in life and in business
Kellogg: nourishing families so they can flourish and thrive
IAG: helping people manage risk and recover from the hardship of unexpected loss
Amazon: to be the Earth's most customer-centric company—a place where customers can find and discover anything they want to buy online at the lowest possible prices
Starbucks: to inspire and nurture the human spirit, one person, one cup and one neighbourhood at a time

benefiting everyone from suppliers to consumers to owners' ('Danone re-thinks' 2018). As reported in the Financial Times (20th September 2018) Danone has also committed to achieving B-Corp certification for its business as a whole and argues that taking measures to improve its Environmental, Social and Governance (ESG) performance will help it become more genuinely sustainable in the long term. If correct, this should attract lower long-term risk rating, thus cutting the cost of capital. That is to say that ESG performance is increasingly being linked to lowering long-term risk ranking thus cutting the cost of capital. Danone appears to be the first big multinational to tie borrowing to ESG performance. Led by these role models, boards today must think of governance as embracing a wider range of issues than in the past, and while preservation of shareholder wealth remains an important board objective, it cannot be at all costs, let alone exclusively. The next step for boards is to convince investors that such measures ensure that the capital employed is working harder and thus should be rewarded.

To summarise, directors face numerous competing and often conflicting challenges: addressing the concerns of activist investors, meeting their responsibilities to the company as defined by law, meeting the demands and high expectations placed on them by stakeholders and delivering on ESG commitments (such as those that are part of the UN's 2030 Sustainable Development Goals). At the same time, societal disquiet is rising and trust in business (and in capitalism more broadly) is declining.

Boards and investor engagement

An important theme of activist investors is a desire to get closer to the board, not just the chair and chair of the remuneration committee. With so many of the challenges facing companies today, it is only reasonable that investors are keen to have a better handle on the quality of each director. They recognise that all directors in aggregate represent an effective board. Professor David Beatty, corporate governance expert and experienced director has argued that investor relations is becoming a board, rather than management role.

Whilst current practice has chairs spending around 10 per cent of their time with investors, and much of that in the days leading up to the AGM, there is a growing demand that this changes in two ways: first, the chairman should be spending considerably more time with investors and that should be spread throughout the year; and second, *all* directors should meet with investors on an ongoing basis, thereby giving investors a greater feel for the quality of the board. BlackRock's CEO, Larry Fink, in his annual letter to CEOs, summed up the need for change:

> The time has come for a new model of shareholder engagement, one that strengthens and deepens communication between shareholders and the companies that they own. Engagement needs to be a year-round conversation about improving long-term value.

Larry Fink, echoing a growing sentiment, calls for a rethink on the part of boards to engagement with shareholders, which contrasts with the traditional paradigm followed by the majority of boards in Anglo-Saxon markets. There is now a case for a pause for reflection and a question as to whether this traditional paradigm is fit for purpose today.

Investors need convincing that all board members understand how the market perceives their company and to better understand what each director (especially committee chairs) brings to the board. In turn, directors get a better appreciation of how investors think and what they want to see.

As discussed in this chapter, the traditional mindset reflects a pejorative view to shareholder engagement and a sense that 'activism' is damaging to capitalism. A fresh view needs to be taken to shareholder engagement to ensure it is neither occupying the passive realm at one end or the hostile realm at the other end. Engaging with shareholders to co-create holistic change is key.

Letter to the board

Dear Directors,

Industries are facing unprecedented change and no sector appears immune. Revolutionary changes in technology have lowered barriers to competition and allowed a continuous stream of globally based new product innovation. The internet, the digital world, rapid globalisation, artificial intelligence and the rise of new technology-savvy competitors from markets like China have the potential to affect business models and economies in the same way that electricity and transportation (railways, cars and aeroplanes) did in centuries past. As business and industry models are changing, so too is the investor community, but for very different reasons.

Today, as investors, we are becoming more active in demanding higher returns (sometimes, it must be said, with a short-term horizon); however, we are also increasingly concerned about a wider range of issues such as corporate culture, executive remuneration, reputation, social and environmental concerns, and climate change and more generally society's growing mistrust of business and capitalism and corporate governance. We see all these issues as an integral part of enterprise risk and tied in a fundamental way to a company's *social licence* to operate. Some directors and boards might not be fully convinced that these are all legitimate concerns, but they can no longer be ignored and need to be understood.

The reality is that the winds of change have never been louder or stronger and now more than ever there is a need to re-evaluate the way in which companies, and their boards, engage with the investors like us —the owners of the company.

Increasingly, as investors, we have worried about the threat to the *social licence* that businesses have and how societal mistrust towards business may encourage greater government and regulatory scrutiny, potentially leading to sometimes misplaced intervention. In Australia, the 2018 Royal Commission into the banking industry highlighted deep cultural problems that violated any measure of ethical behaviour and, in some cases, extended to breaking the law. It is no wonder that double digit declines in trust in banks have been reflected in the Edelman Trust barometer for 2018.

Indeed, the examination into corporate governance at Australia's largest bank, the CBA, which is ranked the 13th largest bank in the world by market capitalisation (2018 Statista world rankings), highlighted issues that have parallels in other institutions in the UK, US and Europe. The Australian Prudential Regulatory Authority (APRA) found that 'there was a complacent culture, dismissive of regulators, an ineffective board that lacked zeal and failed to provide oversight, a lack of accountability and ownership of key risks by senior executives, a remuneration framework that had no bite' (White 2018, p. 23). This regulatory review of CBA found:

- a widespread sense of complacency throughout the bank, starting at the top
- that the bank was reactive in dealing with risk
- that a slow, legalistic, reactive and, at times, dismissive culture characterised many of CBA's dealings with regulators
- that the bank was insular. It did not reflect on and learn from experience and mistakes, including at board and senior leadership levels
- a remuneration framework that had little sting for senior managers when poor risk or customer outcomes materialised (White 2018, p. 23).

These hard-hitting shortcomings are not unique to CBA or Australia. Parallels can be drawn with RBS, Barclays and Lloyds/HBOS in the UK and Wells Fargo in the US. In many cases, boards have attempted to distance themselves from cultural problems within companies by claiming 'no knowledge' of them; however, boards can no longer rely on this defence, as regulators have ruled that ignorance is no defence.

A number of recent cases demonstrating lapses of judgement by boards and their oversight of management painfully illustrate the disappointing level of attention, performance and conduct of many companies—far too many. This explains, at least in part, the current deficit of trust in business, particularly large business, and growing tendency for shareholder activism, sometimes aimed at individual directors. The rise of activism to some extent is addressing a governance failure of boards and, therefore, is both legitimate and welcome in a societal sense, even though many boards resist what they see as unwelcome intrusion.

The first thing to be clear on is that boards and individual directors have two core duties: a duty of loyalty and a duty of care. The duty of loyalty is that each director and the board must act in the best interests of the company—not just for today but for the long term. To fulfil your duty of care as directors you must exercise a high level of due diligence when making decisions. This means that directors must discover as much information as possible and consider all reasonable alternatives when reaching a decision that is in the best interests of the company. In exercising their duties, boards have traditionally assumed a posture of 'nose in, fingers out' (NIFO); this means that while the board keeps a close watch on how management is performing and seeks information to validate its performance, it 'keeps its fingers out', leaving the day-to-day operations to management. This balancing act requires considerable skill. We agree that the board must not undermine the authority of the CEO; however, it must also be actively engaged, particularly with regard to the strategic options open to the company. We believe in strategically active, not passive, boards.

As engaged investors, we have a legitimate role to play, including joining the board of a company in need of change. We believe we are well placed to ensure that boards show greater sensitivity to well-reported failures in corporate governance. We desire to forge a closer relationship with the board, not just the chair and the chair of the remuneration committee.

While current practice has chairs spending around 10 per cent of their time with investors, and much of that in the days leading up to the AGM, there is growing pressure to change this in two ways: first, we believe the chair should spend considerably more time with us as investors and that should be spread throughout the year; second, *all* directors should meet with investors on an ongoing basis, giving us a greater feel for the quality of the board as a whole. As an active and engaged investor we want a sense of the breadth, depth and rigour of the governance process within a company; from a succession point of view, they also want a better understanding of the depth of knowledge and expertise among board members.

As engaged investors, we believe that it is important that all board members understand how the market perceives their company and that each director be provided with an opportunity to explain what they bring to the board. In turn, directors get a better appreciation of what investors think and want to see. The time we believe has come for a new model of shareholder engagement, deeper more regular and constructive conversations about improving long-term value.

Many of the issues explored in this letter call for a rethink of the nature and quality of engagement we have with you.

Given the growing disquiet among investors in general about the role boards play in strategy we ask that you outline clearly to management the role that the board plays in the stewardship of shareholders' wealth, the societal purpose that underpins its legitimacy and the role that investors can play in board effectiveness and renewal. Our expectations are that the board be explicit about how it executes these responsibilities, while also being clear on some of the natural limitations that it faces. To meet changing expectations, we believe a fundamental re-examination of the role and structure of the board is likely to be necessary. In a world in which almost everything is changing, it is entirely appropriate to ask 'how should boards change in the future?' If this question is not seriously examined, then boards can become susceptible to the 'boiled frog syndrome'. This is not a sudden revelation; it has, like the proverbial train, been getting closer and closer overtime.

In summary, we seek your attention on the following:

- that director search and selection methodologies are made more robust to ensure that directors are appointed on merit and have deep and relevant commercial know how and knowledge of the industry that the company operates in (while not blind to the strengths of other industry models)
- that the board play an active role in all C-suite appointments, remembering that executives tend to gravitate towards hiring people who remind them of themselves—similar backgrounds and sometimes even similar schools, similar styles and so on. Boards that allow CEO's a free hand in appointing C-suite executives are abdicating responsibility.
- that the board leads work on creating a clear and compelling corporate purpose that unifies internal and external stakeholders, anchors organisational practices and is used by the board and top team as the filter through which key strategic decisions are run through
- that the board take the lead on strategy formulation, co-creating strategy with management not simply endorsing strategy management brings forward, engaging in its own independent stress testing of the strategy; ensuring that the strategic direction and investment decisions of the company are positioning the business for success tomorrow as well as today (and, in this context, have a clear view on the impact of digitalisation, emerging competitors on the business and its strategic future)
- that the board exercises more control over executive pay to hold key leaders accountable, ensuring that a tighter correlation exists between pay and performance, and reviewing bonus structures to promote long-term decision-making; removing sales incentives that are having the propensity of distorting behaviour; and allowing for variable rewards to be forfeited, further deterred or clawed back under certain circumstances
- that the board explore ways to build a deeper understanding of company culture beyond the periodic review of aggregated employee engagement surveys; that it has its fingers on the pulse of the company and has a clear understanding of the enablers and impediments of a healthy vibrant culture, including subcultures. In this regard, boards must ensure credible feedback loops are in place. This may include board exposure to the top 30–40 of the most talented executives over the course of the year in semi-structured dialogues which will allow the board to get a more intimate sense of how these executives are led and how they lead others
- that changes are made to board process to ensure that a cluttered and time-pressured board agenda (which crowds out time on the strategic futureproofing of the company) is avoided and that conversations about strategy are ongoing and not once a year event-based conversations
- that the company is proactively monitoring and measuring how trust is being earned, retained and strengthened in relation to its social licence;

that it sets and commits to ESG goals and ensures that these are actually translated into business practice

- That an externally run board effectiveness review is conducted once every two years. A board is only as effective as the working relationships directors have with one another. The more work the board does on itself the more effective a decision-making body it becomes

We look forward to continuing to actively engage with you and build on a dynamic, productive and trusting relationship.

In conclusion

This chapter has covered a number of commitments engaged, active investors expect from the board. It reflects the complexity and challenges of corporate governance in the contemporary era in which societal demands and expectations of businesses are changing in quite a dramatic way. Big companies often hold privileged positions in society and have to earn and grow the trust that position comes with. When well-known companies, using market power to maximise economic rents or optimise legitimate tax loopholes, are not paying what society sees as their fair share of taxes, they are in danger of jeopardising their social licence. This type of behaviour helps to explain why society's regard for, and trust in, business is at a concerning low, and why the risk of legislative and regulatory intervention in the affairs of business is high. Regaining lost societal trust is not easy, as trust arrives on the back of a tortoise and leaves on the back of a galloping horse. Management may at times be conflicted dealing with these complexities: boards should never be.

Today, the nature of shareholder activism is both growing in scale and changing in nature. Investors are genuinely interested not only in achieving at least a satisfactory return covering the risk-adjusted opportunity cost of their capital, but also in having a greater say in the scope of governance and how a company meets its ESG commitments and societal obligations. Social licence and purpose are not perfunctory themes; they are substantive and have the potential to result in significant change in the way that companies operate. In all of this, a constructive tension with engaged investors is welcome in particular in determining if the board is up to the task of navigating many of these complexities ahead. The quality of the board is an integral part of a company's 'human and social capital'; therefore, it is appropriate that there should be greater transparency in terms of the value each director brings to the company. Engaged investors want to better understand how each director and the board as a group will position the company for the future.

Today, investors and society rightly expect much more from boards in the strategic leadership they provide and so they should.

References

'Activist investor Bramson lays down marker on Barclays' 2018, *Financial Times*, 9 August, p. 1.

'BHP told that bending to shareholder activists pose risks for debt investors' 2017, *Sydney Morning Herald*, 19 October, p. 22.

'BT investors call on next boss to consider break-up of business' 2018, *Financial Times*, 21 August.

'Danone rethinks the idea of the company' 2018, *The Economist*, 9 August.

'John Menzies hit by shareholder revolt over executive pay' 2018, *Financial Times*, 23 August, p. 19.

Edelman Trust barometer 2018. http://cms.edelman.com/sites/default/files/2018-03/ Edelman_Trust_Barometer_Financial_Services_2018.pdf.

George, B 2018, 'Op-Ed: why BlackRock CEO Larry Fink is not a socialist', *Working Knowledge*, 12 March. https://hbswk.hbs.edu/item/op-ed-why-blackrock-ceo-larry-fink-is-not-a-socialist.

Jenkins, P, Arnold, M & Binham, C 2018, 'Activist pressure brings out blue sky M&A thinking at Barclays', *Financial Times*, 24 May, p. 22.

Kay, J 2012, *Kay review of UK equity markets and long-term decision making*, July. https:// assets.publishing.service.gov.uk/government/uploads/system/uploads/attachment_ data/file/253454/bis-12-917-kay-review-of-equity-markets-final-report.pdf.

Mooney, A 2018, 'Bond investors discover powers of persuasion on governance', *Financial Times*, 18 June, p. 27.

Porter, ME & Kramer, MR 2011, 'Creating shared value', *Harvard Business Review*, Jan/Feb, pp. 57–65.

White, A 2018, 'Complacent, reactive, insular', *The Australian*, 2 May, p. 23.

9   The future of governance and the 'fit for future' board

This chapter in summary

This chapter asks whether boards today are 'fit for the future'. Building on some of the themes from preceding chapters, it suggests how directors, boards and governance might prepare for a more unpredictable future and considers some of the more emergent and agile ways in which boards can govern.

The responsibility for steering and stewarding companies through what is an increasingly uncertain environment is in the hands of both investors and boards. This responsibility is not only about today's, next month's or next quarter's earnings, but also anticipating and preparing for opportunities and challenges further ahead. Regulation is not the only issue causing boards to change. The demands on boards today are profound. These reflect the combined effects of complex regulatory environments, geopolitical factors, economic uncertainties made more complex by Brexit, the rise of populist maverick leaders, accelerating cyber-attacks on businesses and governments, demographic changes, growing wealth inequalities, globalised competition and emerging technology on company strategy. These pressures are forcing organisations to focus on being future-fit and strengthening their capacity to adapt. In 2016, 48 per cent of 400 US public directors surveyed felt that economic uncertainty was one of the biggest challenges facing corporate boards (WDT report 2016, NYSE Publications).

The key to a sustainable future for companies is the ability to adapt. Those who have not adapted fast enough have become irrelevant, sometimes gradually and sometimes more suddenly. Over half of the top 100 biggest companies in the world in 1912 had disappeared by the late 1990s (Harford 2011). Between 2014 and 2015, 23 new entrants replaced companies in the UK's FTSE 350 (Thornton 2015).

Those companies that have adapted successfully have understood the following two truths:

- what made the company successful to date will not make it successful going forward and core assumptions have to be continually challenged
- the practice of vigilant scanning and paying attention to weak signals (both internally and externally) before they emerge as major issues is vital for on-going success.

Boards need to determine whether the company is moving quickly enough to adapt at two levels: how it is transforming its own ways of working and culture, and how it is driving change in the broader organisation. Both will require a reframing of the role of corporate governance. This chapter explores both levels of change. Somewhat ambitiously, it not only provides guidance on where and how boards should focus their change efforts but also attempts to predict what 2030 (and beyond) will require of boards.

The unstoppable winds of change in corporate governance

In response to some notable high-profile cases of complacent, negligent, over-optimist or ill-informed boards, calls have increased for better accountability, more rigour and greater independence across the corporate world. This section summarises some of the changes that are already underway in corporate governance. Taken together, these suggest a momentum that requires boards everywhere to sit up and take note.

Accountability for culture and strategy emerged as key issue in the wake of the GFC as noted in the book's introduction. Boards were perceived as spending too much time looking in rear-view mirrors and not enough time looking forward or thinking about the systemic risks that may flow from their decisions. In recent years in the UK, the Financial Reporting Council (FRC) has been encouraging companies to focus on broader aspects of governance, such as culture and strategy. Companies are now required to include in their annual reports a strategy report that provides a holistic view of their business model, strategic priorities, market position and future prospects. Additionally, the FRC also requires UK boards to outline how they are developing and reinforcing corporate cultures and setting the tone from the top. In Australia, the 2017–2018 Royal Commission into Misconduct in the Banking, Superannuation and Financial Services Industry ('Royal Commission') has produced unprecedented public analysis of the banking sector's internal governance and has left much to worry about in terms of culture, especially the role of sales incentives and other remuneration practices in driving the wrong behaviours.

The role of proxy advisors in corporate governance monitoring and reporting has also grown in recent years. The increasing influence of these advisors, combined with the lack of regulation of such advisors, is concerning to the director community and is receiving more than passing interest from regulators. In the US, steps have been taken by the Securities and Exchange Commission to change this, with proxy advisors facing more accountability. This will be a growing area of focus for Australia also.

The disclosure of information regarding the representation of women on public company boards and in senior management has also received attention in respect of board renewal efforts in Canada, Australia, UK, Norway and Spain. Some countries have set clear quotas for gender representation; for example, in Norway, for boards with four–six members, each gender must be represented by at least two members; six–eight member boards, each gender must be represented by at least three members; nine member boards, each gender must be represented by at least four members; more than nine member boards, each gender must be represented by at least 40 per cent of the members of the board. Spain has followed suit. Australia and the UK, although resisting quotas, have instituted a 'please explain' rule in which justifications have to be provided for why there is a gender imbalance. The UK 30 per cent club, started in 2010 by a group of FTSE chairs and focussed on gender diversity on the boards of the FTSE 100 companies, has reported an increase in female board directors from 12.5 per cent in 2010 to 12.9 per cent in 2018. They have since expanded their aim to increase gender diversity at executive levels from 25 per cent (which is what it is today) to 30 per cent.

In developing countries, similar winds of change are blowing. The recent large and high-profile corporate frauds in India have precipitated moves to increase the responsibility of board directors and auditors to better oversee systemic weaknesses in their companies. South Africa has focussed on integrated reporting and developed new standards for taking a stakeholder inclusive approach to effective management.

APRA (The Australian Prudential and Regulatory Authority) has mandated a board's responsibility for risk cultures. The published standards require boards to understand and measure the current state of risk cultures within their organisation and develop and implement initiatives to build and improve risk culture. At the same time, ASIC (The Australian Securities and Investment Commission) has called for greater civil penalties for executives responsible for promoting poor culture. Further, as noted in Chapter 8, the 2017–2018 Royal Commission into Banking in Australia increased the volume on calls for boards of financial services companies to take charge of the risk and reward culture of the companies they steward, a criticism that was explicitly levelled at Australia's largest bank, the CBA ('How an Australian bank laundered money for Hong Kong drug gangs' 2018; 'Probe exposes Australian bank's abuse of customers' 2018). In addition to addressing risk, how companies and boards create greater transparency in the context of public interest issues matters also.

There is recognition in the UK that the *Public Interest Disclosures Act 1998* (brought in as a result of the collapse of Barings and BCCI) does not adequately protect whistle-blowers. It seeks to protect individuals who call out allegations of wrong doing by the company. A groundswell of whistleblowing cases in the UK following the GFC revealed large-scale breakdowns in corporate cultures and ethical leadership. This has resulted in calls by the European Commission for whistleblowing protections to be strengthened for all businesses with more than 50 staff and revenues in excess of 10 million Euro. This marks a cultural shift globally in legislators and regulators' approach to issues of transparency and non-retaliation. The role of whistleblowing in shifting cultures is discussed further on in this chapter.

No corporate governance jurisdiction will be unaffected by these winds of change. To stay ahead of the curve of regulatory intrusion, boards will need to think more systemically about their driving purpose, role in culture and strategy, and how to earn the respect of the communities their companies serve. These issues are considered in the following.

The 2030 board

At the end of 2015, the International Review Board surveyed the board community across five major regions (North America, Latin America, EU, Developed APAC, Emerging APAC, Africa), seeking to discover the focus areas they felt were likely to increase in support of business growth over the next 10 years. Four issues topped the list consistently: development/reinforcement of corporate culture as the top issue, followed closely behind by strategic planning horizons, sustainability and digital economy expertise.

To properly reflect these future-focussed issues, how will the board agenda need to change? Generally, board agendas look much the same as they did a decade ago. Time is spent on performance reports, audit reports, compliance reports, legal obligations and risk management. As discussed in Chapter 6, on some boards, as much as 70 per cent of meeting time is focussed on these issues. Rather than consider matters of strategic direction, business culture, sustainability and core purpose, boards tend to focus on what is *counted* and may not reflect as often on what should really *count*. Some critics argue that the root cause of poor corporate governance is incapable of being addressed, at least in board agendas and mandates as we know them. At the same time, and particularly over the last decade, the oversight responsibilities of the board have become increasingly more complex, with questionable value add, as discussed in Chapter 6.

Echoing Carter and Lorsch's (2004) sentiment in *Back to the drawing board*, a decade later Barton and Wiseman (2015) declared that 'boards aren't working'. Their analysis highlighted how, despite a wave of guidelines and support from legal and regulatory reforms, most boards are not delivering on their primary mission of monitoring and guiding management in creating a future underpinned by a healthy corporate culture that drives sustainable performance across a range of measures, including financial outcomes. The Mckinsey & Company 2017 survey of global governance asked the 1,100 participating directors about the presence of nine potential business disruptions on their boards' current agendas and their agendas from two years ago. Their survey found that boards' knowledge of these disruptions is highly variable. Across the nine disruptions, they rated changing customer behavior as somewhat or very good. Disappointingly, most reported a poor understanding of cyber security, activist investors, geopolitical risk and digitization. For each of the nine disruptions, there was a strong correlation between those who said they understood the topic when they also said it appeared on the agenda.

While all directors understand their fiduciary duties, even today too few would feel an obligation to focus on disruptive strategies other than reacting to management-led initiatives as shown by subsequent research studies (BCG Publications, June 2016)

Boards will have to work harder and faster to pursue new knowledge and their own education on emerging topics. They will need to take deliberate steps, either individually or collectively, to expose themselves to new markets, new technologies, renowned experts and so on. This raises the question of whether full-time directors (in respect of larger public companies) will become necessary. It also raises the idea of establishing an 'Office of the Board' that would serve as a full-time independent team to provide NEDs with independent analysis to utilise in their deliberations. Given the enormous pressures that governing complex organisations now represents, nominations committees may want to consider a Nordic style points system to determine director workloads to ensure that NEDs are not taking on more than they can reasonably be expected to handle.

Replacing the once a year strategy off-site with a more fluid strategy development process may also be necessary so that strategy is no longer a once or even twice a year contemplation. If the value of boards is in bringing broader strategic horizons to the table, and guarding against the narrowing of strategic horizons, should boards be asking management for a menu of strategic options with pros and cons of each? Should they also be asking management to disclose strategic options they discarded and why, rather than the current practice of having a well-formed strategy brought to the board for approval?

The selection of directors must be driven by a conversation about the sort of organisation envisioned five years hence. Questions need to be asked about changes in skills (i.e., what board and management skills are critical now that will become less critical in the future and what board and management skills are not critical now but will emerge as critical in the future). Other questions might include: How might advisory panels be of use to boards as the complexity of running a corporation escalates exponentially? Can the board agenda be structured to build a more forward-looking mindset while at the same time not blurring the line between management and board duties?

To deliver a forward-looking agenda, five areas are proposed that we may need to rethink and change. These are described in the following.

Achieving a healthy corporate culture

The board is ultimately responsible for the culture within an organisation. Therefore, it is disappointing that only about half (47 per cent) of business leaders surveyed worldwide agreed that developing and reinforcing corporate culture should be a focus for boards over the next 10 years (IBR data Q3 2015). Culture is to a company what character is to a person and what history is to a nation. It is defining. Consequently, it is very difficult, if not impossible, to sustainably change culture without a major revolution or transformation in thinking and practices.

Ensuring a healthy corporate culture starts at the top, with the board. Jensen (1993 cited in Sacconi et al. 2015) described board culture as the source of the underperformance problem: 'Board culture is an important component of board failure.' He was referring to the persistence of 'the old-boy network' in appointing directors, not least because the courtesy born of such connections frequently comes at the expense of truth and candour in board discussions. While the embededdness and exposure of directors in broader social circles is key to their board capital, as noted in Chapter 2, certain board networks have been shown to be far too narrow. As noted in Chapters 2 and 3, the unspoken rules of reciprocity can be pervasive, and an NED may be reluctant to challenge another NED or chair that has been instrumental in recommending their appointment to the board. This is damaging not only to the quality of debate but also to the integrity of the final decision. There is often an implicit expectation of collectivism and solidarity on boards; as a consequence, poor business decisions may sometimes be defended by claims that 'the board was unanimous'. Social norms and routines within a board are appropriate; however, they should not take priority over the dynamic tension of rigorous and constructive debate, thoughtful analysis, challenging management (even if occasionally upsetting the CEO) and decision-making. Chairs need to create a culture where constructive dissent is expected and not viewed as disloyalty to the collective. The disappointing truth is that what Jensen observed in 1993 has changed very little today. There are some notable exceptions, such as the courage Archie Norman showed when he was appointed chair of Marks & Spencers. As the new chair of Marks & Spencers, Norman said he wanted arguments and debate, not harmony in the boardroom. According to one commentator, Norman 'didn't join [Marks & Spencers] to be a governance chair. [Marks & Spencers] has not failed to turn around in the past because of a lack of talent. It is because the culture hasn't changed' (Hipwell 2018, pp. 34–35). In a similar vein, Lou Gerstner, who was hired to turn around a failing IBM in the 1990s famously stated: 'The last thing IBM needs is a strategy, it needs to fix its culture.' Gerstner added:

> Transformation of an enterprise begins with a sense of crisis or urgency. No institution will go through fundamental change unless it believes it is in deep trouble and needs to do something different to survive ... the thing I learned at IBM is the culture is everything.
>
> (Lagace 2002; see also Gerstner 2002)

Management guru Peter Drucker is purported to have said that 'culture eats strategy for breakfast'. What Drucker meant was that the power of a company's culture will be defining regardless of the elegance of its strategy, a belief echoed in Gerstner words. A more nuanced version of the frequently cited Drucker quote may be that culture might eat strategy for breakfast, but leadership talent ensures there is food on the table. The existence of a healthy corporate culture and the leadership to advocate and role model the behaviours (implied by the desired culture) is a core responsibility of the board, but it is not something that most boards devote enough attention to, beyond reviewing the headline results of annual employee engagement surveys.

While employee engagement surveys are valuable in revealing disconnects between the executive team and the wider workforce, such documents rarely provide answers about the causes of the disconnects. Depending on the nature of the company, insights can be gleaned by examining how closely different divisions and functions within the company cooperate and the extent to which they have common goals. A lack of cooperation and common goals can be an endemic problem in large companies, fostering the creation of silos. Engagement surveys will provide insight into one dimension of the problem only. Boards will have to find ways to gain deeper understandings of the dynamics in the company, including power dynamics—how power is used and abused and how the company's desired identity may be undermined by powerful subcultures within the business. These issues are discussed in some detail in Chapter 3. The best way for boards to develop a deeper understanding of the culture is to walk amongst the company's customers and partners and employees. This may include being exposed to 30–40 of the most talented of executives over the course of the year. While some board committee chairs will ordinarily have such contact, these interactions are generally task-related, and it is difficult to assess the quality of strategic thinking at this level or to assess the breadth of capability and behavioural alignment more generally. Some companies create a calendar of events at which executives the next level down from the C-suite are deliberately exposed to board members in semi-structured dialogues, allowing directors to get to know the leadership talent more intimately. In monitoring culture, there are no shortcuts to directors spending time with their finger on the pulse of the company and understanding the 'tone' by meeting employees, speaking to customers and suppliers, making site visits, listening to the market and investors, and looking for indicators of potential problems—not in a perfunctory manner as is sometimes the case, but in a substantive way.

Tell-tale signs that help a board to understand how a company's culture is viewed both internally and by external stakeholders include:

- overly confident and domineering personality of the CEO—often mistaken for charisma
- lack of openness to challenge prevailing ideas and assumptions
- strong visible subcultures (e.g., dealing room culture at some banks)
- casual attitude towards regulators and compliance
- the absence of bad news
- poor evidence of diversity (beyond simply gender)
- average employee engagement
- executive remuneration design that is potentially flawed
- high employee turnover, especially in key roles
- failure to conduct exit interviews or failure to address recurring themes

- customer complaints that recur and continue unabated
- defection of key customers, accounts or contracts.

The chairman and CEO of advisory firm Seawick provides another window into culture, highlighting the micro-behaviours that say a lot about a culture in the following statement:

> Surprisingly, the markers of declining culture are often on plain sight: not returning phone or email messages, cancelling meetings without explanation, promise to arrange meetings or to respond to requests that never eventuate, unilateral changing trading terms and treating stakeholders with disdain or contempt, just to name a few of these, all signify a culture of arrogance, self-importance and standing, and deluding themselves into believing that they can exercise those attributes indiscriminately.
>
> ('How to stop' 2018, p. 25)

Boards should be alert to such micro-behaviours and alert also to executives who seem to take the importance of culture lightly, particularly those schooled in fact and rule-based disciplines such as law and accountancy. Culture is anchored in unspoken norms, behaviours and social patterns; therefore, many executives consider it a secondary concern in the way they behave and communicate, seeing it as part of the mandate for HR, rather than them.

With regard to corporate culture and internal risk management, an important control mechanism for boards is the role of whistleblowing and whistle-blowers as noted. Whistle-blowers have become a critical part of financial fraud enforcement worldwide. In the UK, the *Public Interest Disclosure Act 1998* (PIDA) is the key piece of legislation protecting individuals who 'blow the whistle' in the public interest. In addition to the law, most companies have detailed policies covering whistleblowing. The UK's Financial Conduct Authority has rules that aim to encourage a culture in which individuals raise concerns and challenge poor practices and behaviours within financial institutions. It is important that a company's whistleblowing policy is reviewed by the board and communicated throughout the organisation. Trust in the integrity of the whistleblowing framework is key. Employees that raise concerns must do so in the knowledge that their identities will be protected and that their concerns will be taken seriously. This fundamental premise was at the centre of a scandal that engulfed the CEO at Barclays Bank when he attempted to find the name of a whistle-blower ('Barclays CEO fined' 2018). The strength of a company's commitment to enforcing whistleblowing policies provides important insights into the culture of the company ('UK decision about Jes Staley in Barclays whistle-blower case' 2018). A company's whistle-blower policy serves as a check and balance mechanism within the overall governance of a company ('The man who blew the whistle on CBA' 2014).

Steps boards can take to strengthen corporate culture

- Re-examine how much time the board is actually spending on issues pertaining directly or indirectly to corporate culture.
- Spend more time with the executive beyond the CEO in semi-structured conversations to understand the kind of climate they create within their respective businesses and functions.
- Initiate where possible group discussions at which the degree of constructive contention of ideas among members of the executive is visible
- Take a keener interest in corporate culture indicators such as customer complaints and reasons for customer defections rather than relying on aggregated scores in surveys.
- Take a closer look at the existence of strong subcultures rather than focussing on aggregated employee engagement survey results.
- Pay more attention to employee exit interviews and understand more deeply why key people are leaving and seek to identify trends.
- Review and refresh the whistleblowing policies and ensure that practices are being adhered to that make it safe for people to speak up and out, and psychologically safe for bad news to be delivered at all levels of leadership.
- Take a close look at the decision-making rules within the company to ensure that decision-making principles are adhered to on three levels (Steare 2013):
  - ethics of compliance (what do the rules say?)
  - ethics of reason (what does the situation demand?)
  - ethics of care (who will this decision hurt/harm and who will it benefit?).

Reframing the guiding purpose and retaining the social licence

As noted in Chapter 8, a clear, compelling and worthy purpose is the glue that binds groups of individuals and an organization together and helps to define its place in the broader ecosystem of stakeholders. It is the foundation on which the collective 'we' of a real team, such as a board, is built. Purpose plays a critical role because it is the source of the meaning and significance people seek in what they do and it starts from the top.

When organisations have lost their way, it is often because they have strayed from their guiding purpose. Chapter 8 reviewed companies that had made their guiding purposes clear and enduring. As with culture, some boards give purpose a light touch, treating it as a philosophical concept loosely linked to what the business does. At its core, purpose provides a clear overriding reason as to why the company exists—employees know why they come to work, customers are motivated to buy the company's products/services and investors can see the long-term business case for investing. Given the magnitude of these effects, a guiding purpose should be used as a touchstone for a whole range of options and decisions; 'how does this (decision) fit with our purpose, our values and, by extension, social licence?' Clarity of purpose allows boards to navigate complex (and sometimes-conflicted) decisions regarding shareholder value and stakeholder considerations. Thankfully, unlike a decade or so ago, few companies would describe their purpose as that of maximising shareholder wealth. With clarity of purpose, internal and external communications on strategy are provided meaningful context. Importantly, customers resonate with a purpose that serves society and is contemporary and grounded in values. Purpose is also important when operating in any market, and it is particularly important when operating internationally, far from the parent company's home base. Some businesses have expanded internationally and, in adapting to local conditions, have not always followed the moral compass that clarity of purpose provides.

The strength and clarity of a company's purpose remind directors and staff that they have a moral as well as fiduciary responsibility in conducting the affairs of the company. Building a purpose-led organisations should be viewed through the prism of opportunity, in particular the opportunity for attracting investment funds and for bigger profits. For example, a 2018 study by J P Morgan found that socially responsible investment is becoming mainstream and is now worth USD 23 trillion globally. Unilever's Sustainable Living Brands which include Vaseline, Rexona and Dove are growing 40 per cent faster than the rest of their business and delivered 70 per cent of the company's turnover in 2017. A general shift towards a more conscientious approach to capital allocation is underway and accelerating and here to stay. Black Rock is now one of the largest suppliers of sustainable exchange-traded funds (ETFs) inclusion the largest low carbon ETF. Companies such as BNP Paribas, HSBC, Aviva and Norway's sovereign funds have committed to help carbon intensive companies transition to a lower carbon future. These actions on the part of these companies are very much part of their guiding purpose relating to supporting sustainable growth and go beyond simply PR or marketing spin. Their purpose guides the decisions they make about what they will invest in and what they will not invest in. For these powerful reasons, ensuring that the guiding purpose of a company is both clearly defined and visible for all to see is a core responsibility of a board that is focussed on the future.

As well as a guiding purpose, a modern company, particularly a large company, also needs a *social licence* to operate. When there are scandals and other major failures in governance, that licence is subject to review. In this regard, modern sentiment is very similar to that espoused by US President Teddy Roosevelt in 1935:

> I believe in corporations; they are indispensable instruments of modern civilisations; but I believe that they should be supervised and so regulated that they shall act in the interests of the community as a whole.
>
> (Micklethwait & Wooldridge 2003)

What Roosevelt was referring to was the obligation of companies to operate under a *social licence*, which society, in extremis through government and its agencies, could amend or withdraw. The precarious nature of a social licence can be seen in the banking sector in the US, UK and Australia. In the UK, post-GFC regulatory reforms (Edmonds 2013), such as the separation of commercial banking from investment banking, are examples of social licences being amended. In Australia, the establishment of the 2018 Royal Commission to consider, inter alia, the conduct of commercial banks, their abuses of customers and rent-seeking behaviour underpinned by an oligopoly industry structure is, in many ways, a review of the *social licence* of banks. Consequences for banks—their boards and executives—from the findings handed down in 2019 have yet to play out in full. This Royal Commission serves a similar purpose as the 2011 UK Vickers Report, which investigated and then make recommendations on ring-fencing commercial banking from investment banking, and the 2010 US Dodd-Frank Wall Street Reform and Consumer Protection Act (Dodd-Frank), which recommended restrictions on certain banking activities. The banking sector is not alone in having its social licence amended by government when there is evidence of scandal or market power abuse.

At the heart of investor and societal disquiet with business is concern about the quality of corporate governance. As the following report from the *Financial Times* makes clear, these concerns have been around for a long time:

> At the heart of the Enron scandal is a failure of corporate governance … an audit committee that signed misleading accounts. A Board that was ineffective in supervising senior management's actions. These failures are all too common … they exist, too, in companies where there are no scandals, merely poor performance or entrenched mediocrity.
>
> ('Same old problems' 2002, p. 14)

This has prompted many questions about the quality and effectiveness of corporate governance, which, in turn, has raised questions about board design, competency, motivation, incentives and culture. The effect these issues have on a board's effectiveness are described in Chapter 7.

Steps boards can take to strengthen their guiding purpose

Boards need to ask three questions to determine their guiding purpose:

a   Why are we here and what are we here to do?
b   Who are we doing it for and why?
c   How are we moving the organisation closer to its strategic goal?

Using the board effectiveness review approach advocated in Chapter 7, boards can engage in a facilitated conversation about the role of the board to ensure that a shared view is collectively developed. Without a shared view of the role of the board, a guiding purpose is unlikely to develop.

A focus on all forms of diversity

> I like Bartok and Stravinsky ... it is discordant sound ... and there are discordant sounds within a company. As President you must orchestrate the discordant sounds into some kind of harmony. But you never want too much harmony. One must cultivate a taste for finding harmony within discord, or you will drift away from the forces that keep a company alive.
>
> Takeo Fujisawa, co-founder of Honda Motor Company

When decision-making groups are diverse, decisions and debates are not one-sided and thinking horizons are extended beyond the here and now. This is because like-minded thinkers progressively bring less and less new information to the table. Challenges and opportunities of the future will be less visible to homogenous boards than to those that comprise a range of life and career experiences and socio-economic backgrounds.

As disruptive forces quicken their pace, profoundly affecting current business models and platforms, only boards that prioritise and role model all forms of diversity in ways that reflect the desired culture, markets and customers will not be left behind. Building a truly diverse board is not an easy task.

The issue of gender balance at board and TMT levels has received significant attention over the past decade. Although there have been few significant changes in this area, numerous studies and data show the link between gender balanced leadership and revenue, profit and productivity. By contrast, there is much less information about the effect of ethnic balance on boards. Recently, the University of Singapore compared the performance of companies with and without ethnic diversity on their boards. The study found that boards that comprised at least two ethnic groups scored much better than those that did not, with an average return on assets of 2.9 per cent versus 0.8 per cent, respectively.

Diversity also includes generational diversity. Digital natives (generally from the millennial generation) instantly recognise the transformative value of digital technologies to business, yet few boards access this kind of diversity. Digitally agile board members are critical, as proficiency with digital technology has become a core competency expected of every business. The potential for digital technology to reconceptualise business models and innovate products and services is only just becoming known. This aspect of diversity is dealt with more fully in the following.

Another key aspect of diversity, absent on many boards (which tend to favour the appointment of consultants, lawyers, accountants and bankers), is experience as entrepreneurs and start-up talent. Boards face huge challenges in attracting and then integrating entrepreneurs and their thinking into the existing culture. Some entrepreneurs and start-up talent who have joined incumbent companies and then exited by choice cite cultural resistance to new ideas. This suggests that it is not enough to simply bring these skills in. An accompanying culture change agenda to fully leverage the value these new hires bring is also needed. Entrepreneurial skills are critical to the success of many businesses today, especially those confronting inflection points in their growth trajectory. However, the governance rules and responsibilities that come with being a director are singularly unattractive to most entrepreneurs. This raises an important question: why do successful entrepreneurs avoid joining boards of public companies? This is a problem that boards of the future must address with the active engagement of investors. The time is right for a fresh approach—one that acknowledges that the current model of board governance in Anglo-Saxon markets is no longer fit for purpose and looks to alternatives, such as the so-called 'German model' or a derivative of it, as a better way forward. Such a model would allow for greater stakeholder engagement and may be more appealing to entrepreneurs who might find advisory responsibilities more appealing than the compliance-related obligations of being a director.

German model

Greater diversity of thinking can be encouraged on a board via the German model of corporate governance. Depending on the range and complexities of stakeholders, and the nature of the social licence held by the company, there is merit for some companies to explore a variation of this model. The German model is also known as the two-tier board model—the two tiers being the supervisory board and the operating board. The supervisory board meets quarterly to focus on strategy, economy, culture, social licence, management bench strength and stakeholders. At the next level is the operating board, which is the traditional board; it focusses on operating matters, compliance, risk management and the day-to-day. A much more societally oriented model than the unitary shareholder-centric model in Anglo-American economies, the German model has the potential to increase diversity of thinking on a board. A precise copy of the German model is not being advocated. Rather a suggestion that the two-tier board may go some way towards addressing current problems, especially the need for boards to become more strategically active as described in detail in Chapter 6.

There is also merit in the argument that the boards of companies that hold special privileges within society—such as major banks, telcos and utilities— could have investors, customers and employees (including a tech savvy employee under 35 years of age) as representatives on a 'advisory board' ('Call for customer' 2018). This model has the potential to involve other stakeholders beyond shareholders. However, an important caution is that simply hiring difference onto a board does not mean that the difference will be fully leveraged by the existing board dynamic. This issue is extensively explored in Chapters 2 and 3 in terms of how boards might become more alert to dysfunctional aspects of the existing board culture and what actionable strategies they may consider employing to improve it.

Swedish model

Further insights can be gleaned from the Swedish model of corporate governance, which has been described as a model in best practice ('Sweden sets an example in corporate governance' 2016) by the investor-led International Corporate Governance Network (ICGN). Under the Swedish model, investors largely control the boards of individual companies by controlling the nominations committee. Shareholders sit on nominations committees and have the right to approve or reject directors each year. By contrast, under the Anglo–American model, nominations are made by director-controlled nominations committees, with shareholders granted rights that are largely constrained to the processes and protocols of the AGM. The ICGN recommends that 'shareholders should be able to nominate candidates for board appointments'. Similarly, the OECD recommends that 'effective shareholder participation in … the nomination and election of board members should be facilitated'.

The Swedish model of corporate governance is touted as being a key factor in the consistently strong performance in value creation of companies in the Nordic region compared to their counterparts in both Europe (including the UK) and North America. A study by the BCG shows that from five-, 10- and 15-year perspectives, Nordic countries outperform on a total shareholder return basis. BCG characterised the Nordic corporate governance model as follows:

> Despite country-specific variations, the Nordic corporate-governance model is distinctive for establishing a powerful nonexecutive board that is separate from the executive management. The model establishes a direct hierarchical chain of command running from the shareholders general meeting to the board to the management. This structure gives the board a unique role, empowering it to act with the shareholders mandate to directly control the management. Through this mechanism, the Nordic region aligns the management incentives with those of the shareholders and strikes an effective balance between risk taking and stability. The nonexecutive board also has a clear role in determining the company's overall goals and strategy.
>
> ('Nordic boards' 2016)

In summary, blending people with diverse backgrounds and experience onto a board brings a broad range of views and ideas to the table, creating the potential for an environment for good decision-making and debate. As explored throughout part 1 of this book, this potential will only be realised in some circumstances. The role that social identity and power plays in if and how influence attempts are mounted and how they are responded to, has been dealt with extensively in part 1, in particular Chapter 3, recommending actionable strategies to counteract its adverse effects on the decision-making culture.

Steps boards can take to strengthen diversity

- Challenge the tendency to point to the 'lack of women with requisite sector experience' as the sole reason why change is impossible, as it simply perpetuates under-representation.
- Ask if you may be too reliant on existing networks to notice female candidates, again perpetuating inherent network biases.
- Explore reasons why some credible female candidates choose not to join board life, thereby facilitating a deeper understanding of an aspect of board culture that may be turning strong candidates away.
- Broaden out from gender to include other forms of inequality that will increasingly receive societal attention. Prioritise groups in which representation does not yet reflect your organisation's make up, moving beyond the more visible attributes of diversity such as gender, ethnicity and age.
- Challenge and widen the board's pool of talent and experiences to meet emerging skillsets.
- Invest in mentoring schemes that will allow aspiring directors to learn from the voices of experience; invest also in reverse mentoring schemes through which experienced directors can learn from rising stars who perceive the world differently and are less attached to 'the way things have always been done'.
- Use the approach to conducting board effectiveness reviews (outlined in Chapter 7) to assess how open the culture of the board is to new and diverse thinking and address the effects of power imbalances that can potentially subvert a healthy decision dynamic despite a diverse board composition

Responding to the digital economy

The board plays a pivotal role to help the company get ahead of the digital disruption – not just anticipate it, but lead it and help accelerate change.

(Stevens & Strauss 2018)

Research suggests that most pre-digital incumbent executives do not have the necessary experience to lead their company's digital transformations. While board members will not themselves need to be digital experts, they will need to have intimate understanding of how digital can transform existing business models and challenge current paradigms to ensure that management is sufficiently prepared. According to the Korn Ferry Institute, only 1.7 per cent of NEDs on the FTSE 100 index would quality as digitally competent. In 2017, Calastone investigated the composition of executive leadership at ASX 100 companies and found that only 40 per cent have a technologist on their TMT, let alone digital experience. This lack of digital proficiency requires urgent attention from boards.

Table 9.1 Levels of digital experience

Digital thinker	This person has had little direct experience managing or working on a digital initiative but understands at a high level what it means to be digital. This individual may have consulted or advised a digital business, but they were not born digital
Digital disruptor	This person has deep expertise in all things digital, which often comes from experience working for a big technology company or a digitally native business. This type of leader is likely to have less management expertise
Digital leader	This leader has had experience within a pre-digital incumbent that has embraced digital at a strategic and operational level. They are likely to have had greater exposure to digital and disruptive innovation as a leader
Digital transformer	This person has had a leadership role as part of the transformation of a pre-digital incumbent business. He or she may not be as senior as a digital leader, but they are likely to be more digitally savvy and experienced

Source: Stevens and Strauss (2018).

Stevens and Strauss (2018) identified four levels of digital expertise that may provide a useful framework for boards to consider when thinking about their management's fitness for the future (Table 9.1).

However, for business to truly succeed in the digital economy, it is not simply a matter of hiring executives with skills and/or experience to operate in one or more of these domains. The culture, energy and pace also needs to be fit for purpose. A number of 'cold economy' incumbents have hired digital experts without paying sufficient attention to culture and these talent acquisitions have experienced 'organ rejection'. New ideas require the freedom to be tested and to fail; a future-ready board understands this. Boards must allow for missteps at the executive level, embrace the learnings that come from those missteps and proactively provide directional advice.

Steps boards can take to lead the digitisation of their businesses, products and services

- If not already started, commence an ambitious plan to educate the board as a group on the new economy—its opportunities, challenges and threats to the business. This kind of education agenda can be challenging for those who are not digital natives and will be very uncomfortable for some. Organise a board 'deep dive' session that all board members attend to ensure their understanding of digital (the intention is not to turn them into digital natives but to help them see the implications of digital on current business models). Buy an annual subscription for all directors on a leading global publication that is at the forefront of digital change and thinking.
- Create a technology advisory board or panel to gain new insight and fresh thinking from a diverse range of relevant technology, digital and start-up

expertise. As well as looking at ways to boost digital expertise around the table, this will ensure that you are making the most of external advice and counsel.

- Identify current board members that are not digitally savvy and address, as a matter of urgency, their new economy education and digital fluency. Adding a digital savvy NED is no longer the answer—all NEDs have to be brought up to the same level of understanding of digital technologies and the new economy.
- Find out whether the person entrusted with corporate strategy within the TMT (i.e., the head of strategy) is digitally experienced. If their strategy experience is predominantly in the pre-digital era, ask if a change is required to ensure that your strategy is digitally agile.
- Have regular conversations with the executive exploring new forms of revenue that may come from digitising the business to ensure they are continually thinking about the harnessing of digital capability; coach leaders on how they might question norms and outmoded business practices.
- Ask if the culture of the company allows experimentation with new business models and platforms, thereby developing a better understanding at board level of the cultural enablers of a digital economy.
- Recognise that a full spectrum of technology skills exists and ensure that the board is opting for the right kind of expertise; for example, technology mainframe expertise is different from cloud-based expertise.
- Assess the ways in which your business is using data to drive research and development, and investment and business development strategies. Could it be doing more?
- Given the global nature of malicious cyber-attacks, make cyber risk a key focus of the risk committee and ensure that global collaborations intended to address cyber security issues are actively encouraged. If there is no cyber strategy currently in place, waste no time in developing one. Then, if it is not already, make cyber strategy a standing agenda item for every single board meeting. Staying one step ahead of cyber criminals will be a necessity.

Existential risk, sustainability and scenario planning

Boards are now required to keep and monitor risk registers. These generally cover various classes of risk, such as market risk, credit risk, operating risk and reputational risk. However, discussions about risk in organisations rarely centre around existential risks, such as catastrophic transgenerational risks and risks whose effects cannot be undone. These include risks associated with the earth's warming, hostile artificial intelligence, destructive biotechnology or nanotechnology, engineered or natural pandemics, nuclear terrorism, cyber-attacks on electric grids and so on.

Following Shell's lead in the 1970s, some companies now run regular scenario planning sessions on such risks. Table 9.2 describes the focus of such a process and some of the things to watch out for when scenario

Table 9.2 Scenario planning

Stages	Focus	Red flags to note
Scenario generation	• Identifying driving forces in the industry/market • Identifying plausible and rigorously constructed events (qualitatively and quantitatively) • Identifying critical 'what if' uncertainties impacting performance • Identifying critical questions faced by decision-makers	• Limiting the focus to what is already known • Assuming the future will look very much like the past • Giving too much weight to unlikely events
Scenario planning	• Assessing impact of each scenario • Developing strategic alternative for each	• Overconfidence or excessive optimism about likely impacts • Resisting the urge to shut down free and open debate
On-going	• Instilling discipline of *'what if'* thinking to retain alertness about evolving environment	• Focus on systems, processes and capabilities to the exclusion of underlying planning assumptions that may no longer hold

Source: Thuraisingham (2018).

planning. While the chances of any of these events occurring is small (other than the earth's warming, which is underway), scenario planning exercises have been shown to broaden the strategic horizons of participants and build the strategic muscles of board members. Therefore, it is important to ensure that scenario planning becomes a habitual practice not just at the board level but also at the executive level. Scenario planning moves beyond probable futures and starts with 'what if' questions, challenging assumptions about certainties and mental models. It builds long-term organisational resilience.

In conclusion

Corporate boards are among the most important institutions in capitalism as they lie at the heart of governance and are key to mitigating the principal-agent costs facing shareholders. While no system of corporate governance is perfect, the record of boards is mixed; some would argue they are one of the weakest links in the capitalist system. Despite numerous reforms, the core role of the board has remained largely untouched for over a century. At a fundamental level, board reform remains legalistic, regulatory and astoundingly conservative.

Boards in the Anglo-American world are not futureproof. Board members may be more diverse today than they were 10 years ago but they remain, in the main, a composite of part-timers (in some cases worryingly, part-timers in pursuit of a life style change following executive life), largely drawn from the same shallow gene pool. Importantly, it may be argued that the way boards are currently set up makes it difficult to ensure attention is properly paid to monitoring value creation strategies effectively. Legendary investor Warren Buffet summed up the situation well:

> The requisites for board membership should be business savvy, interest in the job and owner-orientation. Too often, directors are selected simply because they are prominent or add diversity to the board. That practice is a mistake. Furthermore, mistakes in selecting directors are particularly serious because appointments are hard to undo: The pleasant but vacuous director need never worry about job security.
>
> ('Qantas chair from a shallow pool' 2018, p. 40)

As institutions, boards are responsible for ensuring that our major economic assets and much of our investment wealth are subject to sound steward-ship. Does the current governance framework and practices satisfactorily meet the highest possible standards of stewardship? In some cases, clearly not. The primary goal of the board should be to determine how best to position the company for future success. To do this it needs to be clear on purpose—the company's raison d'être, the glue that unites its stakeholders in support of its goals.

This chapter suggested five themes that boards should pay more attention to, but it did not suggest that these should be universally important for every governance jurisdiction. Some countries have more established, sophisticated approaches to governance than others. Nevertheless, boards everywhere face the same fundamental challenge: how to lead change and stay nimble and strategically agile in the face of uncertain times.

References

'Barclays CEO fined $1.5m for trying to unmask whistle-blower' 2018, *Reuters*, 11 May, pp. 5–7.

'Call for customer representatives on boards' 2018, *Australian Financial Review*, 21 May.

'How an Australian bank laundered money for Hong Kong drug gangs' 2018, *Financial Times*, 14 March.

'How to stop the rot within: fix your culture' 2018, *The Australian*, 26 July, p. 25.

'Nordic boards are the best in the world: here's why' 2016, *Business Insider Nordic*, 17 June. https://nordic.businessinsider.com/boards-of-directors-in-the-nordics-are-the-best-in-the-world-2016-6/.

'Probe exposes Australian banks' abuse of customers' 2018, *Financial Times*, 1 May.

'Qantas chair from shallow pool' 2018, *Australian Financial Review*, 29 June, p. 40.

'Same old problems with corporate governance' 2002, *Financial Times*, 19 February, p. 14.

'Sweden sets an example in corporate governance' 2016, *Financial Times*, 11 April, p. 24.

'The man who blew the whistle on CBA' 2014, *Australian Financial Review*, 28 June.

'UK decision about Jes Staley in Barclays whistleblower case is a disaster' 2018, *Forbes*, 7 May.

Barton, D & Wiseman, M 2015, 'Where boards fall short', *Harvard Business Review*, January–February.

Carter, CB & Lorsch, JW 2004, *Back to the drawing board*, Harvard Business School Press, Boston, MA.

Edmonds, T 2013, *The independent commission on banking: the Vickers report*. https://researchbriefings.parliament.uk/ResearchBriefing/Summary/SN06171#fullreport.

Faeste, L et al. 2016, 'How Nordic boards create exceptional value', *BCG Publications*, June.

Gerstner, LV 2002, *Who says elephants can't dance? Inside IBM's historic turnaround*, HarperBusiness, New York.

Harford, T 2011, Adapt: Why success always starts with failure, Picador, New York.

Hipwell, D 2018, 'The retail wizard putting M&S under his spell', *The Times*, 23 April, pp. 34–35.

Lagace, M 2002, 'Gerstner: changing culture at IBM', *Working Knowledge*, 9 December. https://hbswk.hbs.edu/archive/gerstner-changing-culture-at-ibm-lou-gerstner-discusses-changing-the-culture-at-ibm.

Micklethwait, J & Wooldridge, A 2003, *The company—a short history of a revolutionary idea*, Modern Library, New York.

Sacconi, L, Blair, M, Freeman, RE & Vercelli, A (eds) 2015, *Corporate responsibility and corporate governance*, IEA, New York.

Steare, R 2013, *Ethicability: (n) how to decide what's right and find the courage to do it*, Roger Steare Consulting Limited, London.

Stevens, A & Strauss, L 2018, *Chasing digital: a playbook for the new economy*, Wiley & Co, New York.

Thornton, G 2015, *UK corporate governance review and trends*. https://grantthornton.co.uk.

Index

Note: **Bold** page numbers refer to tables and *italic* page numbers refer to figures.

absentee owners 152
accountability 110, 167; board 10, 12, 20–4,
    56, 125; for culture and strategy 167;
    exercise of 110; formal and informal
    forms of 21–2; as goal and process
    20–4; informal practices of 4; informal
    processes of 21; process of 39–46
active board, strategically 123; board
    capital 124; curse of legacy thinking and
    conservatism 127–9; from dance floor
    to balcony 132–3; incumbency and case
    for change 125–7; from ineffective ones,
    distinguishing 137–9; monitoring and
    adapting strategy 133–4; NED exposure
    to disruptive forces and diverse thinking
    130–2; strategic clarity, developing
    134–5; strategic effectiveness, defining
    135–7
active investors 151, 162, 164
active listening 111, 113, 117
activism 150, 151, 153, 155, 160, 161;
    growth of 151–2; shareholder 13,
    152–6, 164; threat of 156
activist shareholder 152; agitation 156;
    long-term investors and 1
advisory role 5, 10, 57, 132
agency theory 10, 22
Airbnb 126
Andrus, J. 139
Anglo-American model 179
Anglo-Saxon markets 5, 160, 178
anti-competitive market structures 127
anxiety 20, 41, 74, 113
APRA *see* The Australian Prudential
    Regulatory Authority (APRA)
'archipelago' style of board 108

Argyris, C. 87
aspirational gap 145, *146*
Australia 14, 128, 130–2; activism 151;
    banking sector in 127; commodities
    market in 114; Royal Commission
    160–1, 167, 168, 176; *Two Strikes
    Rule* in 154
The Australian Prudential Regulatory
    Authority (APRA) 161, 168

Baron, R.A. 94
Barrick, M.R. 94
Bartlett, Christopher 157
Barton, D. 169
Beatty, David 159
Bednar, M. 38, 139
'bet the farm' decisions 22
black box 2, 3
black hat 109
Black Rock 157, 159, 175
blockchain technology 126
blue-sky thinking 109
board: accountability 10, 12, 20–4, 56,
    125; chair 4, 101, 102, 106, 147, 148;
    character 58–65; contribution to
    strategy 13–15; cultures 4, 52, 58–65,
    92, 95, 96–8, 171, 178, 180; director
    motivations 39–46; factional 63, 64;
    'fit for future' *see* 'fit for future' board;
    governance 11, 12, 178; group effects
    65–7; leadership of *see* leadership of
    board; role of 10–13; nomination
    committees 72; strategy-shaping
    context 15–20
board capital 29, 70, 124, 148;
    behavioural variations in NED use

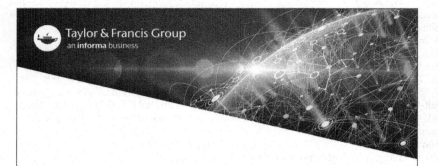